The Private Sector in Development

Entrepreneurship, Regulation, and Competitive Disciplines

Michael U. Klein
Bita Hadjimichael

THE WORLD BANK
Washington, D.C.

First printing May 2003
1 2 3 4 06 05 04 03

ISBN 0-8213-5437-X

Library of Congress Cataloging-in-Publication Data

Klein, Michael U., 1952–
    The private sector in development : entrepreneurship, regulation, and competitive
    disciplines / Michael U. Klein, Bita Hadjimichael.
        p. cm.
    Includes bibliographical references and index.
    ISBN 0-8213-5437-X
        1. Industrial policy—Developing countries. 2. Trade regulation—Developing
    countries. 3. Entrepreneurship—Developing countries. 4. Capitalism—Developing
    countries. 5. Competition—Developing countries. I. Hadjimichael, Bita, 1958– II. Title.

HD3616.D452K54 2003
338.9′009172′4—dc21

                                                                    2003043294

Contents

Figures

Foreword

Following the debt crisis of the early 1980s, the failure of many import substitution experiments, and a fading belief in centrally planned approaches to economic development, private sector development has become a prominent theme in the development debate. The 1990s then saw revolutionary changes in many former communist economies, and a wave of privatization experiments took place around the globe. Private sector development became almost synonymous with privatization. Today, following a degree of disenchantment with privatization and because of corporate scandals that have occurred worldwide, private sector development is again called into question.

Throughout the years, the very concept of private sector development has remained only loosely defined. For some, it expresses a belief in market solutions; for others, it stands for privatization. Still more people believe that private sector development is about various types of activist industrial policy, particularly for small and medium-size enterprises. In the moral debate, at one end of the spectrum are those who see private sector development as an approach that feeds greedy private entrepreneurs at the expense of poor people. At the other end of the spectrum are those with the view that the last thing the private sector needs is for public agencies to carry out its development.

Given this backdrop, this book tries to lay out a view of what constitutes the private sector development agenda and to introduce coherent ways of thinking about the concept that are useful for defining the role of development agencies.

Peter Woike
Executive Vice President, International Finance Corporation
Managing Director, World Bank

Acknowledgments

Many people from the World Bank helped us in the preparation of this book. We are indebted to Neil Roger for his many insights and suggestions. We gratefully acknowledge contributions from Syed A. Mahmood and Chiaki Yamamoto and production support from Jocelyn Tan Dytang. We also would like to thank the following individuals for their valuable comments and contributions: Geeta Batra, John E. Besant-Jones, Tyler Biggs, Penelope J. Brook, Gerard Caprio, Asli Demirgüç-Kunt, Simeon Djankov, David R. Dollar, Philip D. Gray, Kristin Hallberg, Jeffrey S. Hammer, April L. Harding, Timothy C. Irwin, Ada Karina Izaguirre, Emmanuel Y. Jimenez, Ioannis Kessides, Sunita Kikeri, Daniela M. H. Klingebiel, Aart C. Kraay, Peter F. Lanjouw, Elizabeth L. Littlefield, Magda Lovei, Deepa Narayan, Helen Panaritis, Harry A. Patrinos, Guillermo Perry, Guy P. Pfefferman, Alexander S. Preker, Omar M. Razzaz, Susan Rose-Ackerman (Yale Law School), Apurva Sanghi, Warrick P. Smith, Lyn Squire, Andrew H. W. Stone, Bernard W. Tenenbaum, David R. Wheeler, and Jacob Yaron. Finally, we are grateful to the Office of the Publisher for the design, editing, and production of this book.

Abbreviations and Acronyms

CDC   Commonwealth Development Corporation
CFCs   chlorofluorocarbons
CIS   Commonwealth of Independent States
FDI   Foreign direct investment
GDP   Gross domestic product
HDR   Human Development Report
IFC   International Finance Corporation
OECD Organisation for Economic Co-operation and Development
PM   particulate matter
SPM   suspended particulate matter
UNDP United Nations Development Programme

1

The Private Sector
and Poverty Reduction

A New Swedish Model?

Over the past 10 to 15 years, the world underwent revolutionary change. The communist regimes of Eastern Europe and the Soviet Union collapsed. Privatization swept the world, undoing many of the nationalizations of the 1960s and 1970s. Private capital flows were liberalized and, by the turn of the century, dwarfed official flows to emerging markets, despite severe financial crises in emerging markets.

At one level, there is a consensus on the desirable economic model that never existed in the past century. There just is no articulated alternative to some form of market economy. Even among the different forms of industrial market economies there appears to be some basic convergence. At the risk of speculation, one might see the emergence of the "New Swedish Model." Sweden, the Netherlands, and a number of other industrial and emerging economies have been trying since the 1990s to promote vigorous competition in the productive sectors. At the same time, these countries have been trying to establish regulatory frameworks that safeguard social and environmental standards and to maintain or build effective social safety nets. In essence, such efforts are not fundamentally different from so-called

Anglo-Saxon capitalism—at least by the standards of ideological debates in the 20th century.

At another level, new doubts have emerged. Attempts to adopt a market economy approach have not always been successful. Privatization has been abused by powerful groups. Deregulation of financial markets has increased risks to poor citizens in a number of countries without necessarily delivering sustained growth. More than a decade of market reforms in Latin America has yet to show significant positive results in many countries. Most parts of the former Soviet Union have seen living standards decline for a decade. African incomes have slid backward for several decades. More-successful economies have been remorselessly shaken by a series of financial crises. It is now clear that market reform and privatization alone are not enough.

It is a world where the glass appears half full to some, half empty to others. Over the past decade, more people than ever have escaped the worst of poverty, and the percentage of poor people in total world population has declined a little. Yet the absolute number of poor has risen, and global income inequality may never have been greater, with no improvement in sight (figures 1.1 and 1.2). Some blame unfettered market development for not having lifted the lot of the poor and for having made poor people more vulnerable. At the same time, it is clear that most of the poor (about two-thirds) live in rural areas and in countries that are only weakly connected to the rest of the world.

And what do ordinary citizens have to say about this? What do they think about private enterprise? Some opinion polls show that citizens do not trust large corporations to respect social or environmental concerns (figure 1.3). Corporate villains are a favorite subject in popular books and movies. At the same time, the World Bank's study *Voices of the Poor* finds that poor people seem to think that private enterprise is reasonably important to them and that private firms are quite effective. Compared with all other institutions in urban areas, private enterprises appear least ineffective. In rural areas also, the poor do not accuse the private enterprises of being ineffective. Local shops, in particular, as well as—to some degree—the sometimes maligned moneylenders, are appreciated by most people. Poor people have to deal with and depend on a number of government institutions, but they find those institutions rather ineffective. They appear to rely most heavily on family- and community-based organizations for support (Narayan and others 2000a).

FIGURE 1.1. Number of People Living on Less than US$1 a Day, 1987 and 1998

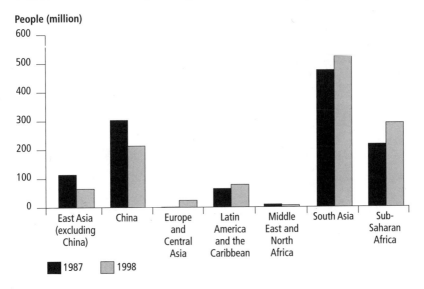

People (million)

Source: Pfeffermann 2000. Reprinted with permission.

FIGURE 1.2. Number of People Living on More than US$1 a Day, 1987 and 1998

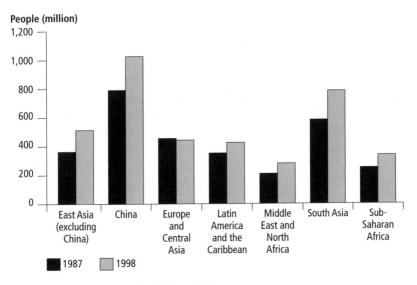

People (million)

Source: Pfeffermann 2000. Reprinted with permission.

FIGURE 1.3. In Whom Do We Trust? Survey of Opinion Leaders on Three Key Issues

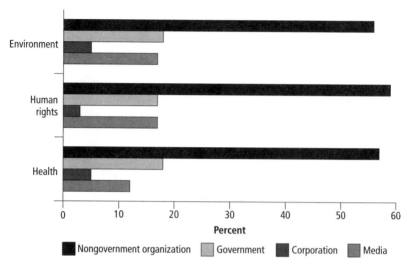

Source: de Jonquieres 2000. Reprinted with permission.

The overall picture might be interpreted as follows. Private firms of all sorts are typically not much loved, but they are recognized as important and quite effective. Central to this scenario is the nature of incentives on private enterprise. The profit motive is a powerful tool and produces effective action. By the same token, it creates incentives to ride roughshod over social and environmental concerns. This observation brings us back to the New Swedish Model. The key to a sound private sector that contributes to development is tapping entrepreneurial spirit through the profit motive while embedding that spirit in disciplines that can harness private initiative for socially useful purposes.

Openness and Competition

During the second half of the 20th century, for the first time in history, it has become possible for poor people everywhere to escape from poverty within a human life span. Before the industrial revolution, income and living conditions in the world changed little for hundreds of years. Up to the

18th century, even under the economic conditions prevailing in the most advanced countries, citizens could not expect to see much improvement in income during their lifetimes. For almost all people, prolonged deterioration of living standards was always possible. With the advent of the industrial revolution, it became possible to improve living standards faster. In the 19th century, the lead country, the United Kingdom, was able to double average per capita income in just 60 years. Today, a wide variety of countries have been able to double average per capita income in about 10 years (for example, Botswana, Chile, China, Ireland, Japan, the Republic of Korea, Thailand) by adopting and adapting technical and organizational advances already invented elsewhere.

Openness and competition are key reasons we can have hope for poverty reduction (figure 1.4). The effective and rapid adoption of best practice requires openness to new ideas and technology. Competition provides incentives to adopt improved practices. Open and competitive markets have proved to be the best mechanism both to stimulate innovation and to spread best practice within countries and across borders. For example, openness and product market competition, particularly in demanding export markets, underpinned much of the growth of East Asian economies (Stiglitz 1998). Growth, driven by such markets, is a powerful prerequisite

FIGURE 1.4. Convergence and Divergence in the 1990s: Per Capita GDP Growth Rates

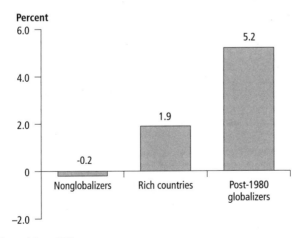

Source: Dollar and Kraay 2001.

for poverty reduction. In most countries, the poor benefit from growth in the same proportion as others (figure 1.5; see also Anand and Ravallion 1993; Barro 2000; Dollar and Kraay 2000a; Gallup, Radelet, and Warner 1998; Gugerty and Timmer 1999; Ravallion 1995, 1997a, 1997b, 2000; Ravallion and Chen 1997; Ravallion and Datt 1999; Roemer and Gugerty 1997; Srinivasan 2000; Timmer 1997). Measures such as connecting the poor to markets by giving them choice, by providing entrepreneurial opportunity, and by building roads and communication systems support the most powerful mechanism for escaping poverty—namely, the ability to adopt and adapt improved practices. Hence, competitive markets are one of the reasons we can even consider international development targets such as halving poverty by 2015. By the same token, we can be upset about the lack of progress in poverty reduction in many countries, particularly in Africa, precisely because growth and, therefore, rapid poverty reduction are now possible, although not automatic. When there is growth, it does not always trickle down across countries or within them (Stiglitz 1998).

FIGURE 1.5. Growth Is Good for the Poor

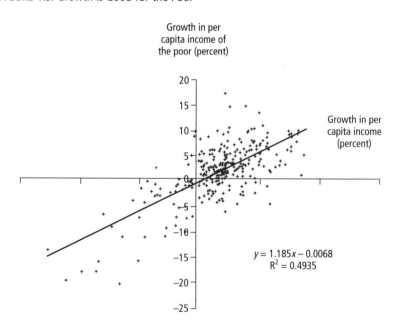

Growth in per
capita income of
the poor (percent)

Growth in per
capita income
(percent)

$y = 1.185x - 0.0068$
$R^2 = 0.4935$

Source: Dollar and Kraay 2000a.

Individual, Institutional, and Social Capability

Openness and competition provide opportunity and incentive to improve performance throughout an economy and across borders. Yet without the capability of economic agents to respond effectively, performance will be disappointing. For example, studies on the effect of foreign direct investment, the most powerful mechanism to transfer best practice across borders, suggest that its contribution is most significant when domestic capability is high (Blomstrom and Kokko 1996; Borenzstein, De Gregorio, and Lee 1998; Caves 1999; Mody and Wang 1997; World Bank 2001b). Capability is a function of human capital, of the state of infrastructure, and of the formal and informal institutional framework in which markets operate (Crafts 2000). The supply of all these forms of capital can benefit from market disciplines.

A decent education and adequate health are required for people to perform. Particularly in low-income countries, the record of health and education systems has been disappointing. The problem is not primarily a lack of resources. The evidence suggests that the resources spent on health and education are not the key factors for creating true capability (figure 1.6; see also Filmer, Hammer, and Pritchett 1997). What matters is the effec-

FIGURE 1.6. Education and per Capita GDP Growth Rate, 1960–85

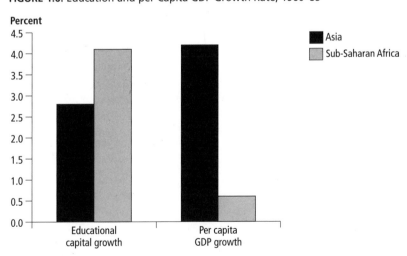

Source: Pritchett 1996.

7

tiveness of service delivery. Private approaches and market mechanisms can help improve service. The same is true for infrastructure.

Individual human capital and infrastructure are just part of capability. As pointed out by the late Mancur Olson (1996), in 1980 workers in Haiti earned about one-tenth of the salaries of workers in Germany. However, immigrants from Germany in the United States earned just double what immigrants from Haiti earned. Although some of the difference may be due to the special characteristics of immigrants from the two countries, overall it seems that special characteristics of the United States had a greater effect than did human capital per se. One might conclude that the higher capital stock in the United States explained the outcome. If so, then moving capital to Haiti should be the answer—the standard prescription of traditional development theory. However, capital and labor are both most productive if another underlying factor is at work (Hendricks 2002). A variety of recent studies suggest the importance of institutional characteristics, such as good governance, social capital, and trust (Guiso, Zingales, and Sapienza 2000). Clearly, the most important form of social capital is peace, particularly the absence of civil strife (table 1.1; see also Olson 2000). The private sector development agenda can only complement efforts to improve social order and trust. But it also matters directly for improving social capability because market-type solutions can help decentralize decisions and establish a balance of power in society. Altogether, effective private sector development renders the state more effective, and vice versa.

TABLE 1.1. Growth in Sub-Saharan Africa in Four Environments, 1995–96

Environment	Percentage of population	Growth rate of output per worker (percent)
Lack of social order	12	0.8
High degree of macroeconomic instability	43	2.7
Inadequate resource allocation policies	12	4.2
Modest levels of social order, macroeconomic stability, and resource allocation	26	4.7

Source: Based on Collier and Gunning 1999.

Market-Type Disciplines for Tax and Donor-Funded Assistance

The amount of potential resources available from donors is now relatively large compared with known poverty dimensions, and the grant element in aid is now about 75 percent of total transfers (World Bank 2002a). For example, in Africa's low-income countries, the average aid level amounted to about 9 percent of gross domestic product (GDP) during the 1990s. At the same time, the poorest 20 percent of people had incomes equivalent to just 4 percent of GDP (World Bank 2000a). Trickle down does not seem to work, even with tax and donor financing.

The world has become so rich that poverty elimination is within practical reach.[1] Money per se is clearly not the problem. Critical are delivery systems with improved incentives such that intended beneficiaries are reached. The most obvious avenue is to disburse donor or tax funds when results are achieved, not when projects are constructed. Desirable results should be responsive to beneficiaries by empowering them to choose. Thus communities should participate in setting goals for collective goods and services. For project execution, competing providers, including both for-profit and not-for-profit organizations, should be allowed to bid for the right to deliver a service and to pay the winning bidder when the service is actually delivered. The role of government would then be focused on critical functions, such as contracting out projects and providing regulation. That is how markets operate. Firms in markets focus on output and results. They are only paid and only survive if they deliver results. If development is to be about results for the poor, private sector development has to play a critical role, and its principles should be applied to aid agencies just as they are to any other types of organization.

Winners, Losers, and Markets

Analyses so far have not been able to identify simple systematic causes that explain why the poor benefit more or less from growth in different cases. Complex social, political, and economic factors interact to produce the outcomes we observe. How, in detail, that interaction functions and to what extent and how one could hope to engineer better outcomes remain unclear (World Bank 2000a). It is clear, however, that effective markets are the fastest and surest way to reduce poverty, because open markets promote catch-up with best practice within countries and across borders. Suppression of markets and exclusion from markets tend to be the reasons for the lack of growth of countries, regions, and population groups within countries.[2]

Yet by their very nature, markets create winners and losers, even though they may "lift all boats" eventually. After all, one of the key functions of markets is to select people and firms that do well and provide incentives for change to those that do not. Not all poor people will benefit equally, and there may be a relapse into poverty for some, even when markets work well. Sometimes, markets can increase the vulnerability to shocks (World Bank 2000f). By the same token, markets are likely to increase mobility in society, including among income groups (figures 1.7 and 1.8). Precise evidence of these effects is limited because of large data problems (box 1.1). Recent

FIGURE 1.7. Shocks and Stresses Causing Downward Mobility, by Gender

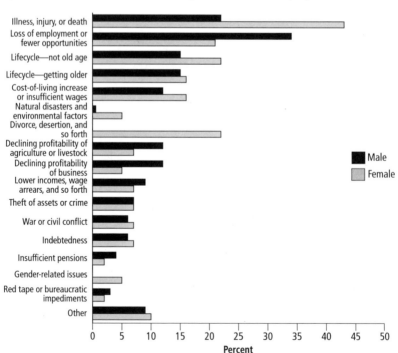

Source: Narayan and others 2000a.

FIGURE 1.8. Factors Leading to Upward Mobility, by Gender

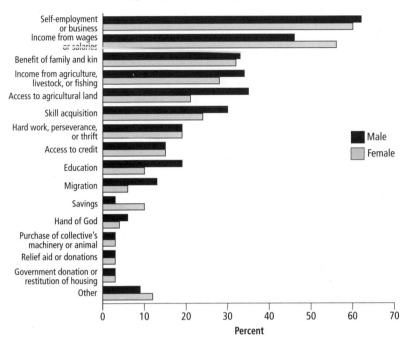

Source: Narayan and others 2000a.

studies comparing Peru with the United States suggest that market reforms in Peru have significantly increased income mobility even beyond that in the United States (table 1.2). The chances for the poor to escape from poverty have thus increased. But market reform does not create equality of outcome. It can help create opportunity by reducing or eliminating bias and favoritism. The main policy interventions that help reduce the vulnerability of people to adverse shocks seem to be effective basic education, particularly for girls, and prevention of disease, for example, through improved water supply and sanitation.

The effect on both winners and losers is likely to be greatest when open markets are created in places where large distortions previously existed. Radically new conditions after reform mean that income distribution can change significantly during reform processes. In several transition economies that were most plagued by large distortions before reform, income distribution and poverty worsened significantly after the breakdown of cen-

---

Box 1.1. Market Systems and Income Distribution

Over longer periods, market economies can experience prolonged improvement or deterioration of income distribution. The best among shaky data on long-term trends in income distribution exist for the United States. From the 18th century until today, income distribution has shifted over many episodes, each lasting several decades (Fukuyama 1999, Williamson 1987). Income distribution data from most other countries in the world show little change in overall distribution over the last half of the 20th century (Dollar and Kraay 2000a). Altogether, there is no evidence that market economies experience systematic deterioration of income distribution, nor do such distributions improve systematically.

---

tral planning. Opponents of market reform may use such outcomes to slow or stall the process of reform.

In a number of cases, the poor suffer not from the effects of markets on income distribution, but from the politics preventing the introduction of markets. For example, the most decisive reformers among former communist countries of Eastern Europe experienced the least deterioration of income distribution—notably Poland, which was arguably the strongest to emphasize free entry and hard budget constraints for firms, and, within the Baltic states, Estonia (Keane and Prasad 2000; Pinto, Belka, and Krajewski 1993). Radical reformers such as Chile and El Salvador improved the situation of the poor. Broadly, a similar picture applies to trade policy reform (Matusz and Tarr 1999). The most complete analyses of 13 episodes of trade policy reform show that effective trade reforms have supported growth and, hence, poverty reduction overall.

A key danger for the poor may thus be either limited reform, which generally leaves incomes low (as in Belarus, the Democratic People's Republic of Korea, Myanmar, and Ukraine), or half-hearted reform, which opens up opportunities that are grabbed by powerful elites and risks doing little for growth while worsening income distribution (as in the Russian Federation during parts of the 1990s) (World Bank 2000d, 2000f).

True market reform empowers citizens and challenges vested interests. Moving toward markets means that those in power give up some of their influence in the interest of creating a "bigger pie" for all. In the process, some incumbents may not do well. Their exposure to adjustment costs,

TABLE 1.2. Relative Income Mobility in Peru and the United States
(percent)

Peru, 1991–2000

Quintile 1991	Quintile 2000					
	1	**2**	**3**	**4**	**5**	**Total**
1	**45**	25	19	6	5	100
2	25	**25**	23	14	13	100
3	16	23	**22**	20	19	100
4	11	18	18	**32**	21	100
5	3	9	18	28	**42**	100
Total	100	100	100	100	100	100

United States, 1979–89

Quintile 1979	Quintile 1989					
	1	**2**	**3**	**4**	**5**	**Total**
1	**61**	24	9	5	1	100
2	23	**33**	28	14	3	100
3	8	25	**30**	26	11	100
4	5	13	23	**33**	26	100
5	3	5	11	23	**59**	100
Total	100	100	100	100	100	100

Note: Numbers may not add up because of rounding. Quintiles for Peru are calculated using equivalence expenditure. Quintiles for the United States are calculated using family incomes. The figures in bold along the diagonal indicate the percentage of those in a quintile who ended up where they had begun.

Source: Graham and Pettinato 2000. Reprinted with permission.

rather than the exposure of the poor to adjustment costs, is often the reason for their unwillingness to reform, which is often cloaked in declarations of concern for the poor (Acemoglu and Robinson 2000; Havrylyshyn and Odling-Smee 2000; Hellman 1998).

Overall, the private sector development agenda for the alleviation of poverty matters in two main ways:

- The creation of effective markets provides the poor with the opportunity to enhance their living standards.
- Market-type mechanisms are key to improving the delivery of basic infrastructure and social services that empower the poor, including services that are tax or donor funded.

In the following sections, these issues are discussed in more detail. Although the private sector development agenda is critical to reducing poverty, it is equally clear that it is just part of the overall equation. Poverty has many dimensions other than economic ones (box 1.2). The state and civil society are critical for poverty reduction. Private sector development is simply a complement to other efforts and is particularly closely related to the governance agenda.

Box 1.2. Poverty's Many Dimensions and Its Measurement

The Voices of the Poor *study presents the world through the eyes of more than 60,000 poor women and men from over 60 countries around the world (Narayan and others 2000a, 2000b; Narayan and Petesch 2002). The study brings out the many dimensions of poverty. Although the nature of poverty varies depending on gender, age, culture, and location of people, there are obvious similarities across countries. Material deprivation; troubled gender relations; discriminating social relations; lack of security; ineffective institutions; and lack of information, education, and health remain the main characteristics of poverty. Defining poverty as multidimensional raises the question of how to measure poverty overall and how to compare achievements in the different dimensions. The education and health dimensions of poverty are measured by conventional social indicators, whereas voicelessness and powerlessness are measured using a combination of participatory methods, polls, and national surveys on qualitative variables such as the extent of civil and political liberties.*

Income poverty is estimated by the World Bank on the basis of data on consumption per capita. These data were collected through household surveys. The headcount measure of poverty is defined as the number or proportion of the population with consumption levels below the international poverty line of US$1 per day—the critical cutoff in income or consumption below which an individual is determined to be poor. On that basis, the share of the poor in world population declined from 29 percent in 1990 to 23 percent in 1999; however, in absolute terms it reached 1.15 billion (World Bank 2002b).

Notes

1. One perspective is provided by data from the annual *Human Development Report* (HDR) published by the United Nations Development Programme (UNDP). For some years, the report has presented estimates of the additional resources it would take to meet all basic needs in the world. The HDR for 2000 puts the number at US$80 billion per year (UNDP 2000). That figure translates to US$1,400 for each of the richest 1 percent of people in today's world. Whatever we may think about the quality of that number, it invites the following thought: if one could credibly promise private donors that one had a foolproof way to meet all basic needs, then surely it would be easy to raise the money just through private donations.

2. See Ben-David (1999), Edwards (1997), Frankel and Romer (1999), Jonsson and Subramanian (2000), Sachs and Warner (1995), Srinivasan and Bhagwati (1999), and Winters (1999) on the link between "openness" and economic growth. See Baldwin (2000), Harrison and Hanson (1999), Rodriguez and Rodrik (2000), and Rodrik (1999b) for critiques of the above.

2

The Investment Climate

The Engine of Growth and Poverty Reduction

The Demise of Centrally Planned Development Models

To escape from poverty, the poor need jobs. As the saying goes, to help the poor one should not give them fish, but a fishing rod and teach them to fish so that they can ensure their own livelihood.[1] Investment is key to alleviating poverty because it is the mechanism that provides jobs (table 2.1).

If it were just a matter of the number of jobs, solutions would be easy. For example, state-owned enterprises could absorb all those in need of employment. The real issue is not just employment, but increasingly productive employment that allows living standards to rise. State-owned enterprises or subsidized private firms have generally failed to deliver sustainable productivity growth (Boardman and Vining 1989; Boubakri and Cosset 1998; d'Souza and Megginson 1999; Earle and Estrin 1998; Ehrlich and others 1994; Frydman and others 1999; La Porta and Lopez-de-Silanes 1997; Macedo

> *First, I would like to have work of any kind.*
>
> —An 18-year-old man, Ecuador

TABLE 2.1. Private Firms as a Source of Job Creation, Selected Developing Countries, 1987–98

Country	Period	Jobs created (thousands)		Ratio of private to public job creation
		Private	Public	
Mexico	1989–98	12,431.0	143.0	87:1
Costa Rica	1994–98	238.0	12.0	20:1
Turkey	1987–92	1,490.0	91.0	16:1
Kenya	1993–98	173.0	13.0	13:1
Guatemala	1994–98	47.0	4.0	12:1
Bolivia	1994–97	181.0	18.0	10:1
Uruguay	1987–92	127.0	27.0	4.7:1
Gabon	1992–96	4.7	1.3	3.6:1

Note: This table is limited to the few countries for which changes over time in job creation are documented for the entire public sector, including state-owned enterprises.

Source: Pfeffermann 2000. Reprinted with permission.

2000; Megginson, Nash, and Van Randenborgh 1994; Pohl and others 1997).

By the same token, simple increases in investment do not produce productivity growth per se (Easterly and Levine 2000). Investment levels in centrally planned economies were exceptionally high at some 30–40 percent of the gross domestic product (GDP). Yet after some initial successes with industrialization, productivity growth and, hence, income growth slowed and eventually declined. Likewise, investment in human capital—for example, education—does not necessarily lead to growth (Pritchett 1996). A series of studies show that, not only in the extreme case of the former Soviet Union, but also in many other contexts, greater use of resources has not led to sustained improvements in productivity—sometimes not even to greater output (McKinsey Global Institute 1999; Young 1992, 1994). The development models that were popular in the 1960s and that influenced the rise of state-led and planning solutions centered on identifying needs and resource gaps to meet those needs. They then proposed resource transfer and the stimulation of investment per se—and performed badly (Easterly 2001).

In short, productivity growth and, hence, the way out of poverty is not simply a matter of throwing resources at the problem. More important, it is a matter of using resources well. Generally, the key driver of strong growth performance is the capability of firms, not the level of saving or investment per se (Sutton 2000). The case is best documented for member economies of the Organisation for Economic Co-operation and Development (OECD). In such economies, the same level of investment produces significantly different levels of income. Using resources well is far from trivial. Otherwise, central planning would work, and all resource-rich economies would do well. By the same

> *Getting a job has nothing to do with what you learn in school.*
>
> —A poor person, Uganda

token, the primary purpose of improving the investment climate is not to raise money, but to create the conditions under which humans innovate and spread improvements in economic performance. Under those conditions, investment then follows.

Innovation and Diffusion of Best Practice

To generate widespread growth, an economic system should fulfill a number of functions. First, the system should generate technical and organizational innovation to provide productivity improvements and, thus, the basis for increased living standards. Second, the system should help diffuse the benefits throughout an economy and across borders, thereby ensuring that scarce resources are used as efficiently as possible everywhere.

Innovation—Choosing among Experiments. Economic growth can be characterized as a process in which humans experiment by constantly recombining existing building blocks in innovative ways (Burke 1995, Romer 1993). For example, the computer built on several preceding innovations, such as the invention of binary arithmetic, symbolic logic, the punch card, the audion tube, and the concepts of programming and feedback (Drucker 1998). The critical element that humans add in the growth process is ideas, not physical resources. Physical resources have always been on earth.[2] In practice, innovation and adaptation require freedom for individuals and firms to try out new ways of doing things, be they technical or organizational.

Not all ideas and experiments can be pursued at the same time for lack of existing capacity. Somebody needs to determine which ones to support and which ones to discontinue. Making such decisions is a key function of the financial system. From this perspective, the financial system encompasses not only banks and capital markets, but also managers of large firms whose core duty is to allocate funds. The financial system is, in part, like the brain of the economy, determining what to do and not to do. A significant part of the value of the financial sector comes from that decisionmaking role, not from the mechanics of moving funds around. The transfer of funds is to some degree simply the outcome of the decision on what activity to back and how to match providers of funds with users of funds.

The role of the financial sector becomes more critical as the complexity of economies increases (box 2.1). In many low-income countries and regions, fairly simple financial sectors are adequate to provide financial services. Even in advancing countries such as the Republic of Korea, for many years a fairly regimented financial system was able to allocate funds reasonably well. In Korea, as in many other industrial countries, the critical financial decisions have often been made within large firms rather than by the formal financial system. A key point is that managers allocating internally generated funds are a critical part of the financial system.

Making decisions on the funding of experiments is a matter of making informed bets. There is no way of anticipating which experiments will be most valuable with any degree of precision (box 2.2). It remains a matter of opinion. The best one can do is to tap the vast amount of knowledge that is dispersed among humans. Competition among people and firms tends to encourage performance better than centralized hierarchies at collecting and aggregating opinions and local knowledge (Allen and Gale 2000), and better performance is a main reason to organize financial markets competitively. The process of convincing dispersed owners of existing resources to back decisions with funds is reflected in the resource mobilization efforts of financial institutions. Again, the true underlying value is not the mechanics of raising resources, but the underlying decisionmaking process.

As economic growth proceeds, the number of building blocks that can be rearranged increases. Hence, the number of experiments increases dramatically.[3] As new experiments proliferate, it becomes harder to sort through them. Improved science can help rule out fruitless experiments. To some extent, firms find ways of increasing the speed with which they sort through a very large number of experiments (as happens, for example, in the pharmaceutical industry). Yet not all of the rapidly increasing number of experiments can be undertaken. Therefore, making the right bet on what

Box 2.1. Financial Sector Development and Poverty Reduction

Financial sector activities strike many people as unrelated to poverty reduction, if not opposed to it. Particularly fancy capital market transactions using swaps, options, and other derivatives evoke images of "casino capitalism"— of outrageous remuneration for obnoxious and greedy traders. Bank-based systems may remind people of bankers with a heart of stone.

Yet more and more studies demonstrate that a well-developed financial system is critical for growth and, thus, also for poverty reduction (figure 2.1; see also Khan 2000). A well-functioning financial system allocates savings to the best possible uses. It is the brain of the economy that determines what gets done and what does not. Central planning—the functional equivalent of the financial sector—has failed. Decentralized decisions in financial markets made by competing actors are the superior way to raise growth—provided they are embedded in an adequate prudential framework.

FIGURE 2.1. Financial Depth Generates Subsequent Growth

Ratio of liquid liabilities to GDP, 1960

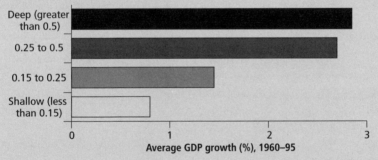

Deep (greater than 0.5)

0.25 to 0.5

0.15 to 0.25

Shallow (less than 0.15)

0   1   2   3

Average GDP growth (%), 1960–95

Source: World Bank 2001d.

There is, thus, little more important for poverty reduction than the development of financial institutions that make sound decisions. It is not clear that any particular type of financial institution works better than others. Bank-based financial systems have advantages, as do systems more based on capital markets. The key is to delegate decisions to financial institutions, to have them compete, and to expose them to the consequences of both success and failure, particularly the ability of shareholders to gain from good decisions and to lose their capital when bad decisions are made.

Box 2.2. The Process of Innovation

There are certain recurring factors at work in the process of change. The first is, as expected, that an innovation occurs as the result of deliberate attempts to develop it. When Thomas Edison began developing the incandescent light bulb, he did so in response to the inadequacy of the arc light. All the means were available: a vacuum pump to evacuate the bulb, an electric current, the filament concept that the arc light itself used, and carbon for the filament.

A second factor, which recurs frequently, is that the attempt to find one thing leads to the discovery of another. William Perkin was in search of an artificial form of quinine, using some of the molecular combinations available in coal tar, when the black sludge that resulted from one of his experiments turned out to be the first artificial aniline dye.

Another factor is that unrelated developments often have a decisive effect on the main event. The existence of a pegged cylinder as a control mechanism for automated organs gave Basile Bouchon the idea of using perforated paper for use in the silk loom.

Motives such as war and religion may also act as main stimulants to innovation. Use of the cannon in the 14th and 15th centuries led to defensive architectural developments, which made use of astronomical instruments that became the basic tools of mapmaking.

Accidents and unforeseen circumstances play a leading role in innovation. When the earl of Dundonald's coal distillation kiln exploded and the vapors ignited, investigation into the gases resulted in the production of coal gas. Physical and climatic conditions also play their part. In the early 19th century, the prevalence of malaria in Florida, spread by mosquitoes breeding in the swamps surrounding the town of Apalachicola, spurred John Gorrie to develop the icemaking machine and air-conditioning system in an attempt to cure his patients, in the mistaken belief that the disease was related directly to summer temperatures and miasma rising from rotting vegetation.

Source: Burke 1995.

experiment to pursue is both harder and increasingly valuable. In a way, the importance of doing the right thing rises relative to the extent to which one is doing things right. A well-functioning financial sector thus becomes increasingly valuable, as do competitive conditions in the financial sector.

Diffusion—Moving Average Practice Toward Best Practice. Once new and useful things have been developed, including products, services and organizational solutions, they can be adopted and adapted elsewhere. Adaptation, which is a form of innovation, is often involved in diffusion processes (for example, when agricultural innovations are transferred to new farming environments). For developing countries, the new options provided by advanced economies allow leapfrogging of whole stages of development by bringing average domestic practice closer to global best practice. A key challenge for policymakers is, thus, to develop approaches that facilitate the diffusion and adaptation of best practices across borders and within countries in response to consumer demand.

Competitive markets are key mechanisms that provide the incentive to adopt and adapt best practice (Blundell, Griffith, and Van Reenan 1995; Frantzen 2000; Geroski 1990; Nickell 1996; Nickell, Nicolitsas, and Dryden 1997; Porter 1990; Porter and Sakakibara 2001; World Bank 2001e). Traditional economic theory assumes that firms embrace best practice quickly and efficiently; such theory considers the interaction of firms in markets as if only efficient firms existed in the market. In reality, firms are highly heterogeneous. At all times, efficient and mediocre firms coexist in markets. Some firms learn, and some do not. Some are lazy, others dynamic. The heterogeneity of firms implies that usually the biggest productivity gains can be reaped by bringing average practice closer to best practice among firms. Various mechanisms achieve this outcome. Sometimes, new and better firms enter the market and drive out old, less-productive firms. In other instances, the market for corporate control improves the match of people, ideas, assets, and cash. In yet other cases, existing firms learn and improve. Most important for the diffusion of best practice appears to be the selection mechanism that, on the one hand, rewards those firms that innovate or adopt and adapt innovations and, on the other hand, forces those that do not do so to change their ways or fail.

Competition and Cooperation

Trust and the Rule of Law. As societies grow wealthy and continue to innovate, the division of labor and, hence, trade becomes ever more complex. Clearly, for production and trade to occur, abuse of power and stealing need to be contained. Yet economic theory has progressed beyond pointing out the need for a minimal state that ensures a modicum of rule of law and sanctity of property rights. An increasing number of trades happen between individuals who do not know each other. Also, in many trades time of delivery and payment diverge (for example, credit-based transactions). A significant amount of trust is required for the system to function, and information must flow well for people to assess whether their trust is justified or violated. If the incentives arising from gains to trade are sufficient, improved information flow can then enhance the division of labor.

Traditional theory assumed that information was equally available to all actors in the economy. It followed that omniscient market participants and omniscient central planners alike could make rational decisions that would optimize welfare for all. In reality, participants in an economy know more about themselves than others do. They often have incentive to disguise their true condition or motive. Others know this and discount the information they obtain. This problem can lead to a breakdown of trade and the division of labor in the sense that some advantageous trades are not concluded and the costs of engaging in trade (that is, transaction costs) rise.

Both innovation and diffusion processes thus seem to benefit from competition as a central mechanism. Like using mechanisms to deal with information problems, maintaining peace and the rule of law requires cooperation. Systems that have overemphasized cooperation, through central planning at the extreme, not only have seen little innovation; they also have failed to spread best practice that has already been invented, even though one might argue that the transfer of best practice would most easily lend itself to centralized decisionmaking. Clearly the feedback provided by customers who vote with their payment and the freedom of entry for new and better firms is crucial for wealth creation in all its forms. The key to effective growth lies in decentralizing decisions, in empowering citizens, and in tapping their ingenuity and their local and tacit knowledge. At the same time, trust and cooperation are required to reduce the potential for breakdown in the division of labor from information problems and abuse of power.

The market is the most-effective institution yet discovered that is able to match competition and cooperation. Competition consists of consumer choice, free entry for new entrepreneurs, and free exit for firms that fail. Cooperation is facilitated by the infrastructure of markets. Markets provide incentives to develop reputation and, thus, generate trust. Furthermore, a number of organizations, such as firms and other intermediaries (for example, consultants, accountants, auditors, exchanges, and arbiters)—as well as economywide rules (for example, the rule of law) and organizations (for example, standards and metrology institutes)—have developed to help markets cope with breakdowns of trade. The rules formalize an underlying system of trust that sustains the complex division of labor. Without that underlying trust, institutions, including markets, would lose legitimacy and fail to perform. Without competition, they would ossify.

For the division of labor to become more complex and to lay the ground for increases in wealth, the effective coexistence of state, community, and markets is critical. In particular, markets are not mechanisms to render the state or civic action superfluous. This book argues for extensive use of competition and market-type disciplines. That position is based on the view that competition, appropriately applied, renders the state and communities more effective—not that it renders them unnecessary. The role of the state thus becomes focused on providing the framework for markets on the basis of private ownership and entrepreneurship. The spirit of the basic approach is captured in figure 2.2, which depicts key mechanisms to enhance state capability. In addition, this book does not take the view that competition systematically undermines the social fabric and thus the very basis on which functioning markets rest. That issue is addressed later.

FIGURE 2.2. Mechanisms to Enhance State Capability: Three Drivers of Governance Reform

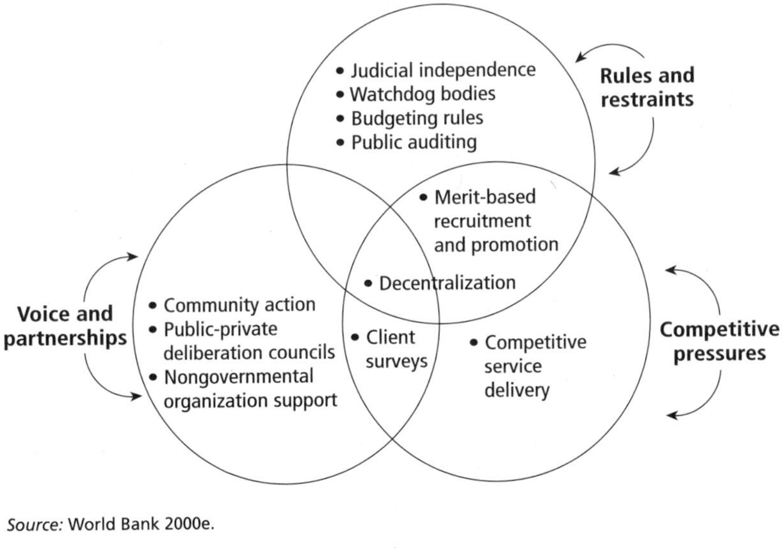

- Judicial independence
- Watchdog bodies
- Budgeting rules
- Public auditing

Rules and restraints

- Merit-based recruitment and promotion
- Decentralization

Voice and partnerships

- Community action
- Public-private deliberation councils
- Nongovernmental organization support

- Client surveys

- Competitive service delivery

Competitive pressures

Source: World Bank 2000e.

25

Even when structural market conditions are propitious, competition needs the appropriate framework set by government and the commercial culture in order to work effectively. The framework includes laws that establish rights to tangible and intellectual property and that create the ability to undertake transactions at reasonable costs; contract law and contract dispute resolution that facilitates striking up flexible and reliable commercial agreements without undue costs and delays; and laws to credibly protect consumers and employees from torts and fraud, not for the purpose of promoting litigation, but to inspire due care and truthful dealings. Other prerequisites for the propitious functioning of markets that are based on private ownership and entrepreneurship involve the business culture and code of conduct, as they are shaped by competition law, enforcement mechanisms, and the social ethics of the business community. It is critical that competing suppliers not conspire against customers by rigging bids, dividing markets, or engaging in boycott tactics.

Overall, establishing the right investment climate includes the task of establishing effective markets, including their institutional infrastructure (figure 2.3; see also Stern 2001). Such markets have the capability to

FIGURE 2.3. The Rate of Investment Is Higher in Indian States with the Best Investment Climate

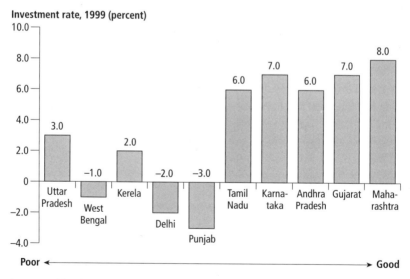

Source: World Bank 2002c.

spread best practice, to support innovation, and to solve the problems of cooperation that arise. They thus create the conditions for successful investment that ultimately brings more and improved jobs to the poor.

The Ecology of Firms

A number of studies have been performed in both industrial and developing economies during the past decade that shed light on how firms in private markets actually perform the functions outlined above. The studies reveal basic regularities among all types of markets in all types of countries.[4] Typically, an industry is created following some innovation. Initially, lots of small, innovative firms enter. Some make it (box 2.3). Most do not survive a phase of shakeout, after which the industry settles into a more regular pattern, in which most people work in small and medium-size firms. In competitive markets, there is a high degree of churning among smaller enterprises. Some 5–20 percent of companies enter and exit the market each year. Often half of these firms do not last for more than 5 years. The fastest-growing enterprises are typically small firms. Some of those firms become large or are acquired by larger ones. Large enterprises do not

---

Box 2.3. Markets, the State, and Innovation

Airspeed Limited was one of the hundreds of small companies that were inventing, building, and selling airplanes in the 1920s and 1930s. Nevil Shute Norway, the owner, estimated that 100,000 different varieties of airplane were flown during those years. All over the world, enthusiastic inventors were selling airplanes to intrepid pilots and to fledgling airlines. Many of the pilots crashed, and many of the airlines became bankrupt. Out of 100,000 types of airplanes, about 100 survived to form the basis of modern aviation. The evolution of airplanes was strictly a Darwinian process in which almost all the varieties of airplanes failed, just as almost all species of animals become extinct. Because of the rigorous selection, the few surviving airplanes are astonishingly reliable, economical, and safe.

The Darwinian process is ruthless because it depends on failure. It worked well in the evolution of airplanes because the airplanes were small, the

(Box continues on the following page.)

Box 2.3. (continued)

companies that built them were small, and the cost of failure in money and lives was tolerable. Planes crashed, pilots were killed, and investors were ruined, but the scale of the losses was not large enough to halt the process of evolution. After the crashes, new pilots and new investors with dreams of glory would always appear. And so the selection process continued, weeding out the unfit, until airplanes and companies had grown so large that further weeding was officially discouraged. Norway's company was one of the few that survived the weeding and became commercially profitable. As a result, it was bought out and became a division of De Havilland, losing the freedom to make its own decisions and take its own risks. Even before De Havilland took over the company, however, Norway decided that the business was no longer fun. He stopped building airplanes and started his new career as a novelist.

The evolution of airships was a different story, dominated by politicians rather than by investors. British politicians in the 1920s were acutely aware that the century of worldwide British hegemony based on sea power had come to an end. The British empire was still the biggest in the world, but it could no longer rely on the Royal Navy to hold it together. Most of the leading politicians, both Conservative and Labour, still had dreams of empire. They were told by their military and political advisers that in the modern world air power was replacing sea power as the emblem of greatness. So they looked to air power as the wave of the future that would keep the United Kingdom on top of the world. And in this context, it was natural for them to think of airships rather than airplanes as the vehicles of imperial authority. Airships were superficially like oceanliners—big and visually impressive. Airships could fly nonstop from one end of the empire to the other. Important politicians could fly in airships from remote dominions to meetings in London without being forced to neglect their domestic constituencies for a month. In contrast, airplanes were small, noisy, ugly, and thought unworthy of such a lofty purpose. Airplanes at that time could not routinely fly over oceans; they could not stay aloft for long and were everywhere dependent on local bases. Airplanes were useful for fighting local battles, but not for administering a worldwide empire.

Source: Dyson 1998.

grow as fast, but they live longer. Multiplant companies live longest. Some large firms fall back into the fray of smaller ones or are bought up.

In advanced markets, large firms are often much bigger than economies of scale in production technique, logistics, or marketing would indicate as the optimal size. Economies of scale tend to explain why some industries consist, on average, of relatively small firms and others of relatively large firms. However, the firm size distribution within any industry is broadly similar. The coexistence of both very small and very large enterprises requires explanations other than economies of scale.

At the birth of an industry, small businesses are critical. In more mature sectors, larger enterprises take on greater relative importance. New small firms entering the market tend to be a little more productive than the ones exiting (Tybout 2000). They enter because, on average, they correctly expect to have a better chance to survive than the low-performing small companies currently in the market. However, most new ones are not able to survive for long and to grow. Large firms tend to be more productive than smaller ones, to pay higher wages, and to provide more job security. Studies of the underlying link between size and productivity suggest that size is not the cause of productivity and growth. In fact, causality runs the other way: more-productive firms grow and become large (figure 2.4). Growth in the size of firms accounts for over two-thirds of all industry growth (Rajan and Zingales 1998). Job growth, in turn, happens mostly in those companies that increase productivity (Batra and Tan 1995).

> *The rich have one permanent job; the poor are rich in many jobs.*
>
> —Poor man, Pakistan, 1996

Advanced economies are characterized by firms of larger size (figure 2.5). Larger enterprises reflect a more sophisticated division of labor among employees than would be possible if the employees formed independent competing businesses. Larger firm size is made easier as the rule of law develops and facilitates complex cooperative arrangements. With increases in productivity, firm size and wages rise. At the same time, the division of labor among companies may become more complex. For example, complex subcontracting arrangements and industrial clusters, such as the upper Italian garment industry or the information technology companies of Silicon Valley, may to some extent be able to combine the advantages of large companies with the flexibility of smaller ones. The most-efficient means to stimulate the creation of small and medium-size firms and their collaboration is, in fact, effective management of cities. From the

FIGURE 2.4. Firm Size and Total Factor Productivity, Percentage Gain in Productivity as Firms Grow in Size

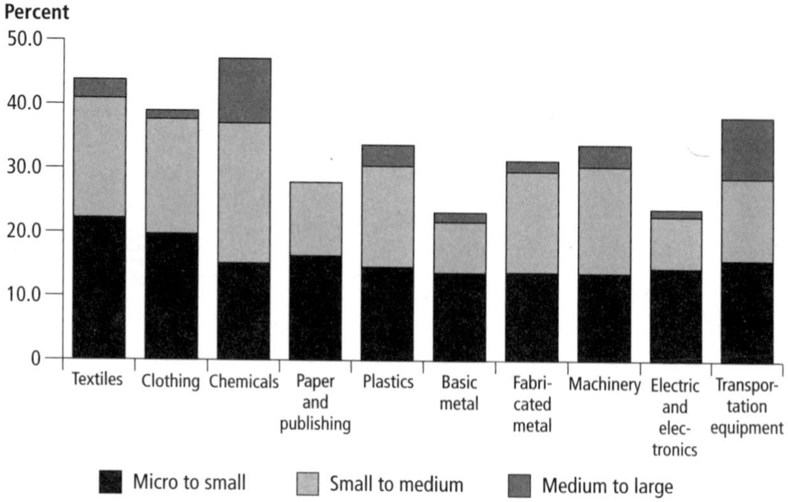

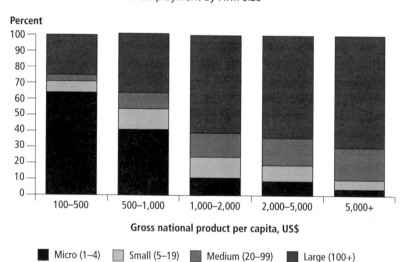

Source: Based on Aw 2002.

FIGURE 2.5. Distribution of Employment by Firm Size

Source: Hallberg 2000. Reprinted with permission. See Snodgrass and Biggs 1996 for more information.

perspective of businesses, cities are agglomerations that support information flow and trade and that enable cooperation, as well as competition, between firms (Glaeser 1998).

Larger firms—whether foreign or domestic—tend to be at the apex of subcontracting chains. Likewise, they are often key to the development of clusters (Nugent and Yhee 2002). They provide credit to subcontractors as well as technical assistance. In particular, where financial markets are not very well developed and where enterprises that are not well connected politically are rationed out of the market, large firms may constitute the key channel to access credit. There is, thus, a clear symbiosis between large firms and small and medium-size firms, with each dependent on the other.

By relying on foreign investment, countries can import more productive companies and stimulate productivity improvements throughout the economy. Foreign direct investment (FDI) is not just the domain of large multinationals but also includes medium-size firms (for example, in textiles and garments). The key point is that FDI can speed up the structural shift in the economy that is required for growth. From this perspective, sound policies that support FDI are among the best ways to develop domestic small and medium-size companies. The main channels for this effect are contracting relationships.

Large firms are institutions that deal with market failures by internalizing certain decisions (Williamson 1975). In particular, they cope with some of the information asymmetries that plague financial markets. For example, outside financiers may have a hard time telling good from bad credit risks. Hence, we observe that most investments are funded from retained earnings. Debt finances only a small part of investments, and equity financing makes hardly a net contribution to investment in most cases (Mayer 1989). In fact, large firms are able to fund subsidiaries that would have a hard time obtaining funds in the open market. Large firms are, in this sense, part of the financial system. The internal market for corporate control matches funds with assets, people, and ideas—again a way of dealing with market failures in financial markets. This issue is also relevant for the argument that small companies embody ideas, the benefits of which may not all be captured by the firms themselves. Large firms— by buying up innovative businesses or by encouraging ideas within their internal market for corporate control—are a mechanism to deal with this issue.

Presumably firms can improve on financial markets because of the long-term interaction between the corporate center of large, long-lived firms and their subsidiaries that gives rise to an interest in maintaining reputation among the players concerned. There is thus an incentive for the subsidiary to reveal correct information, in addition to a mechanism for the corporate center to detect cheating and to punish cheaters over the long haul. Similarly, long-term interaction allows improved technology and skill transfer, as well as cooperation, between large, long-lived firms and subcontractors—again because of reputational interests of the players involved. In all of this process, the fact that large firms live longest is crucial for the functioning of the reputational mechanism.

In advanced economies, reputational mechanisms are enhanced by economywide rules on corporate governance that enjoy legal protection. In developing countries, large firms substitute for such a system of rules and enforcement. Business groups and family networks are the dominant players, economically and often politically. However, when the rule of law becomes more important, on average firms do not become smaller, they become even bigger. The rule of law is a complement, not a substitute, for firm size. At the same time, concentration of market share tends to shrink because value-added grows even faster than firms do. Also, because of better protection of the rights of outside investors, enterprises are able to attract wider sources of capital. An effective legal system thus allows a more equal playing field with more competition, a more complex division of labor within firms, and a more-sophisticated market for corporate control.

There is thus an ecology of firms. Many different and quite heterogeneous companies compete and cooperate. The ecology will do well when the most innovative and efficient tend to survive while the other ones fail. In typical markets, companies evolve ways of dealing with diffusion, market failure, and decisions on which experiments to fund. A more complex division of labor is associated with an overall increase in firm size, and firm size is, in turn, associated with higher wages and greater stability of employment.

For the ecology of firms to work well, it is important that the selection mechanism between good and bad enterprises works well. In particular, entry and exit decisions must be reasonably free of political bias. In practice, in many countries large incumbent firms exert political influence at the expense of small and medium-size firms as well as foreign entrants. This practice leads to a "missing middle" of new and dynamic small and medium-size businesses in both urban and rural areas. Establishing an equal playing field for all types of enterprises is often one of the most politically difficult parts of reform. Neither large nor small or medium-size firms should be favored. What should be favored are competition and the rule of law. Monopoly, stealing, and cheating are the problem, not size per se.

Establishing Competitive Markets: Entry, Choice, and Exit

Entry and Operations

Among countries and within countries, the largest potential for widespread and fast growth lies in bringing average practice closer to best practice. It is well known that productivity levels vary substantially among countries. The cross-border transfer of ideas and best practice happens through multiple channels—imports of new products and capital goods, cross-border flows of ideas and information, education abroad, employment of expatriates and consultants, advice and support from buyers of products and services, and so on.

A particularly powerful mechanism is FDI (Foley 2001). Foreign investors, whether large or small, are able to bundle funds, management expertise, technology, and so on in ways most appropriate for producing particular goods and services. Typically, countries catching up fast with world best practice have opened up trade and used FDI (for example, Chile, China, Ireland, Malaysia, Singapore, and Thailand) to stimulate growth and productivity. It is possible to grow fast without FDI as Japan and the Republic of Korea have shown. Although many countries have tried to imitate their success, none has fully succeeded (box 2.4).

Inside countries, the mobility of people, ideas, firms, products, and services is equally critical for effective diffusion of best practice. It appears that productivity levels among firms and sectors within countries—relative to world best practice—vary less when mobility of products and factors of production is high and when competitive conditions prevail (Blomstrom and Kokko 1996; Elmeskov and Scarpetta 2000; McKinsey Global Institute 1994, 1997, 1998a, 1998b, 1998c, 1999, 2000, 2001, 2002). In a number of cases, local firms fail when more-efficient ones enter from abroad or from another part of the same country. Mobility of labor is then particularly

Box 2.4. Foreign Direct Investment in Africa

Foreign direct investment (FDI) inflows to Sub-Saharan Africa have traditionally gone to resource-based sectors. Sub-Saharan African countries, in general, have not been able to attract FDI because of their small market size, poor infrastructure, political uncertainty, corruption, and restrictive policies toward foreign investment. However, several African countries have recently improved the environment for foreign investment and have managed to attract FDI inflows toward activities in sectors that are not resource based. During 1991–94, only 19 percent of FDI inflows to Sub-Saharan Africa went to countries that were not major exporters of oil or minerals. The share of FDI inflows to those countries rose to about 46 percent in 1995–2000 (figure 2.6). During 1991–94, only 19 percent of FDI inflows to Sub-Saharan Africa went to countries that were not major exporters of oil or minerals. The share of FDI inflows to those countries rose to about 46 percent in 1995–2000 (figure 2.6).

FIGURE 2.6. Foreign Direct Investment in Sub-Saharan Africa, 1991–2000

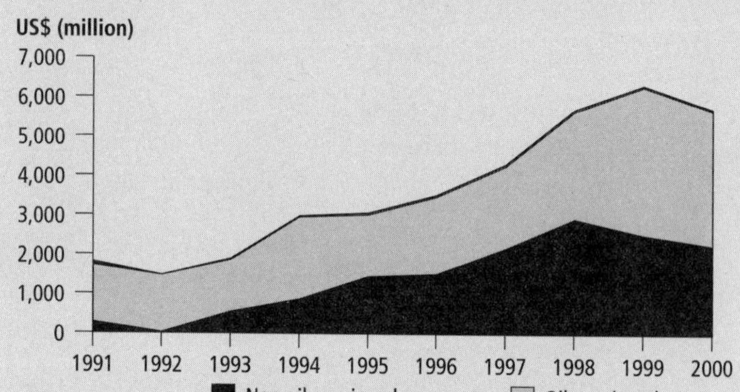

US$ (million)

Source: World Bank 2002a, World Bank World Development Indicators Database.

Countries such as Mozambique, Tanzania, and Uganda, which receive most of the FDI inflows in agriculture, light manufacturing, and utilities, saw sharp increases in FDI inflows in 1995–2000. In Lesotho, FDI has been undertaken to service the market in neighboring South Africa through the Lesotho Highlands Water project (table 2.2).

TABLE 2.2. Foreign Direct Investment Flows in Selected Fast-Growing African Countries, 1991–94 and 1995–2000

Country	1991–94 US$ (million)	1991–94 Ratio to GDP (%)	1995–2000 US$ (million)	1995–2000 Ratio to GDP (%)
Lesotho	11	1.4	230	24.5
Mozambique	29	1.3	153	4.2
Tanzania	21	0.5	163	2.2
Uganda	37	1.0	178	2.8
Total	97	0.9	723	4.0

Note: Data are annual averages. Numbers may not add up because of rounding.

Source: World Bank 2001b; World Bank World Development Indicators Database.

important to provide new jobs that are also likely to be more productive and better paid as the innovations brought by the new entrants spread.

In transition economies, the importance of free entry has been demonstrated starkly during the 1990s. More than privatization of existing assets, entry has been important for the development of dynamic private sectors, as exemplified on the one hand by Poland, where privatization proceeded relatively slowly, but entry was facilitated, and on the other hand by the Russian Federation, where entry was complicated, but privatization of many existing assets proceeded fairly fast (McKinsey Global Institute 1999). China's success is also largely due to opening up entry to domestic quasi-private enterprises (township and village enterprises) and to foreign investors, the latter mostly in the coastal provinces (Graham and Wada 2001, Wei 1995).

Basic policy measures to create external and internal openness are well known—for example, ways to liberalize and deregulate trade and investment (Thomas and Nash 1991). Yet good overall policy may be thwarted by bad implementation, and the devil is, as usual, in the detail. Hence, administrative procedures, such as customs procedures and trade finance regulations and practices, need to be streamlined to support good policy, as well as licensing, registration, tax policies, and so on.

In many developing countries, growth is held back by numerous obstacles that render the operations of firms difficult (table 2.3).[5] Most problematic is macroeconomic instability, which undermines the ability of firms to

TABLE 2.3. Poverty Is Bad for Business: Obstacles to Doing Business in Transition Economies and Developing Countries, 1997

Obstacle	Countries with serious obstacles (percent)	
	Transition economies	Developing countries
Tax regulations or high taxes or both	90	65
Corruption	60	53
Unpredictable judiciary	50	47
Crime and theft	40	35
Lack of financing	30	37
Inadequate infrastructure	10	40

Note: The survey included executives from 20 transition economies and 43 developing countries.

Source: World Bank 1997; detailed results in Pfeffermann and Kisunko 1999.

form reasonable expectations about the future and, thus, to invest. In addition, obstacles include cumbersome registration requirements; restrictions on access to inputs (labor, financing, infrastructure); burdensome administration of taxes and regulations; and so on. As has been widely documented, such excessive regulations and red tape have severely curtailed the performance of firms, be they local small and medium-size enterprises or medium-size to large foreign firms (Brunetti, Kisunko, and Weder 1998; de Soto 1989; Djankov and others 2000; World Bank 2001e). In a number of countries, this problem has created dualistic firm structures—politically well-connected incumbents on the one hand and, on the other hand, numerous small, informal enterprises that are barred from growing and adopting better practices because when they get too successful they get taxed excessively—formally or informally (box 2.5).

Not all restrictions on firms are harmful. Ostensibly, many administrative restrictions serve social goals, such as to protect society from fly-by-night entrepreneurs. Typically, people with criminal records are barred from setting up firms. In some areas, entrants are required to demonstrate competence (for example, medical doctors). However, studies suggest that most entry regulations do not actually serve the public interest; instead they lead to corruption and restrict markets to well-connected firms. Relatively well-functioning markets allow fairly easy free entry (figure 2.8).

In general, good rules for firms are laid down, for example, in a sensible company law and easy administrative procedures. Because bad imple-

Box 2.5. Corruption

There is a vast and growing literature on corruption, highlighting the adverse effect of corruption on economic performance. Mauro (1995) demonstrates that high levels of corruption result in lower levels of investment as a share of gross domestic product. A paper by Tanzi and Davoodi (1997) provides evidence that corruption increases public investment in unproductive projects and lowers the productivity of the public capital stock. Gupta, Davoodi, and Alonso-Terme (1998) confirm that high corruption increases income inequality and poverty through lower economic growth, biased tax systems, poor targeting of social programs, lobbying by the rich for favorable policies that perpetuate inequality in asset ownership, lower social spending, and unequal access to education. Also, see figure 2.7.

FIGURE 2.7. Corruption Is a Regressive Tax: Results from Ecuador

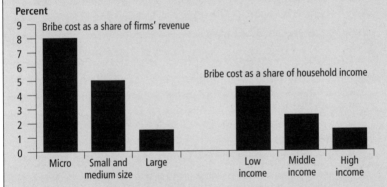

Note: Micro is <11 employees, small and medium size is 11–99 employees, low income is <US$110/month, middle income is US$329/month, and high income is >US$329/month.

Source: Kaufmann, Zoido-Lobaton, and Lee 2000.

A study by Wei (1999) shows that corruption in the host countries has large, statistically significant, negative effects on foreign direct investment (FDI). Wei also shows that there is no robust support for the efficient grease hypothesis—namely, that corruption helps attract FDI by reducing the burden of taxes and capital controls. Drabek and Payne (1999) find that

(Box continues on the following page.)

Box 2.5. (continued)

high levels of nontransparency can greatly retard the amount of FDI that a country might otherwise expect. Countries with relatively high levels of FDI inflows would have attracted even more FDI had corruption been lower.

Abed and Davoodi (2000) probe deeper into the link between corruption and the underlying weaknesses in policies and institutions. They find that progress on structural reforms—defined broadly to comprise the rationalization of state functions, reliance on market-based pricing, and establishment of a sound regulatory environment—is statistically more significant and economically more important than corruption in explaining differences in economic performance as reflected in growth, inflation, the fiscal balance, and FDI. Furthermore, the study shows that structural reform is an important factor in lowering corruption levels; therefore, corruption may mostly be a symptom of underlying policy distortions and weak economic institutions, including missing social trust.

mentation can undermine even the best rules, administrative reform may be necessary. Where excessive interference is the issue, reducing the number of officials responsible for administering rules may be the right approach.

Effective entry and operation also require access to factors of production (labor, financing, infrastructure, intermediate inputs, and so on). Such access requires that the various factor and product markets work reasonably well and that inputs be available on competitive terms. However, competitive does not mean subsidized. Subsidized factors of production all too often destroy value. Many subsidies weaken market discipline and end up supporting politically influential incumbents, thus undermining entry. This problem is of particular importance in the financial sector, which powerful interests routinely abuse in many countries to increase command over resources.

The availability of intermediate inputs is a function of rules governing domestic and international trade. Nondiscriminatory rules are important.

FIGURE 2.8. Regulation of Business Entry

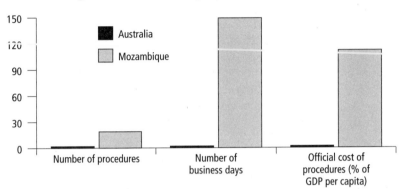

Source: Based on Djankov and others 2000.

In the case of factor markets (for example, financing, labor, infrastructure), openness and competition are key as well. However, in some markets (for example, for infrastructure), competition may not be possible because of bottleneck facilities (natural monopolies) such as networks of pipelines, roads, or wire-based transmission systems. Where natural monopolies exist, the service providers often have weak incentives to render good service. Also, bottleneck facilities are often abused by powerful parties (ranging from some governments to bandits) trying to extract special user fees.[6]

> *We think the earth is generous, but what is the incentive to produce more than the family needs if there are no access roads to get the produce to a market?*
>
> —A poor person, Guatemala

Largely because of bottleneck characteristics, access to infrastructure services such as telecommunications, energy, transport, and water is often a severe constraint for firms, particularly new entrants. In many poor countries, infrastructure costs may add 5–25 percent to the cost of doing business (World Bank 2000a). To the extent that market-type disciplines can be introduced, they promise to improve the provision of infrastructure services. Available options and the contribution of private sector development are discussed in chapter 4.

Consumer Choice and Price Deregulation

The basic points are well known and are equally critical. For markets to work well, prices need to be deregulated. Firms have to be able to set prices that cover all their costs, including the cost of capital. Consumers choose whether to buy goods and services at the price offered. Prices then adjust to balance demand and supply.

If prices are regulated, a number of problems tend to arise. If prices are set too low, there will not be entry or production. Alternatively, quality may be low. When prices are too high, consumers will buy less than they should, entry may be excessive, quality may be excessively high ("goldplated"), or excessive profits may result. Furthermore, when prices are regulated, it is necessary to define prices by product. However, products may be differentiated in myriad ways. Either price controls would impose a straitjacket on product differentiation, or product differentiation would be used to evade price controls. Whatever the precise outcome, price controls shift power from consumers to bureaucrats and tend to protect incumbents from entry by new entrepreneurs.

Although many policymakers have by now acknowledged the wisdom of deregulating prices in markets in which effective competition is possible, a number of concerns actually remain. Relative prices may shift at the time prices are deregulated, creating new winners and losers. Depending on the balance of political influence of the potential winners and losers, governments may be pressured to shy away from deregulation. A typical case is that of petroleum product prices, for which free markets are clearly feasible, but many governments still maintain price controls. Overall, price deregulation typically risks creating unavoidable short-term adjustment costs. Yet such adjustment costs are necessary to allow effective consumer choice and free entry in the long term.

Crucially, social policy goals can be achieved without interfering with the price mechanism. Governments can deploy taxes, subsidies, and quality regulation to achieve desired outcomes in such areas as health, safety, and the environment. In deregulated systems, prices will then adjust to reflect those policy constraints without undermining the basic functioning of the market—hence the trend toward deregulating pricing and entry into traditionally controlled markets such as petroleum products and postal services worldwide. However, price regulation tends to be unavoidable if natural monopolies exist—for example, in infrastructure networks. When other main issues of market power arise, competition authorities may need to take a view on prices and pricing behavior.

Exit

Effective exit mechanisms are part and parcel of effective entry policies. When nonperforming firms are not allowed to fail, they must be propped up with subsidies or other forms of protection. Barriers to exit are, thus, also barriers to entry, because such measures effectively impose a tax on new entrants that do not benefit from them.

Among barriers to exit, we find special protection for labor. For example, some countries render layoffs of workers prohibitively expensive. Typically, such rules benefit a small, relatively privileged class of employees at the expense of new entry and job creation in small and medium-size enterprises. As in the case of entry rules, good exit rules require fairly detailed elaboration, for example, in bankruptcy laws and regulations.

Barriers to exit have been shown to have significant deleterious effects in countries such as India (World Bank 2000c). Hard budget constraints, another term for effective exit mechanisms, have been crucial to the success of the private sector in transition economies, notably Poland (Pinto, Belka, and Krajewski 1993).

Exit is often equated with failure. For example, in many societies personal or business bankruptcy creates a stigma. However, sound exit policies (freedom to fail) are precisely intended to enable assets (people, ideas, funds, and physical assets) to be withdrawn from bad businesses and to be reallocated to better uses. Good exit policies do not destroy assets; bad businesses do. Good exit policies salvage the assets as best as possible and make better use of them—hence the importance of the market for corporate control, which allows assets to be recombined in new and, eventually, more-productive ways (Caves 1998, Klein 2000). Privatization is a key mechanism of the market for corporate control, allowing the transfer of assets from problematic management in the public sector to better management in the private sector.

It is fairly clear what shape effective exit policies take (liquidation, bankruptcy, takeovers, and privatization). However, policies are often hard to implement, especially for larger firms. Large enterprises tend to be politically important and are often able to convince politicians that they are too big to fail. When exit mechanisms fail, they tend to give rise to ballooning, nonperforming assets in the financial system of many countries. Assets thus remain badly used and represent a drag on growth.

Institutional Infrastructure for Markets

Increasing wealth is associated with an increasingly complex division of labor in human societies. A complex division of labor with decentralized competition in markets requires underlying rules, which in turn require widespread acceptance and cooperation among humans. Those rules specify in more or less formal ways the rights and obligations of market participants and, thus, place limits on competitive behavior. Efficient markets always require the coexistence of competition and cooperation.

Key rules are those pertaining to property rights and all forms of regulation—for example, those covering health, safety, environmental, and privacy concerns. To render the rules effective, ways of monitoring them, of settling disputes, and of enforcing judgments are required.

Property Rights

The Importance of Property Rights. It is critical for markets to have a system of property rights that specifies who is able to do what with assets (Barzel 1989). Such a system determines the extent to which people can expect to benefit from the fruit of their efforts and their assets. The minimum prerequisite for effective property rights is some basic social peace. When stealing is rampant—for example, by roving bandits in civil wars or by predatory rulers—incentives to save, invest, and produce are severely reduced, and growth is suppressed. Absence of war and, thus, stealing is clearly an important precondition for development, as is amply clear from studies of the performance of African economies (Collier 2000; Collier and Gunning 1999; Collier and Hoeffler 1998).

Historically, as resources become scarce, some form of property right has indeed tended to develop (North 1982). Such processes of property rights creation in response to increasing scarcity are under way at all times in growing societies, for example, currently in Africa for land rights (Deininger and Binswanger 1999, Deininger and Feder 1999).

Communal rights may develop initially, which specify which member of a community is allowed to use communal property, under what circumstances, and what that person needs to do to maintain the property. Such rights can be very detailed and complex so as to solve the collective action problem raised by the "tragedy of the commons" (Ostrom 1990). They remain prevalent in many traditional societies (for example, the Pacific Islands). The introduction of market-friendly policies in societies with communal property rights requires an adequate understanding of the consequences of such traditional rights for the functioning of markets (Ostrom 1990). Some developing countries initially have informal systems of property rights, such as the rights to profits in township and village enterprises in China, that exhibit some efficient profit-sharing characteristics (McMillan 1995; see also box 2.6).

Greater efficiency can, in principle, be achieved when rights become well defined and tradable by individuals or institutions such as firms. Tradability allows the reallocation of assets to those able to use them most efficiently and not just to those with traditional rights. To some extent, tradability can be established in ways compatible with traditional user rights by making user rights transferable or tradable rather than moving to full private property rights. One of the uses of markets for property rights is that the rights that are put in doubt by bad policy are discounted. Gazprom (Russia's largest company and one of the world's leading gas producers), for example, had a miserable market value of US$6.2 billion in early 2000 at the height of global stock market valuation. With a modicum of good management and protection of the property rights of shareholders, Gazprom could be one of the most valuable companies in the world.[7] Markets can thus reveal policy problems better than many other methods, but, of course, they cannot prevent them automatically.

Creating effective basic property rights is crucial for development (Olson 2000). Various historical studies and econometric simulations suggest that the development of advanced economies out of Europe was based to a significant degree on the emergence of effective property rights (Clague and others 1999; Jones 1999; Rosenberg and Birdzell 1927). A recent study of the 60 poorest countries in the world explores different dimensions of good governance and its effect on growth and incomes of the poor (Dollar and Kraay 2000b). Two key dimensions of governance—democratic choice and respect of property rights—develop broadly in parallel, albeit with significant variations. The study suggests that respect of property rights and contracts contributes to both overall growth and income growth of the poor. Other governance dimensions, such as democratic elections, may provide

Box 2.6. The Emergence of Market Institutions

In traditional subsistence economies, the small-scale village trade exists within a dense social network of informal constraints that are sufficient to facilitate (and regulate) local exchange. Given the limited amount of specialization and the tendency toward self-sufficiency, informal constraints are all the institutionalization that is needed. Transaction costs are low, and the organizational structure of the village is contingent with (and, therefore, tends to perpetuate) the institutional setting. As the market extends to broader areas, regional trade results in sharply higher transaction costs because the dense social network of the village is replaced by less frequent clientization of the players (who are now much more numerous). Hence, more resources must be devoted to measurement and enforcement. Yet institutions are still mainly informal, and, in the absence of any unified political structure or formal rules, cultural norms and religious precepts usually play a key role in setting standards of conduct for the players. In the next stage, the creation of capital markets and the development of manufacturing firms with large amounts of fixed capital entail the need for some form of coercive political order, because as more complex and impersonal forms of exchange evolve, personal ties, voluntary constraints, and ostracism are no longer sufficient to deal with the problems of agency and opportunistic behavior. In the final stage, specialization implies that increasing percentages of the resources of the society will be engaged in transacting so that the service sector now accounts for a large percentage of gross national product.

Realizing the gains from trade inherent in successively more impersonal markets requires institutions that will make possible such impersonal exchanges—not only economic exchanges, but also political ones. Throughout history, most economies have become stuck somewhere along the path. Two critical junctures, for example, where economies have become stuck are as follows:

1. During the creation of economic institutions that would make possible impersonal markets—particularly markets that involve long-distance trade or capital markets that involve contracting over space and time

2. During the development of political institutions that would specify and enforce property rights in ways that encourage productive contracting

Source: de Capitani and North 1994.

some benefits, but they are not associated with the growth of mean income or of the poor (Dollar and Kraay 2000b). Such results remain suggestive and vary by geographic region. In Eastern Europe and the former Soviet Union, for example, democratic development appears associated with economic progress (European Bank for Reconstruction and Development 2000).

The Increasing Complexity of Property Rights. As the division of labor becomes more complex, so do property rights. A case in point is shareholder rights. The overall increase in wealth creates large numbers of people who have some amount of money to invest. The worldwide aging trend reinforces the interest of all these individuals to invest their savings efficiently. Investment in the equity of firms is clearly part of an efficient investment strategy. Small shareholders thus acquire property rights in corporations.

The right of a shareholder is fairly complex. It specifies that, if the firm makes a profit, some agreed upon share of it is due to the small shareholder. Such an agreement requires ways of determining whether, indeed, profit was made and ways of preventing underreporting of income or stealing shareholder property by management. In addition, one has to prevent powerful shareholders from acquiring an unfair share of the profit. Finally, most small shareholders invest through intermediaries such as pension or mutual funds, which act as agents of the shareholders. Again, the behavior of the managers and shareholders of such intermediaries needs to be controlled to render the shareholder's property rights effective. From ultimate shareholder to the manager of firms, complicated agency chains characterize advanced economies (Stiglitz 1999).

Thus, a very complex division of labor is created between savers, fund managers, and managers of firms. Weaknesses in corporate governance lead to expropriation of minority shareholders, reduce investment, and enhance the vulnerability of economies to adverse shocks, as in the case of the Asian crisis of 1997 (Claessens, Djankov, and Lang 2000).

Another complex set of rights that grows in importance as economies develop is rights to information such as new ideas, words, or music (that is, intellectual property rights). Once information is generated, the marginal cost of distributing it can approach zero with modern technology. Furthermore, in many cases, as soon as buyers assess information and whether to buy it, they automatically possess it. Without effective property rights that allow the seller to charge for it, valuable information may never be produced. A whole new array of mechanisms to render effective property rights to information is currently being developed (de Long and Froomkin 2000). For example, mechanisms are being tested that destroy information that has been passed to others for inspection if it is not paid for by a specific deadline—"Mission Impossible" style ("this tape will self-destruct in 5 seconds"). At the other end of the spectrum, there are full-fledged intellectual property rights, such as patents, utility models, and copyrights. At the same time, the debate is on about the right balance between property rights protection (a monopoly on information) and the diffusion of new products and services at least cost (without excessive monopoly profits).

Inevitably, the enhanced division of labor leads to more complex property rights, including detailed contractual arrangements. Yet the more complex the rights, the more reduced the ease of trade in such rights and, hence, the ability to use markets. Thus, the growing complexity of property rights is accompanied by attempts to standardize rights such that they can be traded in liquid markets. For example, shares in firms that are publicly traded are subject to a whole series of listing requirements and other standard accounting and auditing rules (OECD 1999b).

Overall, as economies progress, they first develop basic property rights and later more complex ones that lead to intricate trading arrangements. The more complex the arrangements, the greater the society's capability needs to be to establish and use them. Societies where basic rights to physical property cannot be ensured are, for example, unlikely to benefit from the introduction of complex corporate governance principles protecting minority shareholders. However, individuals living in societies with weak governance systems may still benefit from complex property rights to the extent that they are allowed to trade and invest abroad. Using foreign stock exchanges to list local companies, allowing domestic pension funds to invest abroad, and allowing patents to be registered abroad can enhance the division of labor and, thus, benefit individuals even in societies with low domestic capability.

Quality Regulation

Economic activity creates so-called external effects or externalities. For example, production processes may create safety or health risks for workers or third parties. Firms may mistreat workers, employ children, or use prison labor; in some countries, slaves are still found. Consumers may not be able to assess the quality of products adequately. That inability provides incentives for producers to skimp on quality and to cheat. Economic activity may also burden the environment. The free flow of information may hurt the privacy of individuals. In response to these concerns, which are broadly about the quality of goods and services as well as that of production and consumption processes, quality regulations can be put in place.

Wherever quality regulations are meant to help people choose rather than just limiting choice, it is desirable to create optional quality standards rather than mandatory ones. Such standards help consumers recognize what they are buying but leave them the choice of what kind of quality is best for them. Likewise, where standardized contractual arrangements or standardized property rights, such as corporate governance, are established to help investors choose, it is desirable to allow competing bundles of rights—for example, alternative incorporation or listing options for firms that are each associated with (a) differing degrees of reporting requirements and (b) different levels of flexibility for managers and protection for shareholders.

Quality regulations have proliferated, as growth and, thus, increasing wealth tend to be associated with both a more-complex division of labor and greater demand of citizens for enhanced quality. Although prices have been deregulated across the globe, quality has seen enhanced regulation. This development is, in principle, compatible with efficient markets. Prices adjust to reflect the cost and benefits of quality regulations. However, the prior question always remains: does the quality regulation benefit society more than it costs in the first place (Guasch and Hahn 1999)?

Quality regulations modify property rights to take into account environmental, social, and similar concerns. They limit what people can do with their assets. The value of property rights is the present value of expected net benefits. As prices adjust to reflect the effect of quality regulation on property rights, the cash flow due to the owners of property rights changes, thus affecting the value of these rights. Quality regulations thus act as taxes or subsidies, depending on their net effect. Just as very high taxes undermine incentives to work and invest, so do very tight quality regulations.

Markets for Quality. Quality regulations are part of property rights. In a number of cases, one can use this fact and deploy markets to improve the implementation of quality regulations. For example, regulations may limit polluting emissions, they may limit the use of property to allow public rights-of-way to function, they may regulate the right to use water, they may limit the right to build buildings that affect the view from other adjacent ones, and so on. In all such cases, one can redefine the restriction as the right to do things that are not restricted. For example, if polluting emissions are limited to a certain amount, one can equivalently establish the right to emit pollutants up to a total amount. Such rights may then be traded and allocated to those firms that can achieve the overall goals at least cost because they will be the ones willing to pay most for the right.

The last decade has seen a surge in experiments to use markets to improve the implementation of quality regulations. Cases in point are sulfur dioxide emission trading, fishery rights, water rights, radio spectrum rights, and land development rights (Aarland and Robinson 1999; Arnason 1996; Batstone and Sharp 1999; Bernal and Aliagna 1999; Davidse 1999; Haddad 1997; Joskow, Schmalensee, and Bailey 1998; Klaassen 1999; McMillan 1994; OECD 1992b; Renard 1999; Rosegrant and Gazmuri Schleyer 1994; Runolfson 1999; Thobani 1997; Thorsnes and Simons 1999; Wallis 1999). In all these cases, the initial allocation of rights provides the options to governments to obtain the value of the rights by way of auctions—hence, for example, the recent popularity of spectrum auctions, which literally create money out of thin air (Cramton 1995).

An important overall point is that quality regulations established in a command and control fashion are equivalent to other systems: they can accomplish the same goals that could also be achieved through a mix of taxes and subsidies or through a new set of tradable property rights. Yet market instruments, such as taxation of tradable rights, tend to be more efficient in achieving the goals, where such instruments are possible. Private markets are, thus, not only subject to quality regulation; markets themselves, or market-compatible incentives, can also help implement regulations at least cost.

Ownership and Competition

There is no economic rationale for state ownership of property that is traded in competitive markets. In particular, there is no rationale for state ownership of firms operating in such markets. State ownership is not needed to achieve social goals. The judicious use of quality regulation, taxes, and subsidies can achieve desired social goals in a market-compatible fashion.

Yet it is sometimes said that competition is more important than owner-ship. Indeed, without competition it is harder to obtain lasting benefits from privatization. But when one advocates real competition, one advocates real freedom to fail. Without the genuine threat of exit, competition does not work. Exit requires that owners can lose some or all of their investment and, thus, have the incentive to supervise the management of their company or to sell it so that new owners can improve management. It is thus not very helpful to ask what is more important—ownership or competition? Meaningful competition requires freedom to fail, and even the most-determined governments tend to be loath to allow their firms to fail. The public firm will usually enjoy a list of competitive advantages—for example, implicit government guarantees on its financing and exemptions from laws and regulations.

When government officials try to apply private sector–type disciplines to state-owned firms, as in Sweden, for example, they are sooner or later faced with the decision to liquidate or sell firms. Selling remaining assets as part of liquidation or selling the whole state-owned firm is privatization. Privatization is the takeover of a state-owned firm by new owners. Privatization is, thus, part of an effective market for corporate control.

Privatization activity, in terms of number and value of transactions, has grown rapidly over the past decade. By the late 1990s, an average of 500 privatization transactions was taking place on an annual basis (Kikeri and Nellis 2002). The global proceeds from privatization activity reached about US$142 billion in 1999, up from US$33 billion in 1990, with the total proceeds for the decade amounting to US$837 billion. The bulk of the revenues were accounted for by members of the European Union (figure 2.9).

Between 1990 and 1999, roughly US$316 billion of the privatization proceeds were generated in developing countries and were largely accounted for by infrastructure privatization (mainly of telecommunications and power) and by privatization in the petroleum and mining sectors. Latin America accounted for a large share of privatization activity in the 1990s, followed by Eastern Europe and Central Asia as well as the countries of the East Asia and Pacific region (figure 2.10).

Actual Benefits from Privatization. Privatization is a controversial topic (Bayliss and Hall, 2002a, 2002b, 2002c; International Confederation of Free Trade Unions, Trade Union Advisory Committee, and International Trade Secretariats 2001). Hopes in the magic powers to turn around eco-

FIGURE 2.9. Global Privatization Proceeds

US$ (billion)

■ Non-OECD countries ■ EU countries ■ Other OECD countries ■ Total

Source: Based on Mahboobi 2001.

FIGURE 2.10. Privatization in Developing Countries, by Sector and Region, 1990–99

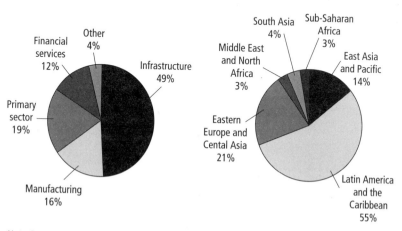

Note: Percentage of total privatization proceeds in developing countries.

Source: World Bank 2001b.

nomic development have been dashed. Several countries that privatized very aggressively have not been rewarded with either quick or sustained growth (for example, Argentina and Russia). In a number of countries, powerful parties have used privatization in its various shapes to grab wealth in kleptocratic fashion. The pitfalls are well known and need to be faced squarely. For example, when privatization of the copper mines of the former Zaire was discussed, parliamentarians correctly argued that the outcome was not likely to be privatization but Mobutuization.

By now, there is a fairly extensive body of evidence on the results of privatization. The basic conclusion is that privatization in broadly competitive markets has, in a large number of cases across all types of countries, yielded better results than the alternative of state ownership. Well over 70 studies have analyzed the effects of privatization, drawing on several thousand privatization cases (Megginson and Netter 2001). Countries all over the world are covered by these studies. They include OECD countries; transition countries; middle-income countries such as Brazil and Mexico; large developing economies such as China and India; and low-income countries such as Bolivia, Côte d'Ivoire, Kenya, Nepal, and countries in the Caribbean (Bernal and Leslie 1999; Boardman and Vining 1989; Boubakri and Cosset 1998, 1999; d'Souza and Megginson 1999; Earle and Estrin 1998; Frydman and others 1999a, 1999b; Havrylyshyn and McGettigan 1999; Jones, Jammal, and Gokur 1999; Kikeri and Nellis 2002; La Porta and Lopez-de-Silanes 1997; Macedo 2000; Megginson, Nash, and Van Randenborgh 1994; Newbery and Pollitt 1997; Pohl and others 1997; Sachs, Zinnes, and Eilat 2000; Sheshinski and Lopez-Calva 1999; Shirley and Walsh 2000). Most of these studies have examined the financial and operational performance of enterprises before and after privatization and have found that, in many instances, privatization has improved performance in terms of productivity and profitability of firms. Analysis of employment and labor market effects of privatization also show that privatization does not always result in unemployment (box 2.7).

The biggest issue in evaluating the results of privatization lies in comparing the outcome of privatization with a sensible view of what would have happened in the absence of privatization. As with any other policy reform (for example, deregulation of prices), it is easy to show that there are losers and winners. The real question is whether overall benefits outweigh costs, whether losers would have done better in the absence of privatization, and whether one could realistically have compensated losers. The studies on

Box 2.7. Privatization and Employment

Public enterprises are usually overstaffed. Consequently, there is concern that privatization causes unemployment. But the evidence is mixed, reflecting differences between industries and countries. Highly protected industries have seen significant employment declines: 80, 72, and 50 percent, respectively, in Argentina's railway, petroleum, and electricity enterprises; 82 percent in Brazil's railroads; and 42 percent in Manila's water utility. However, resulting productivity improvements (370 percent in the case of Argentina's railways) have meant higher wages and performance-based incentives for employees who remain. By contrast, competitive firms and firms in high-growth sectors (telecommunications) are often sold with their labor force intact, with private buyers willing to absorb modest surpluses on account of new investments and expansion. More and more studies show that such expansion has increased employment in privatized companies. Sectoral employment has also grown, particularly when privatization is combined with deregulation. Between 1990 and 1994, 26 Asian and Latin American countries saw employment in newly competitive markets increase by 21 percent, compared with 3 percent in monopoly markets (Petrazzini and Clark 1996). Fears of privatization resulting in rising unemployment levels seem to be unfounded. A study of Argentina suggests that the ambitious privatization program was not a major contributor to the rise in unemployment between 1993 and 1995, but the tequila effect of an interest rate shock was a contributor (Chisari, Estache, and Romero 1999).

Although some workers may benefit, others may be adversely affected, and measures to mitigate the social effects become important. Administrative leave and other such arrangements have been used in China and the Russian Federation, where social obligations make separations difficult. Usually, though, labor reductions have been achieved through voluntary departures by providing those who leave with generous severance benefits and employee shares. Such approaches minimize political and social costs, and their financial and economic returns can be high, but the key is to design packages that are both attractive to workers and that are also sustainable. Retraining programs are often adopted to equip workers with skills to shift to other activities quickly, but rigorous evaluations question their cost-effectiveness. Targeted, demand-driven support on a pilot basis with performance-based delivery (as in the former Yugoslav Republic of Macedonia and Turkey) may

> *have better chances of succeeding. In economies where state enterprises dominate and social safety nets are lacking, these efforts need to proceed in parallel with macroeconomic and labor market reforms aimed at eliminating obstacles to private job creation, improving labor mobility, and developing social protection systems.*

these matters, including analyses of more-complicated privatizations of natural monopolies in infrastructure sectors, show that, compared with realistic counterfactuals, privatization efforts have often done remarkably well (Galal and others 1994; see also chapter 4).

Thus, there is clear potential in privatization. And there is, by now, a better, albeit unsurprising, appreciation of why privatization has, in a number of cases, fallen well short of hopes placed in it. In particular, where privatization was not accompanied by effective deregulation of entry and, thus, the creation of effective competition, it has had disappointing results, as in Russia. In such cases, powerful political forces have also been able to obtain assets in ways that may have worsened significantly the distribution of assets. Nevertheless, even in these cases, it seems that, on average, privatized firms have not performed worse than state-owned ones, apparently because of the so-called agency problems of state-owned firms.

Agency Problems in the Public Sector versus the Private Sector. Owners of government firms are the taxpayers. They do not directly and visibly suffer from mismanagement of particular state-owned firms. Government officials thus tend to have relatively ample discretion (in relation to taxpayers) to deal with state-owned firms and their management. Often they are reluctant to let firms go under, and can afford to prevent such failures by providing some form of subsidy or protection, which ends up hurting taxpayers. In other words, the agency chain from taxpayer to manager of state-owned firms typically has weaker discipline than that from shareholders to managers of private enterprises (box 2.8) (Brealey, Cooper, and Habib 1997; see also chapter 5). In short, it pays to insulate firms from political interference.

However, the experience of the 1990s suggests that privatization by selling shares to widely dispersed shareholders in countries with weak corporate governance systems may not improve performance by much.

Box 2.8. Privatization and the Cost of Capital

When evaluating the costs and benefits of privatization, analysts sometimes suggest using cost of capital for state-owned firms that is different from that for privately owned ones. If we consequently discount the net benefits from privatization at a higher rate than the net benefits from alternative state ownership, privatization makes sense only if the performance improvements from privatization more than compensate for the higher cost of capital of the private sector.

Indeed, the interest rate on state borrowing—the so-called risk-free rate— is typically lower than that of credit to private firms in the same credit market. However, the reason is not that the state has a lower cost of capital, for example, because it would typically manage projects better than the private sector. The reason is that taxpayers are called to serve government debt and often, indirectly, that of state-owned corporations when projects or companies fail in the public sector. Taxpayers thus provide an unremunerated form of credit insurance or callable capital. If the insurance or the callable capital were properly priced, the state's ostensible capital cost advantage would disappear (Brealey, Cooper, and Habib 1997; Klein 1997).

From another perspective, the reason private capital markets are not able to diversify risk perfectly and achieve a cost of capital equal to the risk-free rate is partly due to nondiversifiable systematic risk and partly due to agency costs of raising private financing (Grant and Quiggin 1998). Nondiversifiable risk is, in principle, the same for both the private sector and the public sector, unless policy-induced barriers to risk diversification by the private sector exist. As long as there is no reason to argue that public sector agency chains are better than private sector ones, there is again no argument to assume that the cost of capital for the public sector should be lower than that for the private sector. The higher costs of public sector agency chains show up as unremunerated callable capital or credit insurance provided by taxpayers. Finally, one can argue with a reductio ad absurdum. If the state had a lower cost of capital, it could and should then conduct arbitrage deals by borrowing at low rates and on-lending the proceeds to the private sector at higher rates until all private sector credit demand is met in this way. Alternatively, it would be desirable for the state to provide credit guarantees for all sorts of corporations to reduce their cost of capital. Empirically, we know that neither of these approaches makes sense, as detailed involvement of the state in

> *funding activities in areas in which competitive markets can reign has been a dismal failure.*
>
> *Consequently, privatization makes sense when performance of the private firm is better than that of the state-owned firm evaluated at the appropriate risk-adjusted discount rate.*

The key experiments were the voucher privatizations of transition economies, particularly Russia and the Czech Republic. Weak corporate governance systems mean that the property rights of small shareholders are not well protected. Hence, we have seen expropriation of such shareholders by company insiders and weak incentives for managers to restructure such companies. Company insiders—typically workers and managers—have restructured a little more than under previous state ownership, but not much. Worker representation can sometimes help prevent asset stripping, as occurred in Poland, but it is not generally an effective way to govern the corporation (Hansman and Kraakman 2000). When companies in systems with weak corporate governance have been sold to strategic investors (as was the case, for example, in Hungary), results have been significantly better, because such investors exercise control directly and do not suffer from weak corporate governance (Djankov and Murrell 2002; Nellis 1999).

Once shareholders have been expropriated by insiders, insiders have an incentive to look after their assets. As long as budget constraints are hard—that is, as long as the threat of exit is real—better incentives are likely to emerge, provided that corporate control is well in the hands of shareholders. Rather than using this roundabout way of improving company performance, it is possible to structure privatization such that the state-owned companies are liquidated and their assets are passed to new owners—who may, to some extent, be workers and managers; such restructuring is accompanied by hard budget constraints. This approach has been used in Poland, where parts of firms were sold to individual investors and emphasis was laid on new entry rather than the sale of old firms. Meaningful threat of exit requires that entry by competitors is possible, as was the case in Poland but not in Russia. De jure or de facto exclusivity for private firms severely weakens performance incentives because barriers to entry are barriers to exit and vice versa.

Conditions for Successful Privatization. Privatization is thus clearly most effective when markets are competitive: that is, there is free entry, deregulated pricing, and freedom to fail. The fundamental issues of privatization are thus the same as those of creating real competition (entry, choice, and exit) in any market.

Privatization replaces the taxpayer–to–state manager agency chain with a private investor–to–private manager agency chain. Although all private agency chains typically exert better discipline than public sector ones, privatization in weak corporate governance environments risks producing limited or delayed benefits (Dabrowski, Gomulk, and Rostowski 2001).

Efficiency suffers when governments try to maximize fiscal revenues by selling firms with exclusivity provisions, except in the case of reasonably well-managed natural monopolies such as water pipeline systems (box 2.9). Furthermore, any limits on transparency and eligible bidders reduces the likelihood that the most-efficient party will win and increases the chances that vested interests will acquire the company and will thus worsen asset allocation.

Privatization in Transition Economies. At the outset of transition, much was expected of privatization. Internal reformers and external advisers alike saw private ownership of firms, farms, and factories as the very essence of the shift to the market. There was general agreement that privatization was required to cut the links between the state and productive forces, to build a constituency of property owners who would support and promote reform (and help block any threatened return of the communists), and to place assets in the hands of those with the incentives and skills to use them well.

In addition, there was wide (though not universal) agreement that mass and rapid ownership transfer was the optimal privatization policy. How else could the many thousands of existing inefficient firms be placed in the hands of owners who would carry out the restructuring needed to make those companies competitive and able to survive and thrive in a market environment? Selling them on a case-by-case basis would take decades, and would, it was feared, give antimarket forces time to regroup and halt the transition. With strong intellectual and financial support from Western advisers and the international financial institutions, including the World Bank Group, many transition states embarked on mass privatization through voucher schemes.

Box 2.9. Fiscal Space

Privatization is sometimes sold as a way to create fiscal space. The argument goes that selling state-owned enterprises increases revenues for the state that can be used to fund worthwhile social activities such as education and health care. Privatization is thus depicted as a precondition to helping the poor.

The argument about fiscal space may be good political salesmanship, but it has little substance. When a government sells an enterprise, it receives money now in return for giving up future cash flow. As long as the privatized entity generates the same cash flow as before, nothing has changed. The net wealth of the state has not changed. The state need not have sold a company; it could have borrowed to raise money for social programs.

Only when the state has limited capital market access might privatization be necessary to fund extra programs. But when a state that is not credit- worthy spends privatization revenues on current expenditures, it reduces its creditworthiness even more because its net wealth declines. In such situations, it may be more important to use the receipts from privatization to pay down debt, so that the state becomes creditworthy again. Indeed, a number of governments have used privatization proceeds to pay down the national debt (Barnett 2000).

If the private sector can run the entity better and if the entity is sold com- petitively, then the government receives not only the present value of the future cash flow that it would have received under state ownership, but also the present value of the efficiency gains of the private sector. Such a sale is a real gain to society, and in this case the gain is transferred to government. Selling a firm and then paying down debt would actually increase public sector net worth.

Alternatively, governments may use the real gains from privatization to fund social programs. But the real issue about social programs is whether they are best carried out by the public sector or by other means. In those countries where privatization is most desirable because state ownership works badly, the state is also least likely to conduct social policy well. The real debate is about whether the public sector is best able to provide services to the people, not about fiscal space.

In many cases, it was the firm insiders—workers and particularly managers—who ended up as the dominant owners in firms privatized through vouchers. Recent and rigorous empirical evidence in a study by Djankov and Murrell (2002) shows that insiders as owners do restructure more than state-owned firms. But they are far less effective in this regard than concentrated owners—that is, strategic, core, external investors.

 Moreover, the effects of any and all forms of privatization seem to be much more positive in most of the countries in Central and Eastern Europe than in the Commonwealth of Independent States (CIS), where the effect of ownership change, in terms of restructuring or spurring a return to growth, is so far negligible. These differing regional outcomes seem attributable not simply to the use of vouchers, but also to weaknesses in the legal and institutional fabric in economies long isolated from market operations. That is, the problems of weak and ineffective owners resulting from voucher privatization were exacerbated by the new governments' inability or unwillingness to promulgate, monitor, and enforce the basic set of legal and financial rules required for proper market operations. Most important, hard budget constraints enforced by banks operating at arm's length from borrowers are critical for successful restructuring.

To complicate matters, the promise or implication that distribution of ownership would allow citizens rapidly to share in some rosy and imminent capitalist future, looks, in retrospect, hollow. Two key questions then arise:

1. Could other privatization methods have been used that would have increased the number of concentrated owners? Case-by-case methods worked well in a few transition countries, such as Estonia and Hungary, as well as in the territory of the former German Democratic Republic. But these instances were somewhat special, favored by history and geography. Case-by-case methods proved much more difficult to apply in CIS and southern European transition countries, where the legal and institutional frameworks were not—and generally still are not—sufficiently developed to attract large numbers of core investors. For example, a World Bank-sponsored attempt to use a properly structured case-by-case approach worked poorly in Russia because of the government's inability or unwillingness to put a controlling stake in good firms on the market and because of its failure to follow minimally acceptable commercial procedures or allow free and open bidding. Recent changes in Russian privatization practice, as exemplified by the September 2000 sale of the Onako Oil Company, are promising: market watchers judge this sale to have been much better con-

ducted than those of the past in terms of transparency, because it allowed a controlling share to be sold and generated revenues for government. But, once again, foreign bidders were not allowed. Clearly, there is much more to the matter than simply choosing the right mechanical sales method.

2. Should then these countries have kept their firms in state hands, evolving gradually the ownership and market orientation of firms, while they built up the needed institutional framework? This approach is appealing to many because of its apparently successful application in China, which has enjoyed sustained, high growth rates without—until quite recently—allowing much in the way of formal private ownership. There is great debate concerning just how China has managed this achievement. A few things appear clear. China gradually deregulated domestic markets and granted de facto quasi-private control rights to managers and employees of township and village enterprises (Rodrik 1999a). Foreign investors were welcomed and are associated with the dynamic growth of the coastal provinces. The large, industrial state-owned firms remain a drag on growth. These factors seem to reaffirm the importance of freeing up entry.

Yet any attempt to apply this strategy depends on the state or subnational governments (or some other institution) having the incentives and means to monitor the retained firms to prevent the most egregious asset stripping by managers or their allies. But most transition countries in the CIS have undergone a substantial political transformation in parallel with the economic one. This transformation has weakened or eliminated many of the policy and disciplinary mechanisms required to make this approach feasible. For example, officials in Kazakhstan, concerned that privatization through vouchers was not yielding good owners, but recognizing that unaltered state firms were woefully inefficient, decided to contract out management of a select number of key firms to private suppliers. The approach failed to produce positive results because the same political and institutional factors that impeded privatization blocked the government's efforts to design, monitor, and enforce good contracts. .

Clearly, countries in Central and Eastern Europe and the Baltic states generally have managed to reconstruct a functioning institutional base, and they have been able to attract many concentrated external investors. Those in the CIS are having a tougher time of it on both counts.

The upshot is that there is no easy answer. Privatizing in the absence of adequate legal and regulatory institutions is often problematic on equity grounds, and, in many CIS transition countries at least, it does not seem to offer much in the way of short-run production gains. But keeping the enterprises in state hands and trying to reform them slowly over time has not produced positive results either. By avoiding both economic and political change, Belarus and Uzbekistan have so far managed to avoid the worst dislocation and production declines of transition; however, their increasingly costly efforts are unsustainable.

Hope is found in the study by Djankov and Murrell (2002). While demonstrating that the quantitative performance of privatized firms in the CIS is only slightly better than that of state-owned companies, it shows that privatized firms in that region score much better than state firms on qualitative measures of restructuring—that is, adoption of new business plans, marketing departments, sales procedures, and so on. It may well be that those qualitative indicators of restructuring are harbingers of improved production performance to come, especially as the policy and legal frameworks improve. If so, privatization should proceed, in parallel with efforts to strengthen the policy and institutional bases. Every effort should be made to sell to core, competent investors, and every effort should be made to create and sustain the legal, regulatory underpinnings of market operations along the lines described above.

Rules: Monitoring, Dispute Resolution, and Enforcement

Property rights and quality regulations, which may, in turn, be seen as part of property rights, crucially underpin the functioning of markets in economies with an increasingly complex division of labor. These rules need to be agreed upon, monitored, and enforced.

Setting the Rules. Rules are sometimes set by governments, sometimes by industry associations or other, typically nonprofit, organizations (Slaughter 1997). Merchant law itself has, in some rare cases, emerged by agreement among firms without state intervention (Greif 1989; Greif, Milgrom, and Weingast 1994; Milgrom, North, and Weingast 1990). In fact, merchant law was "nationalized" under Henry II of England when the king allowed appeal against merchant court judgments to state courts (Ridley 1998). The critical point is that many rules of the market can and have emerged through the cooperative agreement of private participants in the market. This observation provides hope that even in weak governance environments the mutual interest of market participants may lead to improved systems of property rights and regulations. Today in Somalia, for example, merchants have come together and formed a sort of police to secure critical areas in Mogadishu. Merchants are currently a key driving force to constitute a new government.

Monitoring Principles and Standards. For countries to monitor whether rules are adhered to, relevant information must flow. Principles of property rights registration have developed to clarify important and complex rights (for example, for land and real estate, patents, securities, vehicles, and so on). Measurement standards have been developed to assess conformance with quality regulations. Accounting standards have developed to assess the performance of firms and, hence, their compliance with obligations in relation to creditors and shareholders.

Such basic principles and standards are public goods. Implementation can be contracted to private agents. Some systems, such as property registration systems (for example, vehicle registration), need to be provided by monopolists. Others may be competitively provided by private agents (rating agencies, accountants, auditors, laboratories, credit information services, and so on), which may or may not need accreditation. These agents are examples of the generic point that the private sector can, in principle, be used to provide any service, once the rules are agreed on.

Dispute Resolution. Of course, disputes may and do arise about ownership and adherence to quality standards. The nature of legal systems appears to be of importance for the effectiveness of dispute settlement in a way that supports efficient markets (Glaeser and Shleifer 2001, La Porta and others 1996a).

Although the legacy of history may, to some extent, determine the effectiveness of judicial systems, systems can be reformed. Even without wholesale reform of legal systems, firms and individuals can obtain dispute settlement through a variety of options. Most disputes are, in any case, settled out of court using a variety of arbitration and dispute settlement mechanisms (Aubert 1969). Within countries, alternative dispute settlement mechanisms are available that may present procedural and cost advantages, including "rent-a-judge" systems, in which both parties to a dispute agree to employ a judge among several competing ones. International arbitration systems allow parties to import a dispute resolution mechanism to improve on locally available options. Within the judicial system itself, it is thus possible to benefit from private provision and competition. Although such options for dispute settlement are available, the state-run legal system provides a backstop system that shapes private forms of dispute resolution.

Enforcement. The best rules, monitoring, and dispute resolution are ineffectual if there is no enforcement capability. Decent police forces are important. Some policing tasks can be contracted out to private agents. In a number of countries, more than half the policing activities are contracted out to private security firms (box 2.10).

But markets arose even before decent police forces existed, and they continue to function in areas beyond the law. Enforcement of rules such as the privately agreed-upon merchant law was possible in medieval days because market participants had a continuing interest in participating in trade. A reasonable flow of information is required for violations to be detected. Violations led to outcasting from the trading community and,

---

Box 2.10. Private Security

In the 1990s, private security companies with publicly traded stocks grew at twice the rate of the Dow Jones industrial average. In the United States, more than twice as much money is spent on private security as on law enforcement, and private firms employ three times as many people as public agencies. Public security companies are taking on functions once performed by governments. For example, many U.S. embassies and consulates are guarded by employees of DynCorp, a private contractor based in Virginia.

Since 1984, the number of security firms in Germany has doubled; their payrolls have more than tripled. In the United Kingdom, the number of people employed by security firms rose from 10,000 in 1950 to more than 250,000 in 2000. About half of the growth in the global security industry has been new business and about half substitution, as large corporations contract out for security services they once provided in-house.

Source: Kelly 2000.

hence, the loss of gains from future trade as punishment. Such reputational mechanisms underlie contract and property rights enforcement in many societies. Notably, special ethnic groups (such as traders in Morocco and moneylenders in India) or large groups of families (for example, Chinese family enterprises) are particularly effective in running such enforcement systems, because information flows well among the related parties and outcasting can be enforced (Akerlof 1976, Greif 1989).

It bears stressing that interest in participating in future trade or future access to financing is a powerful incentive to play by the rules. Any effective legal system relies heavily on voluntary compliance (Aubert 1969). Even in illegal markets, enforcement is—contrary to myth—typically not enforced by knee-breaking but by the interests of parties to deal again in the future (Reuter 1984).

Next to outcasting, collateral simplifies contract enforcement. Collateral rights provide a creditor with rights to property that can be attached relatively easily. The credit may then support activities with cash flows, the rights to which are hard to predict beforehand and are difficult to determine and enforce afterward. Even if collateral rights are hard to enforce in practice, the fact that the borrower actually owns property typically renders the borrower more interested in observing the rules of the game than if he or she were a footloose type (*The Economist* 2001, World Bank 1998).

Functioning markets thus facilitate enforcement of trading and property rules because they create an interest in future transactions. The fact that property rights create long time horizons on the part of asset owners also helps. As usual, private solutions are also available to contract out policing activities.

At the global level, cross-border enforcement of property rights is typically hard, even if contracting parties have agreed to binding international arbitration. Among responsible countries, domestic police forces enforce internationally binding rules and judgments. When a country does not enforce such rules and judgments, it may, to some limited degree, be possible to attach assets held abroad. However, responsible behavior among countries depends fundamentally on their interest to do business again in the future—hence, the fear of sovereign default, which may lead to prolonged loss of access to capital markets.

Unsurprisingly, countries are particularly interested in maintaining decent relations when it comes to sovereign credit or to upholding other specific sovereign undertakings. Because countries increasingly turned to introducing market forces and opened up to cross-border trade and investment, outright nationalization largely disappeared after the 1970s. Instead, countries have signed some 2,000 bilateral investment agreements since 1959 (United Nations Conference on Trade and Development 2000). As happened within countries historically, the ever-tighter web of trading and investment relations among countries promises to increase further the effectiveness of agreed-upon rules and standards.

Ownership, Regulation, and Enforcement. It is sometimes argued that regulatory authorities have a hard time enforcing the rules of the game on private firms because firms can disguise their behavior and try to influence the regulator improperly. But the same is true for public firms. Many large public firms are states within the state.

When enterprises are under public ownership, the incentives to enforce regulations tend to be weak, for example, because the politics of prosecuting one part of the government by another can be complicated. Also, government firms may have weak incentives to comply because their fines—even if levied—come from one pocket of the government and go into another. When companies are under private ownership, arm's-length relationships sharpen incentives all around. For example, experience suggests that pollution regulations can be better enforced in the context of privatization, which makes it easier politically to demand transparency and to scrutinize the firm (Lovei 1999, World Bank 1994b).

Some large private firms may be in a similar position as large public firms, with excessively close links to and protection from government. However, the solution is not to choose public ownership but to establish more arm's-length relationships, which are facilitated when there is real competition among private firms.

The fundamental problem is always who guards the guardians. When competition can be introduced, an effective mechanism is at hand, and one can leave discretion in the hands of managers or owners. When a balance of power needs to be created without a good self-regulating system of competition, special costs have to be incurred by reducing discretion and by creating multiple accountability relationships. Doing so increases transaction costs and creates bureaucracy—that is, a form of lack of discretion (Laffont and Tirole 1993). One can try to minimize such costs, but some are unavoidable.

Distribution of Property Rights

The move from freely available resources to communal rights and eventually tradable private property rights has typically important consequences for the distribution of assets and wealth in an economy, as well as for social relationships more broadly. It is useful to remember here that entry rules, quality regulation, and taxation can all be interpreted as features of property rights. Any change to exclusivity rights, to quality regulations, or to taxation (including price regulation) interferes with or adjusts property rights— namely, the expected value of net ben-

> *Kinh people have been applying and writing papers for a year now and still haven't gotten anywhere. The land tenure situation in Vietnam is precarious without official recognition.*
>
> —A poor person, Vietnam

efits their owners could expect (Courcelle-Seneuil 1869). By the same token, there are, thus, numerous possible interventions that can and do change asset distribution in an economy. However, the scope for such interventions is limited by the need to protect existing rights so as to preserve incentives to invest and create jobs.

Disputed and Unclear Rights. Many poor people live on property that they use but do not formally own. In many cases, ownership of such property is disputed or not clearly established. In fact, the situation resembles a little that of communal property with individual use rights, except that uncertainty about use rights may be much higher. Hernando de Soto (2000) estimates that worldwide such disputed property rights that the poor use may be worth some US$9 trillion. Establishing secure title to such property for the poor may enable them to benefit significantly (Deininger and Squire 1997; see also figure 2.11). Secured tradable titles tend to raise the market value of the property, both because uncertainty about ownership and, hence, the duration of the net benefit stream is reduced and because of increased liquidity of markets. Similarly, secured rights provide a greater sense of stability and may induce the new owners to adopt a long-term horizon for their decisionmaking. For example, new owners may become more creditworthy borrowers, even if their property is hard to attach as collateral purely because they now have potentially more to lose by breaking promises and contracts and more to gain by taking care of the property.

FIGURE 2.11. Protection of Property Rights and per Capita GDP

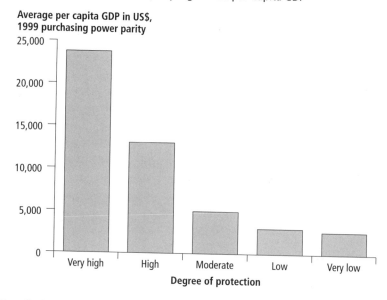

Note: This figure is based on average per capita GDP and the Heritage Foundation's property rights scores for 150 countries.

Source: Hoskins and Erias 2002. Reprinted with permission.

The key to assigning property rights effectively lies in ensuring that rights are, first of all, genuinely unclear and, thus, do not result in simple expropriation of somebody else. Second, streamlined and clear titling and registration procedures are required. In Peru, over 1 million properties have been incorporated under streamlined procedures within 3 years. Gross benefits were estimated at US$1.7 billion.

Privatization and Asset Distribution. Privatization reallocates property rights. Overall, it is desirable that state-owned firms be sold to competent new owners. In principle, these firms should be sold into competitive markets to the highest bidders, whether to strategic investors or to dispersed shareholders. Under such conditions, winning bidders will not earn more than a normal rate of return. The benefits flow to the fiscal authorities. Governments may use revenues from privatization to improve income distribution, for example, using the tax or expenditure system to strengthen the social safety net.

Privatization can also be used to improve asset distribution, for example, by subsidizing share sales to small shareholders. Several governments also hope that such sales to a broad spectrum of citizens establish legitimacy for privatization (popular capitalism). For many developing countries, such approaches are problematic. As discussed previously, the key is a decent system of corporate governance to ensure that small shareholders are not subsequently expropriated by majority owners or managers. The best possible intermediate approach is probably the path taken by Estonia. Estonia sold majority stakes to strategic investors followed by an issue of vouchers to citizens for the remainder of shares. Another mechanism may be to place assets of small shareholders into well-regulated pension funds that can exercise adequate corporate governance, as attempted under the Bolivian capitalization program. As already mentioned, orderly liquidation of failed companies may be used to transfer remaining assets—say trucks—to workers. Such transfers help create new entry and may improve income distribution. When workers subsequently face hard budget constraints, overall efficiency and growth is likely to be enhanced. This model is the basic one used in Poland. Variants are being tried, for example, in Moldova.

New Property Rights. Technical and organizational innovations generate new options to create tradable rights and markets (for example, electricity markets, markets for bandwidth, and so on). When new markets are established through the creation of property rights, these rights should be allocated to those best able to exploit them. Typically, an auction of such rights to the highest bidder is used. However, usually use patterns without formal tradable rights already exist. Firms or individuals may have invested significant capital in the expectation that they would be allowed to continue to fish, to use water, or to use the radio spectrum. New rights, unless they are all grandfathered to existing users, will de facto expropriate incumbents. This problem also exists when communal rights, which tend to consist of complex individual use rights, are rendered tradable. The problem is captured by the old anarchist view that property is theft (Proudhon 1970), which is true in the sense that the establishment of full private property rights may expropriate others who previously expected to be able to use a resource free of charge.

There is, thus, limited scope for reallocating ostensibly new rights, but significant opportunities arise at times. For example, the allocation of some rights to the radio spectrum has generated massive revenues for governments, which can then be used to support social goals.

Existing Property Rights. Interference with existing property rights is problematic because expropriation risks undermining the very basis of markets—that is, the incentive to innovate and invest. Yet interference with existing property rights is not unusual and may take the form of changes in taxation, changes in quality regulation, or changes in competitive conditions in markets (for example, abolition of exclusivity). Outright expropriation also takes place, for example, when land is needed to build highways.

> *Privatizing land consists of wandering between district and national offices for weeks and months at a time.*
>
> —A farm worker, Moldova

Some types of expropriation are compensated. Landowners are compensated for forced land purchases by the highway authority. Utilities losing their exclusivity may be compensated (for example, Singapore Telecom for early opening of the market to competition or electric utilities in the United States for so-called stranded costs—that is, losses from market opening).

If the change to property rights creates overall efficiency gains, it should be possible to compensate those negatively affected and still obtain overall gains for society. This principle is, for example, the rationale for compensating people who are forcibly resettled. However, many changes to property rights through tax adjustments or quality regulations are not compensated. Firms and individuals are expected to anticipate that changes might occur and to adjust early to these prospects. When people do not expect that a particular situation will last, then arguably they never had a property right and, thus, deserve no compensation.

Whether it is land reform or other actions on existing property rights, sound reform requires that, first of all, the intervention enhance overall social benefits. Then, preferably, those who had reason to see themselves as long-term owners of a right should be compensated. Those who should have expected change, however, should not be compensated. It is obviously hard to make that judgment. The creation of a policy process that leads to social improvements and the creation of a reasonably agreed-upon set of expectations as to what does and does not constitute a perpetual right lie at the heart of the issue and have no simple solution. Current new experiments with negotiated approaches to land reform grapple precisely with these issues (World Bank 2000f).

Notes

1. Confucius, 551–479 BC.

2. In a physical sense, resources have not increased beyond what the earth and the sun provide. In fact, there are worries that growth is leading to the exhaustion of natural resources.

3. Building blocks here comprise organizational elements, as well as technologies. In the absence of science, we might hypothesize that the number of experiments increases with the factorial of building blocks (that is, the number of permutations, in which the blocks can be arranged). Just 16 building blocks would give rise to more than 20 trillion permutations.

4. The availability of better data sets gave rise to studies during the 1990s that analyzed the detailed entry and exit patterns of firms. Most of those studies cover OECD countries—mostly the United States—yet another demonstrates that deregulated states produce better data than centrally controlled ones, among other things because there is less political gain from distorting data. But several studies are now also available for developing countries (Audretsch 2002; Aw 2002; Liedholm 2002; Nugent and Yhee 2002). The World Bank's donor-funded Regional Program for Economic Development has generated useful microstudies for Africa over the past decade. See http://www.worldbank.org/afr/findings/french/rped.htm for a list of available studies.

5. Note that administrative barriers to entry do not figure prominently among the complaints of businesses that have already entered the market.

6. Powerful groups, whether officials or private parties are particularly attracted to control of bottleneck facilities—that is, natural monopolies—because such facilities allow them to extract rents. Witness extortion of unofficial road tolls in many poor countries. This problem does not mean that national monopoly companies, whether state run or privately run, should reign supreme and that private entry should be curbed, ostensibly to prevent the entry of mafias. But national champions that may be privately run should be used to compete with other alternatives and to provide choice to consumers. Private monopolies can be just as bad as public monopolies. Unfettered monopoly is the problem—not unfettered markets.

7. Some progress in this direction has led Gazprom's value to rise to US$25 billion by 2002.

3

Public Intervention
to Promote
Supply Response

When reforms have created a good business environment that allows real competition and provides an adequate infrastructure of rules and information systems, one would expect firms to invest and the economy to grow. Yet in many cases economic performance does not appear to improve drastically after reform. The typical debate is whether the cause is incomplete reform or whether the supply response from markets suffers because of market failures. The following debate is equally relevant in urban or rural environments.

Market Failure and Information Asymmetries

A whole series of so-called market failures, like environmental and social effects that are not taken into account in completely unfettered markets, are best dealt with by establishing regulations, taxes and subsidies, or tradable property rights, as discussed in chapter 2. These mechanisms are meant to reshape the incentives of firms and to direct them toward socially desirable goals. All along, it is assumed that businesses recognize what is good for them and do it—that is, they respond to taxes and regulations. The market failures that are at issue when one wonders about adequate supply response are of a different type. In these cases, analysts wonder whether firms do actually recognize what is good for them and then implement it. The general argument rests on information problems. As mentioned before, in reality, market participants know more about themselves than others do. They often have an incentive to disguise their true condition or motive. Their counterparts in transactions know this and discount the information they obtain. Thus, market failure results, in the sense that some advantageous trades are not concluded and the costs of engaging in trade rise (Akerlof 1970, Stiglitz 1989).

The first line of defense against market failure arising from information problems is the institutional infrastructure for markets discussed in chapter 2. Various market intermediaries (for example, consultants, accountants, auditors, exchanges, arbiters) and economywide agencies (for example, standards and metrology institutes, credit bureaus) help economic actors cope with market failure.

Elements of this strategy include the following:

- Developing the policy, legal, and regulatory frameworks that are essential to the creation of innovative financial institutions and instruments, including venture capital, small equity investments, and leasing
- Reducing barriers to entry into the financial sector or subsectors, because a lack of competition in the financial sector invariably leads to the crowding out of financial services to small businesses
- Reducing the risks associated with lending to small businesses, focusing on laws governing the enforcement of contracts, forfeiture and collection of collateral, and use of movable assets as collateral
- Improving information on the creditworthiness of potential borrowers by promoting the establishment of credit bureaus

The second line of defense is firms. Firms are nonmarket organizations that—alone or in concert with other firms—improve on the outcome of hypothetical atomistic markets (Williamson 1975). They are thus institutions that remedy so-called market failure. Extensive evidence from all types of industrial and developing countries shows that when a good business environment is in place, markets select good firms over bad ones (Aw 2002, Tybout 2000). Good firms are the ones that are best able to deal with all business problems, including finding ways to deal with informational market failure so as to conclude all possible profitable trades.

Sometimes firms must grow large so that they can conduct transactions internally that they can monitor better than arm's-length transactions. Sometimes they must form alliances or subcontracting chains that solve information problems. Large firms are typically at the apex of clusters. Generally, the establishment of longer-term relationships with buyers, suppliers, and financiers can help improve on information problems because all parties then have a reputational interest in not cheating too much. At the same time, competitive pressures keep the parties on their toes (Allen and Gale 2000, Hellwig 2000). No particular size of firm is a priori better than the other (Hallberg 2000). Small, medium-size, and large firms form an ecology that solves a variety of business problems. The key to success is that good firms are selected over bad ones through the market.

It is often argued that public sector intervention can add a third line of defense. Even if the government suffers from the same information problems as private firms, it can, in theory, improve on the outcome of private markets—as long as it is efficient, is benevolent, and can deploy instruments that the private sector does not have, such as taxes or subsidies (Greenwald and Stiglitz 1986). However, theory provides limited guidance as to how to proceed in practice.

In both industrial and developing countries, governments have tried and continue to pursue a plethora of interventions, typically consisting of measures such as

- Supplying certain types of financing (for example, long-term credit)
- Providing management and marketing advice to small businesses
- Assisting with the establishment of interfirm linkages and matchmaking programs between foreign and domestic traders and investors
- Supporting technology development through risk-sharing programs and cluster or incubator promotion
- Supporting enterprise-level training

A key question is whether such programs are being pursued because they systematically improve on market outcomes or whether they are politically attractive programs that sometimes may even replace more meaningful reform.

Public Financing for Private Firms

Subsidized and Directed Credit

One clear lesson has emerged from decades of attempts by public agencies to improve the flow of financing to firms. Whether the goal is to provide long-term financing or to help specific small firms with credit, programs that subsidize such financing tend to fail. Normally, powerful players appropriate such subsidies. Overall, the evidence is clear. Although private firms demand subsidized forms of financing, such financing results systematically in net negative economic outcomes (figure 3.1).

Theory also suggests that normally subsidies for financing have no role in subsidizing financing. The central argument about market failure in the credit market is that information problems make it hard to recognize and

FIGURE 3.1. The Effect of Subsidized Long-Term Debt on Enterprise Growth

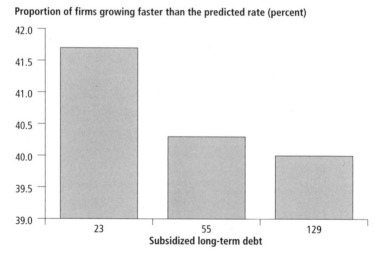

Note: The y-axis is the proportion of firms growing faster than predicted rates. The predicted rate is the rate at which a firm can grow by relying only on retained earnings and short-term credit. The 26 countries for which data were available were divided into three groups (9, 9, 8) on the basis of a ranking of the extent of subsidized long-term debt obtained by multiplying average ratios of long-term debt to total assets of firms by the ratio of government subsidy to gross domestic product. Group A = Austria, Belgium, Brazil, Finland, India, Italy, the Republic of Korea, Norway, and Sweden. Group B = Canada, France, Germany, Malaysia, the Netherlands, New Zealand, Pakistan, Spain, and Switzerland. Group C = Australia, Japan, Mexico, Singapore, Thailand, Turkey, the United Kingdom, and the United States.

Source: Caprio and Demirgüç-Kunt 1998.

assess credit opportunities and, thus, lead to some good deals being left on the table. If one can overcome these information problems, the additional deals that would be concluded can be expected to earn the full, unsubsidized cost of capital. Neither in theory nor in practice is there an argument on efficiency grounds to provide publicly subsidized financing (including guarantees) for firms.

These arguments imply, at a minimum, that taxpayer-supported agencies that try to enhance the flow of financing to private parties should be expected to earn the full cost of capital. As discussed in the context of privatization, their full cost of capital needs to be the risk-adjusted average weighted cost of capital for private financial institutions exposed to similar risks.[1]

In particular, one cannot argue that public sector financial institutions have a higher tolerance for risk than private ones and should, therefore, provide credit enhancements to the private sector that private financial institutions would not provide. Of course, it is true that managers of public financial institutions may in fact be willing to take greater risks than private ones, but only because the taxpayer–to–public sector manager agency chain places weaker disciplines on the managers than the private sector agency chain would. In fact, if public sector financial institutions exhibit greater tolerance for equivalent risk than private parties, one may argue for their privatization for precisely that reason.

The evidence on directed credit is slightly less clear (Batra and Mahmood 2001; World Bank 1993a, 1995). Although directed credit may not systematically lead to negative outcomes, it often does. The instances of positive outcomes may well arise because the credit targets were not truly binding. The balance of evidence suggests that directed credit does not outperform credit provided in reasonably deregulated financial markets (Caprio and Demirgüç-Kunt 1998).

In fact, a main conclusion is that general financial sector reform is the most effective way to support good firms and projects. The abolition of distortions in the credit market, the ability of new players to access financing, and the end of preferences to powerful incumbents are clearly desirable. In particular, efficient exit policies matter. In many countries, well-connected incumbent firms borrow but do not actually pay back, as reflected in high nonperforming assets in the portfolios of financial institutions. The de facto subsidy provided to powerful incumbents easily exceeds the credit support provided to small and medium-size enterprises in most countries.

This practice also creates a strong bias against equity financing and, thus, improved risk-sharing in the economy.

Also, many lending practices that governments try to improve on through public intervention already make sense and do not lend themselves to improvement through such intervention. Character-lending and requiring collateral from small firms rather than trying out cash flow–based lending make sense because of uncertainty about the future of small businesses, which typically depend on one or two people. Those people may suffer sudden personal setbacks or may be tempted, at some stage, to take the money and run.

Short-term lending is also sensible to establish discipline (Harris and Raviv 1990). Well-performing firms can expect rollovers, but more shaky businesses may need to be kept on a tight leash. Such practices are by no means restricted to developing economies and to very small firms. On the contrary, the development of corporate financing in industrial countries was based on these principles—for good reason and with good results (Mayer 1989). When public sector agencies provide financing beyond what the market is willing to provide, they risk undermining credit discipline and growth, as demonstrated by the decidedly mixed results of various financial support schemes to large and small enterprises (OECD 1997a, Nugent and Yhee 2002). In particular, when financial markets have not been reformed, it is dangerous to relax credit discipline further in a system that does not tend to allocate funds to efficient uses. Term financing is not always bad (Demirgüç-Kunt and Maksimovic 1996). On the contrary, long-term financing is highly valuable. However, there is no clear argument for subsidizing the provision of term financing. Large firm size helps improve credit and, thus, helps attract term financing. Large enterprises are effective at overcoming the market failures that plague smaller ones.

Is there then no argument for public sector credit support to firms? The answer has to lie in what public sector financial institutions can do better than private ones. As argued above, they have no risk-bearing advantage. Also, they do not systematically have better ideas or insights. In fact, their commercial acumen may suffer from weak performance incentives. Their potential advantage must lie in their special position as part of government and their ability to offer instruments that are not available from the private sector, not in the imitation of financial instruments used in private markets (Greenwald and Stiglitz 1986).

Political Risk Insurance

Public sector institutions may, in certain cases, be less subject to political risk—that is, some form of expropriation risk (expropriation, creeping expropriation, breach of contract, or currency transfer and convertibility)— than private parties. This lower risk is arguably the case for multilateral development institutions, which operate across borders, where property rights enforcement may be weak. Such institutions can then, to some degree, provide political risk insurance for private parties. This insurance may take various forms. It may be pure insurance. Alternatively, it may be bundled with other financial products. For example, joint lending with private parties may de facto provide political risk insurance, as is reflected in the ability of public cross-border colenders to extract special terms that reflect the implicit political risk insurance.

As discussed in chapter 2, in the past decade, the increasing worldwide web of commercial relations has reduced incentives to expropriate willfully. In a sense, expropriation is now more of a random event, and remedies have been enhanced, for example, through bilateral investment treaties. As a result, private political risk insurance has grown substantially. Private markets now are able to provide coverage against the same types of risks as public institutions do (West and Martin 2001). Insurance capacity overall and per project exceeds that of public institutions. Consequently, political risk insurance products provided by the public sector can potentially add value only for high-risk countries or projects.

The extent to which public institutions should provide political risk coverage in one way or another should be limited to their actual special advantage in dealing with political risk. They should be able to earn a return on capital no lower than that of private parties. The question then is whether they should charge rates or fees up to what the market will bear or whether they should charge just enough to be able to expect to cover their appropriate risk-adjusted cost of capital.

Is political risk insurance provided by public institutions actually a protection racket? There is a tricky issue here. To the extent that public institutions have a special advantage in covering cross-border political risks, it derives from their special relationship with governments. De facto, they substitute for a weak or nonexistent cross-border mechanism to enforce property rights. After all, contracts can always be written to rule out expropriation, and international arbitration can be agreed on to obtain proper dispute resolution. The extra value-added from public institutions offering cross-border political risk coverage then comes from their special ability to prevent risks from arising or to enforce payment when due.

If public institutions exploited their special standing by charging what the market will bear, they would, in fact, behave like protection rackets. After all, we do not want governments to charge for security of our property rights up to the maximum we would be willing to pay, but to charge—typically through taxes—only what it costs to establish law and order. Hence, public institutions should charge no more than their cost, including the full cost of capital. The private insurance companies may, however, sensibly charge what the market can bear, because they need to operate on insurance principles, not on the basis of being an extension of government. It may thus happen that public risk insurance products are cheaper than what the private sector would require to cover the risk, but the public sector involvement is part of a process, which is eventually to lead to the establishment of proper cross-border enforcement of property rights. Always, when government institutes better policy, some private activities that were meant to compensate for bad policy will lose demand.

In practice, translating those principles into operation is not straightforward (James 2001, Moran 2001). It is almost impossible to assess what exactly the risk-adjusted costs of insurers are with any degree of precision, given that the frequency and severity of claims cannot really be predicted. Pricing for guarantees has some elements of cost considerations and elements of pricing in response to what clients are willing to pay. However, two practical implications follow. First, when an official political risk insurer is the only provider of certain types of political risk insurance, it should not hold auctions for remaining insurance capacity as some private insurers do occasionally. Second, if private insurers complain that the rates charged by official insurers are lower than the rates obtained at such auctions, this situation is not necessarily a sign that official insurers inefficiently underprice private ones; it may simply reflect limited competition in private insurance markets.

Other Rationales for Public Financial Support to Private Firms

Support for Policy Reform. One might also argue for a financial role of public institutions if their provision of financing would help bring about sensible policy reform. Again, such an outcome might be possible because of their special relationship with governments that could help overcome political resistance. For example, the introduction of country funds by the International Finance Corporation (IFC) was a first step in opening up capital markets in several countries. Arguably, IFC was well placed to initiate this first step of reform. Also, when a public institution is able to enter a market where no arm's-length private financiers operate, it may be that the institution is allowed to provide instruments that are, at that time, otherwise not available. As in the case of political risk insurance products, it is not clear why financing is required to fulfill the public interest role. The true contribution to the policy reform process comes from a certification function that provides political cover for the host government and a political risk coverage role for the private coinvestors. Both functions could, in principle, be fulfilled separately from provision of financing. But it may be that bundling financing with the special contribution of an organization such as the IFC or the European Bank for Reconstruction and Development is a practical way to proceed that also allows a charge for the service.

Information Advantages of Public Agencies. Public agencies may historically have been the first to enter certain markets. By virtue of this first-mover advantage, they may understand a market better than new private entrants may. For a transitional period, while private financial institutions attempt to enter a new market, they may be able to play a signaling or rating role for private parties that goes beyond the political risk insurance function. The question is, again, whether this role should be unbundled. A straight rating service would not compete unnecessarily with private financiers.

Support for Sustainable Business Practices. Public financial agencies may also try to promote improved business practices (for example, better environmental, social, and corporate governance standards). If those practices are not costly, they should not affect the ability of the public agency to earn a competitive return. If, however, the standards that the public agency promotes impose an extra cost on private firms and place them at a disadvantage in relation to other competitors, then some form of subsidy may be appropriate until the host-country government upgrades social and environmental standards for all investors—foreign or domestic. It is not clear, however, why such a subsidy needs to be bundled with financing. Alternatively, a straight subsidy could be available for any business that subscribes to special standards.

Special Relationship of Public Finance Agencies

Thus, public financing for private firms may make sense for several reasons. Yet it is not clear that provision of financing is required. The core functions to be fulfilled are political risk insurance, rating and certification functions, and subsidy provision. Although these functions may, in practice, be difficult to unbundle, the critical element is the special relationship between public finance agencies and governments at home or abroad.

This special relationship presumably requires that public finance institutions be expected to operate in a manner similar to nonprofit or limited-dividend companies. With nonprofit companies, the issue arising is how to deploy net income when a return on equity is earned but is not distributed as dividends. Like nonprofit companies, public financial agencies should presumably remain immune to private takeover threats to preserve their special political relationship.

Public Support to Business Development Services for Private Firms

Surely, beyond establishing a sound business environment and adequate market infrastructure, the public sector should put in place policies and measures to provide firms with necessary infrastructure (telecommunications, transport, energy, water) and social services (health, education). Functioning cities, for example, are the best of all incubators or clusters as they help firms, particularly small and medium-size ones, establish themselves, grow, and create employment (Audretsch 2002, Glaeser 1998).

Beyond these services, public agencies in most countries try to provide some type of business development services to private firms. Private players can and do provide such services, but they may arguably be underprovided in private markets. For example, public agencies may provide management, accounting, or marketing advice to fledgling entrepreneurs; help suppliers find buyers and vice versa; support the development of business incubators or clusters; or assist with worker training.

In the past, public interventions have rarely been properly evaluated for cost-effectiveness (Nugent and Yhee 2002). Evidence suggests the following. Public sector institutions have often provided advice for many firms at low price, effectively subsidizing the cost of supplying those services. In those cases, the services and advice offered have typically not been sufficiently specific, relevant, or responsive to demand. More resource-intensive public interventions can help, but they tend to be excessively expensive (Nugent and Yhee 2002). Until recently, many interventions have thus been supply driven.

The experience is disappointing for agricultural extension services as well as for support services for nonfarm small and medium-size enterprises in both urban and rural areas (Dinar and Keynan 1998; Evenson 1998; Feder, Willett, and Zijp 1999; Gautam 2000; Purcell and Anderson 1997; Umali-Deininger 1997; Van der Mheen and Nilsson 1997; World Bank 1989, 2000b). A few countries report successful public agencies supporting firms operating in domestic markets or firms producing exports. The usual list of countries includes the Republic of Korea, Singapore, and Taiwan, China (Keesing and Singer 1990, Thomas and Nash 1991). But even in Korea, recent evaluations of available evidence cast doubt on success stories (Nugent and Yhee 2002). Interventions have also been of doubtful economic benefit in most member countries of the Organisation for Economic Co-operation and Development.

To improve the incentives offered by public agencies and to be more responsive to market demand, a number of business development programs have experimented with demand-side subsidies such as matching grants or vouchers; under such schemes, businesses pay for a substantial part of the service. Also, tax breaks have been used extensively. For companies with pretax profits, the two systems are equivalent. As in most other areas of support to small and medium-size enterprises, very few evaluations of actual programs exist. A tentative evaluation of a program in Mauritius has not been able to document success (Biggs 1999). However, on a more hopeful note, a new study of a matching grant program supporting some 7,000 small and medium-size enterprises in Mexico documents clear benefits (Tan 2001).

Governments have also tried to create industrial technology clusters in the image of Silicon Valley or the small industry clusters of northern Italy. Undoubtedly such clusters can be powerful drivers of growth. However, engineering them beyond providing decent infrastructure and a good general business environment has proved elusive (Janovsky 1986).

A similar story holds for schemes to support enterprise-level training. Training employees is critical for productivity growth (Batra and Tan 1995). Theoretically, enterprises might underinvest in worker training because they are not able to capture the full benefits of training programs when the workers leave. It is unclear how important that effect is in practice. In many cases, in developing and industrial countries where wages are flexible, job seekers accept positions that are paid relatively little because they think they can learn. In many firms, average time in the job exceeds a decade and, thus, the likelihood is strong that employee training will actually benefit such firms. Overall, various training support schemes, whether completely subsidized or on a matching grant basis, have shown few convincing results.

The emerging consensus is that lasting subsidies are undesirable and that business development services should be market oriented and privately provided. Private firms have powerful incentives to seek out advice and to search for better partners. When the market selection mechanism works well, firms that find ways to obtain such services grow, and those that do not fail.

Proponents of public support for business development services for private firms still argue that special subsidized services should be provided to enterprises that are currently poorly served. For example, they claim that small and medium-size enterprises should be helped by subsidizing the development of credit assessment systems or management toolkits. In such cases, the argument for subsidy is focused on one-time initial subsidies, with follow-up activity and discipline left to the market. If this argument is pushed to its logical conclusion, public intervention should focus on the enabling environment for firms, including basic market infrastructure such as credit bureaus, but should abstain from direct support to individual firms or intermediaries.

Nevertheless, proponents of public support for business development services currently argue that the public sector can help accelerate market development of such services through short-term subsidies that are

- Designed to achieve specific market development objectives
- Focused on supporting private providers
- Based on a clear exit strategy and vision of how the market will eventually operate without subsidies

Overall Implications for Special Public Support Schemes to Private Firms

Given both the widespread use of enterprise support schemes—for example, for small and medium-size enterprises—and the equally widespread doubt about their effectiveness (Lanjouw 1999), it would appear that they are heavily driven by politics rather than by pure efficiency rationales. The powerful political attraction of providing myriad support schemes and exemptions is, indeed, apparent across the globe. Witness, for example, the continued interest in microfinance schemes (box 3.1) despite significant amounts of undisbursed credit lines for such schemes.

For the special case of support schemes for small and medium-size enterprises, this observation does not mean that such enterprises do not play a significant role or that they do not deserve to do well. In fact, in many countries, small and medium-size firms are disadvantaged compared with powerful incumbents and are often driven into informal means of doing business. It is thus important to lean against the political wind and support reforms of the basic business environment that place small and medium-size enterprises on an equal playing field with other firms.

What is really critical is to have the basic market selection mechanism right. Thus, good firms can enter the market and drive out worse ones. In such an environment, the basic selection mechanism will make reasonably sure that public resources are ultimately put to good use. Hence, the same story that applies to aid-effectiveness overall also applies to public support schemes (Burnside and Dollar 1997, Collier and Dollar 2000). When the policy environment is right, some extra help may enhance it. When it is wrong, extra resources may simply be wasted or, worse, create damage.

However strong the case against firm-level intervention is, frustration with market outcomes will likely remain and will drive the call for special support schemes. Many feel that the market cannot be left entirely to its own devices. They believe it may need to be jumpstarted to reduce the time required to obtain effective development. Some analysts typically find cases where there is a "need" for more long-term capital or a "need" for better support services to small enterprises. Of course, one can always find that a bit more would be good to have and the demand from private parties for subsidies is limitless. To some extent, the call for special support rep-

Box 3.1. Facilitating Access to Markets: The Example of Microfinancing

In recent years, a particular innovation to help poor people tap the power of markets has been microfinancing. Microfinance institutions of various types provide small loans in the order of several tens to several hundreds of dollars. Although efforts to improve the playing field for small and medium-size enterprises help stimulate growth and employment in general without specific targeting of the poor, microfinancing tries to reach the poor. However, many microfinance schemes provide credit for consumption purposes rather than for investment. Of course, financing by itself is, in any case, insufficient unless the poor have adequate investment opportunities. Hence, the effect of microfinancing is likely to be greatest when sensible, market-friendly reforms create a good business environment.

By now, millions of people worldwide benefit from access to microfinancing (Morduch 1999). Various factors matter for success. Customer density appears to help. Hence, microfinance institutions in Latin America are primarily urban based, whereas there are more rural ones in Asia. Credit disciplines, including short repayment periods, are of importance, as are cost-effective delivery systems. Critically, interest rate ceilings undermine the viability of microfinancing. For example, the reform of usury laws may be important to allow microfinance institutions to charge rates that cover the cost of capital. Thus, the broad lessons about the design of financial products for private parties also apply to microfinance institutions. The basic rules of markets apply as elsewhere.

Microfinance institutions mainly reach people who are around the poverty line—not the very poor and not people in remote areas with low population density. Most people served continue to rely on subsidies, and risks of excessive subsidy dependence are clear (Gugerty and Kremer 2000). Because other subsidy systems also have trouble reaching the extremely poor, the subsidy provided to microfinance institutions may, however, be comparatively effective. Again, as in the case of other public interventions to support firms, sound cost-benefit analyses are missing. It remains to be seen whether current hopes for microfinance schemes translate into sustained benefits or whether a period of disenchantment will come, as in the case of any larger-scale support schemes for businesses.

The greatest challenge is, thus, how to scale up the provision of micro-financing on a sustained commercially viable basis. Small entrepreneurs are willing to pay relatively high rates. Repayment performance appears good and much better than that of large, influential clients in many banking systems. This achievement is partially due to community responsibility schemes and partially due to other forms of collateral. More broadly, however, it may be attributed to the typical reputational interest of borrowers to retain access to financial services that are provided under decent disciplines.

The existing microfinance schemes have highlighted the possibility of expanding credit for the poor. Large-scale solutions are, however, unlikely to be sustained unless larger financial institutions are able to downscale their operations and serve the market for small credit and financing on a commercial basis—independent of continued subsidy. Improved information systems on borrower performance such as credit bureaus are likely to be part of the answer. Advances in information and communication technology may help, together with market innovation. In industrial countries, the typical micro-credit instrument is the credit card. Low-income countries may soon be in the same position. For example, it may be possible to use utility payment records to enhance information on creditworthiness. Prepaid electronic cards play an increasing role in poor countries for access to metered utility services. They could become vehicles for credit history. Information technology, combined with innovative local organization by larger domestic financial institutions, appears to hold the greatest promise for scaling up microfinancing. Improved property rights for the poor that allow financial institutions to collateralize loans also appear to be part of the eventual solution.

resents a throwback to the old resource-driven and state-led development paradigm, in which wise planners detect a need, throw resources at it, and attempt to microengineer outcomes instead of accepting the decentralization of decisionmaking that markets represent.

In fact, there is no simple way to set policy among these conflicting rationales and interests, even though there is little hard evidence from the past to support the case for public intervention. Short of abandoning public intervention, the key options for policy design arise from some basic observations.

The typical rationales for public support of private firms that have some basis in both theory and evidence suggest that such assistance should be transitional—that is, until the private firms and markets function on their own. There is no clear rationale for sustained public support of private firms. Hence, as a minimum, sunset clauses should figure prominently in these schemes.

The biggest danger of public support schemes is that taxpayers may be forced to fund subsidies that are not delivered in accordance with sound disciplines. Hence, doubts arise about corporate welfare provided by public financing agencies. There is thus a case for the following. Most rationales for public support imply that such assistance can help businesses conclude good deals that would be otherwise left on the table. By implication, the public agencies offering such support should then be able to earn their risk-adjusted cost of capital. Policymakers should thus have the option to require normal market return targets from public agencies aiding private firms, thereby ensuring that subsidies are not abused. Meanwhile, the activity of public agencies should be focused on remedying those problems in fledgling markets, where they can achieve better results than private firms can.

When policymakers do decide that subsidies are required, subsidy delivery should be unbundled and subjected to better, preferably output-based financial disciplines. Given the disappointing results of many public sector efforts to support private firms and the supply response of these firms, it appears imperative to build into any subsidy program a better, cost-effective method to determine the subsidy equivalent or the subsidy dependence of the scheme and its effect.

Note

1. It is particularly intriguing how some public sector development banks can, on the one hand, promote privatization, while on the other hand, be systematically content with returns from their financing to private firms below their cost of capital.

4

Private Participation and Markets for Basic Services

Private Participation and Markets in Infrastructure

A big policy surprise of the 1990s was the popularity of private infrastructure schemes. During the late 1970s and 1980s, a few countries—notably Chile and the United Kingdom—introduced competitive markets and private participation in various infrastructure sectors. During the 1990s, such reforms exploded, with 132 developing countries trying out private participation in infrastructure in various degrees. Between 1990 and 2001, private sector activity in infrastructure sectors of developing countries involved about 2,500 projects and investment commitments of more than US$750 billion. The strongest growth in private sector activity was experienced between 1990 and 1997, when investment flows rose from US$18 billion to a record US$128 billion (Izaguirre 2002; Roger 1999; see also figure 4.1). This dramatic move to private participation in infrastructure reflects the search for improved governance mechanisms that allocate risks to those best able to bear and manage them (Irwin and others 1997).

FIGURE 4.1. Investment in Infrastructure Projects with Private Participation in Developing Countries, 1990–2001

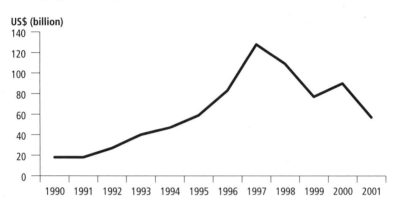

Source: World Bank Private Participation in Infrastructure Project Database.

Competition in the Market

Evidence so far suggests that the biggest gains from reform in infrastructure sectors come when real competition (competition in the market or head-to-head competition) can be introduced where none existed before, as in the gas and transport markets of the United States or the electricity markets of the United Kingdom (Gray 2001; Newbery and Pollitt 1997; Winston 1993). A key insight is that significant benefits result from innovations that arise under competition (table 4.1).

TABLE 4.1. Estimated Gains from Deregulation of Infrastructure Sectors in the United States

Sector	Extent of deregulation	Estimated annual gains (1990 US$ billion)
Airlines	Complete	13.7–19.7
Trucking	Substantial	10.6
Railroads	Partial	10.4–12.9
Telecommunications	Substantial	0.7–1.6
Total		35.4–44.8

Source: World Bank 1994c; see Winston 1993 for more details.

These benefits would have been technically possible under monopoly ownership, but normally monopolists have weak incentives to innovate—notwithstanding their frequent and vigorous claims to the contrary. For this reason, it is not normally possible to say exactly what benefits will arise from competition before its introduction. But also, where competition is not feasible, private participation in infrastructure can lead to significant gains. One of the main reasons for such gains is the clear separation of the new private firm from the public purse. When it is clear that the public sector will not interfere with commercial decisions and will not treat the cash flow of infrastructure firms as part of the budget, private investors will not fear expropriation in some form. Thus, incentives to invest will be strong and will lead to beneficial output expansion (figure 4.2).

More broadly, a series of studies suggests that contracting out public services (including many infrastructure services) can—if done right—yield efficiency gains equivalent to 10–30 percent of previous cost (Bartone and others 1991; Carnaghan and Bracewell-Milnes 1993; Domberger and Piggott 1994). However, when real competition is not or cannot be introduced,

FIGURE 4.2. Welfare Effects of Selling State-Owned Enterprises

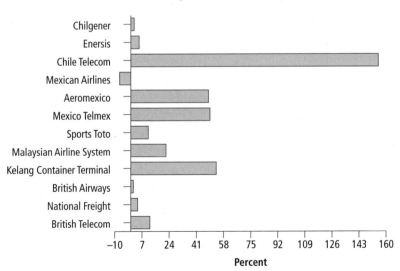

Note: Welfare gains are presented as a percentage of annual sales in the last year before privatization.

Source: Galal and others 1994.

it is more likely that privatization is mishandled, and well-run public firms may do as well as private ones (Kwoka 1996). Even in such cases, many private projects have outperformed public enterprises—for example, in the water sector in Argentina, Chile, Côte d'Ivoire, and Guinea (Clarke, Menard, and Zuluage 2000; Noll, Shirley, and Cowan 2000). This is not to say that they have all achieved perfect results. On the contrary, many problems exist, but compared with plausible alternatives, privatization appears to have been quite successful in many cases. Overall, in the noncompetitive infrastructure segments, it appears that public sector firms do not have systematic advantages, whereas privatization holds promise for genuine improvement.

The key to successful reform in any sector is, therefore, an adequate reform of market structure to maximize the potential for real competition. Market structure reform tries to distinguish—and to varying degrees separate—the true natural monopoly elements of a system from the competitive segments. Typically, networks of pipelines (gas and water), wires (electricity and telecommunications), road, and rail—as well as rights of ways and common facilities in ports or airports—are the prime candidates for natural monopolies. In many cases, it makes no sense to have duplicate physical networks (pipes, wires, and so on) serve the same customer—hence the expression natural monopoly.[1]

In fact, effective forms of head-to-head competition can be introduced in telecommunications, electricity, and natural gas. The precise ways of doing so depend on the relevant technology, size of the market, and public sector capability (Bacon 1994). A variety of options exist to phase in competition. For example, in electricity systems, competition among generators may initially be based on infrequent cost-based bids or be restricted to the wholesale level (box 4.1). Effective competition can also be introduced in the market for freight transport in many countries by deregulating trucking and by not regulating freight rail services that compete with trucks.

In some cases, the network itself is not a natural monopoly. In networks, in which the optimal size of individual transmission channels are small relative to the size of the network, competing transmission channels between producers and consumers may be desirable. For example, in telecommunications systems all over the world, competing infrastructure for wireless transmission makes sense, as do competing wires in some cases. In large natural gas systems, free entry into the long-distance pipeline business can make sense, for example, in the United States, as

---

Box 4.1. Market Design

Market structure reform may also need to unbundle in some detail the various functions of the markets that are newly created. Consider the familiar example of airline seats. We buy airlines seats for travel at some future date. In other words, plane tickets are typically sold in forward markets. When we go to the gate, the plane may be overbooked. An auction may then be held at the gate, which offers just enough money to passengers who are willing not to fly to match demand with the actual capacity of the plane. Last-minute discount sales cope with the opposite problem of filling up seats in underbooked planes. These sales represent the balancing market. Then the plane takes off in line with the instructions of the air traffic controllers. Air traffic control is the dispatch system. Typically, the forward markets are competitive segments, whereas balancing markets and dispatch systems are natural monopolies. The analogy applies to other sectors, including the electricity, gas, and water markets.

---

can competing transmission providers. There is a large potential for such competition in several Eurasian gas and electricity systems (box 4.2).

It should be noted that the attempt to introduce competition in the rail system, as in the United Kingdom, by separating tracks from train operations and by creating multiple train operators, has limited potential to create head-to-head competition. The problem is that there is no effective way of establishing competition between different railway tracks, and competition over the existing network is highly limited because the freight and people transported are not homogeneous products. In contrast, in the case of electricity or natural gas, it does not matter which path electrons or molecules take through the system. This homogeneity of product and path independence allows treatment of the transmission systems for gas and electricity as single marketplaces, where buyers and sellers meet. In the case of railroads, the actual path that freight and people take through the system matters, however, and rail track systems cannot be treated as single marketplaces (Klein 1998a).

That said, the privatization of British Rail reduced government outlays and both freight and passenger traffic increased over 30 percent between 1994 and 1999. The resulting strains for the infrastructure, the lack of

Box 4.2. California Electricity Market

Although the introduction of competition may, in principle, be feasible, it is not automatic, as the plight of California's electricity sector reform reminds us. Reformers promised that deregulation would lower prices. But a shift to markets may not lower prices. A decade-long lack of investment in power generation, partially because of regulatory barriers for new investment predating deregulation, combined with growing demand to create a precarious demand–supply balance. A number of other factors aggravated the situation, notably rapidly rising natural gas prices that increased costs and decreased availability of hydropower. When deregulation happens in this context, market forces drive prices up to what the market will bear. After all, rationing in markets happens through price adjustment, not through quantity restrictions. But policymakers in California also did not allow full price rationing, although they capped consumer prices. In addition, power sales were forced into the spot market, where desperate and strategic bidding can drive prices up excessively. As a result, utilities have been squeezed between rising generation prices and low consumer prices, while some level of quantity rationing continues.

Nordpool, the Scandinavian electricity market, on the other hand, shows how comparatively smooth the introduction of competition in electricity can happen. Also, several developing countries have introduced forms of competition in electricity generation effectively, notably Argentina and Chile. The latter countries use a market design that minimizes options for strategic price manipulation by market participants with effective market power. Instead of continuous daily auctions, they rely on marginal cost estimates provided by power plants in half-yearly intervals.

clear incentives to build out and improve infrastructure, and the high transaction costs in the highly fragmented railroad system help explain current service problems. As in so many cases of privatization, detailed analysis may show that privatization compared well to reasonable counterfactuals, but it failed to meet some expectations raised in the beginning (Mellitt n.d.).

Competition for the Market

In segments in which real competition is not feasible, prices charged by natural monopolists are not held in check by market forces. In a few cases, it is possible to create repeated competition for the market or franchise bidding—in effect bidding for a concession—that achieves similar results as competition in the market (Chadwick 1859). For example, garbage collection service (Bartone and others 1991) and bus routes may be auctioned off repeatedly on the basis of the lowest price to consumers (box 4.3). However, when the potential for effective head-to-head competition has been exhausted, the remaining natural monopoly elements typically require some form of price regulation. For example, frequent repeat auctions of water pipeline systems can be problematic. If the incumbent loses, it is not economic to dig up the old pipeline system and take it elsewhere, as one can do with garbage trucks when losing a concession. Hence, when the incumbent fears the loss of the concession in the next auction, his or her incentives to invest and maintain the system may suffer. Although there are now theoretical schemes that might be able to solve this problem (Klein 1998b), and while occasional repeat bidding still makes sense, prices will normally need to be set by regulators rather than by competitive forces.

Box 4.3. Contracting Out Public Services

Beyond infrastructure, a number of governments are contracting out other public services (for example, inspection services, registration services, testing services, tax collection, security services, legal services, and jails). Also, regulatory or monitoring services may be contracted out. A case in point is the agency that monitors performance of the Gaza water company. The simple fact is that everything can, in principle, be provided by private parties and has been at one time or another somewhere in the world. As long as the government is able to regulate private parties adequately, there is the potential for performance improvements. A number of studies suggest that performance improvements equivalent to about 10–30 percent of cost may well be obtained (Domberger and Piggott 1994, Fouquet and Pearson 1999). Obviously, the results depend on the prior state of the public service and the ability of government to contract efficiently.

Entry and Exit in Natural Monopoly Segments. When considering how to approach regulation of a natural monopoly, one must first ask whether the natural monopoly requires legal protection—that is, some form of exclusivity. When the structure, albeit not the level, of prices charged by the regulated monopolist can be set freely, there is no serious argument for providing exclusive rights (Webb and Ehrhardt 1998). For example, regulators may set a cap on the weighted average of prices for the different services provided by the monopolist, such that the monopolist is ex ante expected to earn about the cost of capital overall. Within this price cap, the monopolist can then be given freedom to set individual prices so as to respond efficiently to both cost and demand conditions. When such a system exists, efficient first movers or incumbents can always undercut new entrants in any business segment—otherwise there would not be a natural monopoly. But when they are inefficient, free entry provides them with an incentive to shape up and provides consumers with extra choice and protection. Hence, for example, the Mexican government decided to provide only 3 years of exclusivity in the 15-year natural gas distribution concessions in the country, and the Chilean government set a policy not to provide any exclusivity at all for the gas transmission pipelines into Chile.

The key point from the perspective of poverty reduction is that free entry into natural monopoly segments allows small and medium-size providers of infrastructure services to compete with large traditional utilities and holds promise to improve access and reduce costs for the poor (Baker and Tremolet 2000; Brook 2000; Brook and W. Smith 2001; Brook and Tynan 1999; Collignon and Vezina 2000; Ehrhardt 2000; Estache, Gomez-Lobo, and Leipziger 2000; Komives, Whittington, and Wu 2000).

Telecommunications. Effective service improvements in telecommunications in Africa have occurred in Somalia, precisely because of a loss of power by the central government and the entry of three (now four) competing providers (Maas 2001). Service has improved, and rates are falling. Today, these benefits are made possible by the ability of service providers to use wireless technology and to hook up to international services by way of satellite. Service providers can thus import international services, including interconnection service. Free entry into all parts of the telecommunications sector is clearly the way to

> *The well-off have telephones, car,... computers, access to services.*
>
> —A poor woman, Brazil

go, as shown in numerous countries (Wellenius 2000). Free entry also holds the key to bridging the digital divide. Studies show that today in Africa, the use of the Internet is as high as in industrial countries, relative to the number of phone connections available (World Bank 2001c). The trick is, thus, to deal with the dial-tone divide by promoting free entry.

Electricity. Even in sectors in which technology has changed less, free entry holds promise. Average connection rates to public electricity systems in Africa are in the order of 10 percent. The reason is that African countries, as do many other countries, legally protect the natural monopoly of their national electricity companies. Citizens are also allowed to use standby generators when the public system fails, as it often does. However, the legal protection of the national company implies that citizens are not allowed to string wires from their standby generators to anybody else, thus sharing the benefits of any economies of scale in small-level generation.

In a few countries, some degree of free entry into the wires business is allowed. In the Republic of Yemen, several thousand small electricity systems provide power to at least 10 percent of the population, in addition to the public system, which supplies about a quarter of the population. Each private system tends to have established a monopoly in its area, as would be expected with a technology that has natural monopoly characteristics. Customers pay high prices—sometimes up to 60 cents per kilowatt-hour, about five to eight times the retail price in industrial countries. Service is intermittent and is concentrated during evening hours. Given the country's low per capita income, consumers do not buy a lot of electricity. But they have voluntary access, and the cost of having electricity is still lower than not having it (for example, some health benefits result from using electric light instead of kerosene lamps).

Some other countries, such as Cambodia, are now allowing some degree of free entry into the electricity business. Somalia has five competing power providers. Also, proponents of alternative energy tend to promote some degree of free entry, particularly in areas not connected to the national grid.

Energy planners worry that such anarchic system development will render the development of the national grid difficult. Indeed, the development of unconnected power systems in the early days of electricity later led to complicated processes of system integration. However, when national systems have bad track records over several decades, extra choice for consumers and options for free, small-scale entry are clearly beneficial. There are plenty of options to allow entry at least into unconnected areas and to impose minimal technical and safety regulations that would improve service (W. Smith 2000). In any case, national utilities that are capable can always underbid small-scale entry as long as pricing is flexible. National utilities, thus, have no excuse to fear small-scale entry. They need fear only themselves.

Water. Decent water supply is particularly important for the poor and for their health. The poor typically rely on natural sources of water or various forms of water vendors. The opportunity cost of fetching water or the prices paid to vendors are typically 10–40 times as high as the cost of water to citizens connected to more-modern water systems. The big issue for the poor is thus not any type of subsidy for water, but market-type incentives to connect them to more-efficient water systems, including standpipes, bore holes, and so on. Informal water companies such as the *aguateros* in Paraguay can represent a valuable alternative to public sector water companies. The aguateros supply water more cheaply than traditional vendors by using simple plastic pipe systems (Solo 1998; see also box 4.4).

> *Water is life, and because we have no water, life is miserable.*
> —A poor person, Kenya, 1997

Box 4.4. Private Participation in the Water Sector: Results from Selected Countries

In the late 1980s, the poor performance of state-owned urban water utilities in many developing countries prompted governments to consider reforms that involved promotion of private participation in the sector. A representative sample of such reforms is analyzed by a World Bank study (Shirley and Menard 2000) that examines the experience with reform in large cities in six developing countries. Three of the reforms involved the introduction of private sector participation: a concession in Buenos Aires, Argentina; a lease in Conakry, Guinea; and service contracts in Mexico City. In Abidjan, Côte d'Ivoire, water rates were changed, and the existing private operator's investment responsibilities were strengthened by the government. In Santiago, Chile, and Lima, Peru, the plans to introduce private sector participation did not materialize. Santiago introduced all the planned regulatory changes, whereas Lima introduced only a few of the regulatory reforms planned under the proposed concession. Both cities kept their water utility under public ownership.

For the most part, the reform of the water sectors in the cities studied led to improvements in water access, labor productivity, and the overall economic welfare of the parties involved. Water access in Santiago and Mexico City was already high before the reforms. Coverage in Buenos Aires, Conakry, and Abidjan improved with the increase in private sector participation, whereas the reform of the state-owned operator failed to increase coverage in Lima (figure 4.3).

FIGURE 4.3. Effects of the Reforms on Access to Water: Change in Coverage, by City

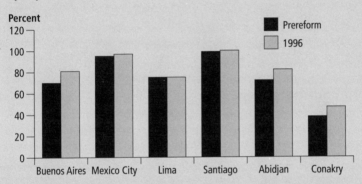

Source: Shirley and Menard 2000.

Labor productivity improved in all of the above cities following the implementation of water sector reforms. Santiago, which had the least number of employees per 1,000 connections before reform, did not experience a large gain in labor productivity. The most-dramatic improvement was in Conakry, where labor productivity was substantially lower than in the other case study cities before reform. The World Bank study included detailed cost-benefit analyses for four of the cases. Among the four cities, the largest welfare gains were observed in Buenos Aires, which implemented the most-extensive reform, handing over responsibility for both operations and investment to the private

(Box continues on the following page.)

Box 4.4. (continued)

sector. The welfare gains from reform were also large in Santiago, even though the reform did not involve an increase in private sector participation. The gains in Conakry were small compared with those in Santiago or Buenos Aires, but they were significant in that per capita income is far lower in Guinea than in Chile or Argentina. The gains from the reform in Lima, which also did not involve increased private sector participation, were small (figure 4.4).

FIGURE 4.4. Welfare Gains from Reform of Water Systems, by City

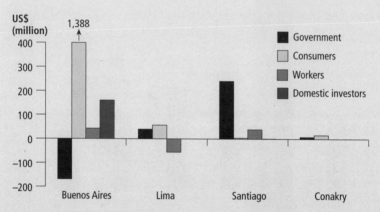

Source: Shirley and Menard 2000.

There are also more recent examples of private sector activity in the water sector—some successful and some not quite successful. Bolivia's first major private contract in the water and sanitation sector, a 25-year concession for the cities of La Paz and El Alto, was implemented in 1997. The average rate for water was raised by about 20 percent in real terms before the concession to ensure the financial sustainability of the concession. The annual rate of new connections to water services in La Paz and El Alto increased by about 66 percent from 10,469 during the period before the reform (1993–96) to 17,187 during the period following the reform (1997–99). More than two-thirds of new water connections were made in poorer areas of La Paz and El Alto. In 1999, a private operator was granted a concession to provide water and *sanitation services to Cochabamba. The government chose a more-expensive scheme, which was backed by municipal and regional interests over a less costly project. The high cost of the project required an immediate rate increase of 38 percent, with an additional 20 percent increase after it became operational. The consumers in Cochabamba, with only 4 hours of water per day, felt that they were paying more for the same poor service. In response to violent political riots over the rate increases, the government ended the Cochabamba concession 6 months after it was launched (Foster and Irusta 2001). The stark difference in the experiences of these cities demonstrates that privatization is not a panacea in the face of political interference, bad project selection, and weak management.*

To date, about 50 water utilities in municipalities of various sizes in Colombia have introduced private participation in the water sector. The results in terms of expansion and quality of service have been encouraging, as demonstrated by the dramatic improvement in performance indicators of water facilities in the cities of Cartagena, Baranquilla, and Tunja (table 4.2).

TABLE 4.2. Performance Indicators in Colombian Water Utilities Operated by the Private Sector

Indicator	Cartagena		Baranquilla		Tunja	
	Before concession (1994)	After concession (2000)	Before concession (1995)	After concession (2000)	Before concession (1994)	After concession (2000)
Water coverage (percent)	68	86	89	94	89	98
Number of connections	84,143	113,035	180,717	241,902	23,308	26,139
Connections in poor areas (percent)	—	82	—	58	—	79
Availability (hours/day)	7	24	18	24	12	18
Number of employees/ 1,000 connections	15.0	2.4	5.5	3.4	5.0	3.7
Production capacity (cubic meters/second)	1.6	3.1	7.5	8.2	0.3	0.3
Percentage of metering	30	99	25	60	90	99
Percentage of unaccounted for water	60	38	46	42	53	43

— Not available.

Source: World Bank 2001a.

Water access issues also exemplify a broader point. When there is demand for a service, some form of supply emerges, even if strictly forbidden by policy. Just consider water, drugs, and arms. In some areas of Africa that are torn by civil war, the poor starve themselves to save money to buy water from vendors. Such vendors may have an incentive to prevent alternative entry, including that of competing state-provided systems. Where vendors actually exercise power, because they are the local thugs or otherwise armed bandits, private monopoly power is created and imposed on citizens. Free entry thus requires a minimum of respect for rules. It does not come about in all circumstances in which it is formally allowed.

Disciplines on Natural Monopolies. Whether or not natural monopolies benefit from legal protection, in the end there will be only a single service provider for each segment of customers. The biggest issue is, then, how best to mimic market-type disciplines (box 4.5). Not providing exclusivity leaves at least some discipline from free entry. Equally important is to provide some freedom to fail (exit options) and the possibility for a new firm to take over if the incumbent fails to perform. Clearly, takeover of incumbent firms should be allowed. Takeover allows a more-efficient management to come in. However, given a set of regulated prices, the benefits of such market discipline go to shareholders. To mimic a real market, the regulatory system needs to set prices so as to capture some of the benefits for consumers while not undermining the viability and incentives of efficient producers. Setting effective prices is the core regulatory challenge, and there is no perfect way to meet it. Otherwise, central public sector management of firms would work, and markets would not be needed in the first place. There is also no way around renegotiating the required long-term contracts or arrangements. In normal markets, prices can adjust to reflect changes in underlying demand and supply conditions. In regulated long-term arrangements, renegotiation takes the place of the price mechanism. This situation may be abused by either negotiating party, but it remains unavoidable. It is, thus, critical to define clearly the way in which renegotiation would take place and the principles on which it would be based.

To help cope with this issue, regulatory processes can, from time to time, use rebidding of the right to run a natural monopoly on the basis of the lowest price to consumers to introduce some market-type discipline. Privatization is a typical case when an incumbent, the state-owned firm, loses its rights, and an award is made to a new private firm to run the natural

Box 4.5. Disciplines for Contracting Out Public Services

Both in private infrastructure and contracting out of public services in general, there is a danger that the shift from public to private provision is associated with a breakdown of discipline and corruption. Privatization in various forms requires different parts of government to work together—contrary to the old state approaches—with the private sector. New processes are required, notably processes for awarding projects and for providing government financial support when appropriate. When there are new rules, new players, and new processes, often the whole new system remains ill defined for some time, and opportunities for abuse increase. Many private schemes have, indeed, been associated with corruption in a number of countries.

It, therefore, is important to get the new disciplines right to reap the potential benefits. A number of countries have developed sound laws or guidelines. Useful policies can be found in the concession laws of Chile and Hungary, in the build-operate-transfer (BOT) law of the Philippines, and in the guidelines of the United Kingdom's Private Finance Initiative. Key areas for policymaker attention are the following:

- *Responsibility among government agencies and the processes for decisionmaking need to be clarified.*
- *Proper risk-sharing systems need to be defined to provide the best possible balance of incentives between the private and public sectors. When possible, contracts should specify performance or output for which the private sector is held responsible and then leave it to firms to choose the best method of achieving the goals.*
- *Award procedures need to have the very strong presumption that competitive bidding is the method of choice.*
- *If possible, user fees should be charged because of the discipline and customer-orientation they impose. When social concerns prevail, targeted subsidies are, if feasible, preferable to free provision.*
- *Value-for-money tests should be performed when tax funding prevails (using the appropriate risk-adjusted cost of capital). Such tests try to establish at what price the public sector could provide the service and put a cap on remuneration the private sector can obtain, acting like a reserve price in the bidding process.*

monopoly. Two main issues arise: (1) care needs to be taken not to seriously undermine incentives of the incumbent to invest and maintain the system, and (2) service continuity must be ensured. The first goal may be achieved either by monitoring incumbent behavior tightly or, if such monitoring cannot be done or is overly intrusive, by providing the incumbent with a preference in the bidding process. The second goal can be achieved by requiring the incumbent to provide service until a new firm is in place and by backing the obligation with a significant performance bond. The hand-over is facilitated if the country allows multiple firms to operate similar types of natural monopolies in different parts of the country (for example, water systems).

In general, there are good arguments for using concession-type arrangements to run natural monopolies. Concession-type arrangements include a continuum of solutions ranging from privatization (as in the English and Welsh water system), through full French concessions and leasing or affermage deals, to BOT (build-operate-transfer), BOOT (build-own-operate-transfer), and similar arrangements. Concessions, by definition, have end dates when the right to operate the concession is reawarded. The award should typically be made on the basis of transparent bidding, whether at the time of privatization or when a private concession runs out (Klein 1998b). Only in rare cases requiring extra speed of award should sole-sourcing be considered. In that case, special oversight arrangements are required to prevent corrupt practices. The bidding methodology needs to ensure that both price and quality aspects are adequately taken into account.

Price Regulation

Regulatory Independence. In between any concession awards that may occur, regulators shoulder the burden of balancing consumer and producer interests appropriately. So that they can do so in a way that reduces non-commercial political interference, it is generally useful to provide regulators with an adequate level of independence (Smith 1997a). The institutional and procedural arrangements for regulatory agencies, including their location in the government machinery (branch and tier of government), may be laid down in contracts, statutes, laws, or any other type of appropriate regulation. The mechanics of these different approaches are all variants on a theme. The core issue is to find the best possible balance between autonomy and accountability for the regulator (Smith 1997b).

Rules for Price Regulation. Regulators use rules provided to them to discharge their task. Of prime importance are the rules governing pricing, which establish the risks borne by private parties and the principles of remuneration for bearing these risks, as well as the penalties for nonperformance. There is an extensive literature on appropriate pricing schemes that take into account relevant quality considerations as well (Kahn 1970, Laffont and Tirole 1993).

Three issues merit highlighting. First, it is, in principle, desirable for regulators to set price levels, leaving regulated companies the freedom to set price structures. Regulating prices in this way provides options to reduce exclusivity provisions and tends to optimize resource use (Ramsey-pricing) by allowing the company to respond efficiently to both cost and demand conditions.

Second, there have been endless debates and experiments on the basic rules that set price levels. Broadly, the debate has been between cost-plus schemes (rate-of-return regulation) and incentive schemes (price-cap regulation). Rate-of-return regulation (as practiced traditionally, for example, in the United States and Hong Kong, China) sets prices on the basis of actual costs. The rate base is multiplied with the cost of capital to determine the overall return to the company. Prices are adjusted at more or less regular intervals in response to requests to regulators. Under price-cap regulation, prices are fixed on the basis of anticipated costs, including the cost of capital for a period of typically 5 years. Under rate-of-return regulation, firms may have an incentive to inflate costs and, thus, earn a high absolute return on them. Under price-cap regulation, companies may have an incentive to improve efficiency to benefit from greater profits.

In practice, the differences among sensible schemes are small. No system is purely cost-plus. In rate-of-return schemes, one may test whether money was spent prudently and for relevant items. There is also a lag between price reviews, which may easily be 2 years or sometimes more. Price-cap schemes, at the time of reviews, are based on a cost-plus methodology similar to that of rate-of-return schemes, and many price caps actually contain pass-through provisions for certain costs. Often, review periods are shorter in practice than 4 or 5 years. One reason is that price-cap schemes typically have special provisions to adjust prices if major shocks occur between price reviews. Also, in many countries, important variables such as the cost of capital are hard to estimate for 5 years into the future and, thus, require more-frequent adjustment. Hopes that benchmarks or yardsticks from other companies could provide reasonably clear ways of setting price caps have proved disappointing so far.

In the end, there is no major difference between rate-of-return and price-cap schemes. Rate-of-return schemes tend to provide adequate comfort to investors, and they command political legitimacy because investors are limited to a particular return and cannot make large amounts of money after the fact, as, in principle, is possible under price caps. Price-cap schemes may have better incentives for efficiency improvement, but they run more easily into political legitimacy issues, when, in fact, firms become much more efficient and are seen to exploit the consumer. However, rate-of-return schemes may lose legitimacy if they are seen to allow excessive investment and cost-padding by the private investors. What matters in the end is a sensible regulator who is able to establish credibility while exercising discretion. This brings the key issue back to institutional design of the regulatory regime.

Third, by definition, natural monopolies exhibit substantial economies of scale. In many cases, marginal cost will consequently be below average cost. In general, economic theory suggests that efficiency is maximized when prices are set to equal marginal cost. However, in that case, the company may not cover all its costs. Government subsidies would then be required to get companies to invest. As noted by Adam Smith (1776), the problem with using subsidies to cover investment costs is that the political process—rather than consumer demand—then determines investment. Essentially, when user fees are required to cover all costs, so-called white elephants are no longer possible, or, if private investors construct them (for example, the Euro-tunnel), shareholders lose. In any case, taxpayers are protected, and normally investment will not exceed demand. Average cost pricing is, thus, a critical part of establishing a more-responsive agency chain in private infrastructure monopolies than would be possible under marginal cost pricing (Laffont and Tirole 1993).

Implications for Financing

Financing for investment is, correctly, of major concern to reforming governments. Fiscal problems have been at the root of many reforms introducing some form of private participation into infrastructure. But therein also lies a major danger. Many fiscally constrained governments tried to induce the private sector to fund investments. At the same time, they were reluctant to raise consumer prices to create the cash flow that would ultimately be required to service private capital. The simple matter is that private investors do not pay; they only finance. Only taxpayers or consumers pay. If the government has no funds to invest and is reluctant to raise consumer prices to cost-covering levels (including the cost of capital), there is bound to be a crisis one day. Some governments may paper over the problem for a while by issuing guarantees to hopeful or gullible investors, but in the absence of eventual basic policy reform, problems are unavoidable. Government reluctance to undertake reform has led to such difficulties in a number of countries, most prominently in Asia, where the 1997 crisis laid bare the structural problems of many schemes such as independent power projects that were undertaken without adequate sector-wide reform (Klein 1999).

The simple key to sustainable private financing is sound policy reform that establishes clarity for investors, establishes good incentives through adequate risk-sharing arrangements, and sets consumer prices at cost-covering or, preferably, market levels. If reform is adequate, financing follows (box 4.6). An ostensible lack of private financing is typically an expression of incomplete reform or lack of credibility, which in turn is usually due to inadequate reform. There is no overall lack of financing (Churchill 1995). Not all governments need to reform so as to attract private financing. But if they want to, they can—provided they are willing and capable to reform seriously.

Both investors and many governments like exclusivity provisions. Governments that sell exclusive rights can expect to obtain higher fiscal revenues, albeit at the expense of higher consumer prices and weaker incentives for efficiency in the sector. Most private investors are happy if they do not have to face competition. Hence, private investors and government officials make numerous arguments about why exclusivity is desirable to ensure that investment happens. Although seductive, the arguments are not convincing. When governments have been willing to introduce private infrastructure schemes without exclusivity and under a sensible policy framework, financing has flowed. That is the overwhelming experience of the early days of private infrastructure in the 19th century and that of recent cases, such as those in the natural gas sectors of Chile and Mexico.

Many analysts have also argued that real competition in infrastructure markets would undermine the ability to finance desirable projects. Again,

---

Box 4.6. Regulatory Risk and Project Financing

Recent work on private bond financing for private infrastructure projects has, for the first time, analyzed the effect of regulatory and governance risks on bond spreads. As in all preliminary studies, the work is hardly conclusive, but the results are interesting and plausible. Overall, governance risks are perceived as significant by bondholders—first and foremost the risks of corruption, red tape, and lack of constraints on government action, followed by concerns about more-traditional political risks, such as civil strife, terrorism, nationalization, lack of law enforcement, and military involvement in politics. Empirically, investors appear not too concerned about genuine mistakes in economic management. They seem to be able and willing to diversify such incompetence as long as it is not part of systemic incentives to steal or to break contracts.

If one distinguishes among three types of governments—industrial, emerging, and developing—a clear pattern emerges. If investors are willing to fund projects in developing countries at all, they are concerned about poor macroeconomic conditions and basic governance problems. For emerging markets, macroeconomic risks appear limited or diversifiable, but regulatory risks are of systematic importance. In industrial economies, investors focus mostly on intrinsic commercial risks.

Source: Bubnova 2000.

---

there is no real argument. In sectors such as refining, petrochemicals, aluminum, and so on, it is normal to fund large projects that are exposed to market risk. When the rules of the market are reasonably clear, the same happens in infrastructure markets, as has by now been demonstrated amply for natural gas projects, power plants, and telecommunications projects.

When sponsors assume market risk, typically relatively more equity and less debt is required to fund a project. The consequent increase in the weighted average cost of capital reflects the additional market risk borne by investors. Overall, efficiency and, eventually, cost are nevertheless improved because of better incentives for investors to anticipate and manage market risk. This observation illustrates the point discussed on cost of capital in the context of privatization. A higher ostensible cost of capital simply reflects the absence of recourse to taxation—not truly higher costs.

In this case, absence of exclusivity prevents extra charges (taxes) to consumers.

As market reforms proceed, not only may we see lower leverage at the project level, but, in due course, we may also see a decline in project financing. As new large infrastructure companies develop, they will eventually possess a large portfolio of cash flow generating companies. Financing out of retained earnings will become more widespread. Corporate financing will gain relative to project financing. This pattern is typical in normal competitive industries with large projects—for example, oil and gas or the old-style U.S. investor-owned utilities, which fund 80–90 percent of investment from retained earnings, just like normal companies (Mayer 1989).

The Wheel of Privatization and Nationalization

When done right, private participation in infrastructure holds the potential for significant benefits. However, it is harder to implement and to sustain successfully compared with privatization in competitive markets. The biggest political challenge is sustainable, effective regulation. In the 19th century, most infrastructure projects anywhere in the world began privately. If private infrastructure is such a good idea, why were so many infrastructure companies nationalized? There are many reasons that have at various times prevailed, including concerns about sovereignty, health and safety preoccupations, and industrial policy interests (Foreman-Peck and Millward 1994; Klein and Roger 1994).

But the core reasons surrounding nationalization have to do with regulation. First, usually those companies that were not nationalized accepted the need for some form of regulation of their monopoly power (for example, AT&T in the United States, RWE in Germany, and China Light and Power in Hong Kong, China). When there is regulation, the regulator has a tough challenge. Prices must not be too low, or investment stops. Prices must not be too high, or consumer outrage and political pressure follow. Historically, many times political pressure ended up lowering prices (or not raising them enough) to a degree that it eroded the profitability of private ventures and shifted the burden to taxpayers to fund subsidies. Taxpayers were often not able to fund all the government's programs. Hence, funds were lacking and the commercial disciplines of infrastructure companies weakened. In the end, service suffered and calls for privatization resurfaced.

Now we are at a stage at which many privatizations have again been carried out. Again, questions arise: Will regulators be able to strike the right balance between consumer and producer interests? Or will the wheel of privatization and nationalization (figure 4.5) keep turning? There is no magic bullet to solve this issue. In sectors in which competition is easy to introduce, as in telecommunications, pressures to renationalize are unlikely. In other sectors, several countries have had regulated private companies for more than a hundred years without nationalization. Examples are France (in water); Germany (in energy); and the United States (in energy, water, and telecommunications). What is clearly important is the search for methods to improve regulatory rules further and to support governments in setting up regulatory regimes with the right balance between autonomy and accountability.

Overall, private disciplines are easiest to implement in competitive markets, where consumers have choice and firms can freely enter and exit. They become more difficult when consumers lose choice, as occurs in natural monopoly situations. They become hardest when consumers have no

FIGURE 4.5. The Privatization Wheel

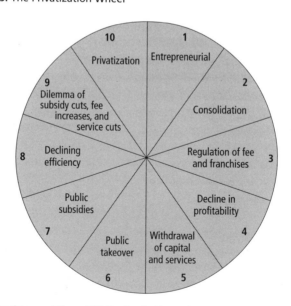

Source: Gomez-Ibanez and Meyer 1993. Reprinted with permission.

choice and taxpayers are forced to foot the bill. These difficulties in establishing discipline are in the nature of the various sectors. They plague public firms as well. The generic question about privatization or contracting out is whether clearer divisions of labor between policymakers, regulators, and private firms can improve discipline and performance or whether the interaction between multiple parties complicates matters to the point that it more than offsets potential performance improvements from contracting (Laffont and Tirole 1993). There is no easy answer. In the end, in any regulatory system there is always the problem of who guards the guardians and, thus, the issue of checks and balances in society. Markets and private sector approaches do not solve everything, but they can make significant contributions to the overall system of checks and balances in society.

Private Participation and Markets in the Social Sectors

Private Participation and Markets in Health

With respect to the role of private sector participation and markets in health, two broad sets of facts stick out. First, in low-income countries broadly between 50 percent and 90 percent of actual health financing or provision is private (tables 4.3 and 4.4). Second, analytical, policy, and project efforts of the development community to improve health standards and outcomes have for decades been directed overwhelmingly at improving the performance of publicly financed and provided health (Filmer, Hammer, and Pritchett 1997; World Health Organization 2000).

The focus on improving public health care is typically justified with reference to a variety of concerns about market outcomes (World Bank 1993b). These include

- Benefits not captured by individuals, such as lower likelihood of infection by others as a result of vaccination (externalities)
- Affordability concerns for the poor
- Local natural monopolies for facilities such as hospitals
- Failures in the insurance markets for health—that is, problems high-risk patients face in obtaining insurance (adverse selection) and incentives for excessive treatment (moral hazard)
- Inability of clients to judge the need for and quality of health care

TABLE 4.3. Percentage of Total Health Expenditures that Are Private

Country or region	Share of private health expenditures (percent)	Number of countries
All countries	53.6	115
Low-income countries	63.1	32
Low-middle-income countries	42.8	36
High-middle-income countries	54.0	15
High-income, non-OECD countries	62.0	10
High-income, OECD countries	32.6	22
East Asia and Pacific	53.2	14
Latin America and Caribbean	58.1	32
Middle East and North Africa	47.4	11
South Asia	74.8	5
Sub-Saharan Africa	59.6	19
Rest of world	29.3	34

Source: Filmer, Hammer, and Pritchett 1997.

TABLE 4.4. Demand for Private Sector Health Care in Five Indian States

Area	Gujarat	Maharashtra	Tamil Nadu	Uttar Pradesh	West Bengal	Weighted average
Rural						
(1) Percentage of treated illness episodes to private providers	69	78	71	91	83	82
(2) Percentage of out-of-pocket expenses to nonhospital treatment	62	64	74	59	74	65
(3) Percentage of out-of-pocket expenses to private nonhospital treatment	48	55	68	51	65	56
Above, (3) as a percentage of (2)	77	86	92	86	88	86
Urban						
(1) Percentage of treated illness episodes to private providers	82	75	69	85	78	79
(2) Percentage of out-of-pocket expenses to nonhospital treatment	61	60	69	57	63	61
(3) Percentage of out-of-pocket expenses to private nonhospital treatment	53	51	62	46	54	52
Above, (3) as a percentage of (2)	87	85	90	81	86	85

Source: Filmer, Hammer, and Pritchett 1997.

At the same time, options for consumer choice in the health market appear larger than is the case, for example, in many areas of infrastructure. Actual practice in a number of countries, as well as theory, suggests the following ways of dealing with the potential market failures while still tapping the power of markets and private discipline.

Externalities, Affordability, and Natural Monopoly. The basic solution for externality issues is to determine the desired level of service politically and then (a) to subsidize demand such that individuals consume the desired amount or (b) to make consumption compulsory as for vaccinations. The service can then be provided privately.

Affordability concerns can be addressed in the same way. Desired service levels for the poor can be achieved by targeting subsidies through a variety of possible schemes to the poor while contracting out provision (see chapter 5).

Just as under public provision, the public sector needs to monitor whether the desired overall targets are achieved. When such targets can be adequately defined and monitored, it is always possible to write contracts, which foresee remuneration to the service provider contingent on achievement of the targets. Funding measurable outcomes in this way provides tougher discipline in achieving public goals than public provision, where inputs are funded.

> *We are not allowed to get sick anymore because we have to pay for medication....*
> *What with?*
>
> —An old man, Bosnia and Herzegovina

The general rules for effective contracting out of public services apply. In fact, matters are easier than for contracting out monopoly services, as many relevant health interventions can be provided in markets of competing providers (Abramson 1999; Abrantes 1999; Ashton 1998; Bennett, McPake, and Mills 1997; Broomberg, Mills, and Masobe 1997; England 2000; Institute for Health Sector Development 2000; Loevinsohn 2000a, 2000b; Marek and others 1999; McPake and Hongoro 1995; Newbrander, Cuellar, and Timmons 2000; Palmer 2000; Preker, Harding, and Travis 2000; Rosen 2000; Sheaff and Lloyd 1999; Slack and Savedoff 2001; Vining and Globerman 1999). In the case of contracting out local natural monopolies, such as hospital facilities in sparsely populated areas, the issues are the same as for contracting out other monopoly services. The issues have been tackled successfully in a number of countries, for example, with voucher schemes for nursing home care (OECD 1997b, 1998a).

Health Insurance. Private insurance markets may leave high-risk patients uninsured (Barr 1993). Voluntary insurance systems may also lead healthy individuals to opt out of the system. When such dropouts fall seriously ill, society is typically faced with demands to pay for care anyway (OECD 1992a). The usual response to these concerns is to introduce a basic level of mandatory insurance, to require individuals to take out minimal policies, and to require insurance companies to insure all individuals (Barrientos and Lloyd-Sherlock 2000; Bertranou 1999; Conn and Walford 1998; Dror and Jacquier 1999; Ensor 1999; Gertler and Solon 2000; Jack 2001; OECD 2001). Such systems may necessitate some level of price regulation to prevent competing insurance companies from shifting high-risk individuals to other insurers, which may then not be able to compete for good risks—the so-called problem of nonexistence of pooling equilibria (Barr 1993; Cutler and Reber 1996; Cutler and Zeckhauser 1999).

The problem is similar to that of privatizing pension systems. Solutions for moving to private pension systems are currently widely shared. Here, as well, it is recommended that basic mandatory insurance should underpin the system, while insurers retain the incentive to attract a mix of good risks (Colombo 2001; James 1996, 1999; World Bank 1994c). More generally, such issues pervade any private insurance market—hence, for example, minimum mandatory vehicle insurance.

The other problem associated with insurance markets is that of moral hazard, the incentive for the insured party to take less care once insured and, thus, to raise the cost of insurance (Gaynor, Haas-Wilson, and Vogt 1998). Any system that subsidizes health care is plagued by the same problem: customers may consume too much. The only solution would be reliance on full user fee financing (Aseno-Okyere and others 1998; Collins and others 1996; Gertler and Hammer 1997; Jimenez 1987; Lewis 1993; Newbrander, Cuellar, and Timmons 2000; Ogunbekun and others 1996; Sharma and Hotchkiss 2001; Shaw and Griffin 1995; Willis and Leighton 1995; Wouters 1995). To mitigate incentives for fraud or excessive consumption, insurance schemes in any market typically require some form of direct contribution from the customer—for example, in the form of a deductible. Optimal insurance schemes would provide lump-sum payments dependent on the patient's illness and would require the patient to cover extra payments. Such arrangements are similar to that of Diagnostic Related Groups in the Medicare and Medicaid systems of the United States

(Schneider 2000; Stover, Quigley, and Kraushaar 1996; Wouters 1998). The issue is the same, whether health care is publicly or privately provided.

Monitoring Quality. Clients of health care cannot easily judge the need for treatment and quality of service. As in any other market, when product quality is difficult to judge, general quality standards and disclosure requirements (for example, labeling of drugs) can help (Jacobzone 2000; World Bank 1993b). However, for a number of services and treatments, quality is hard to judge for the client, and poor quality may have catastrophic consequences. As discussed in the section on quality regulation, the situation calls for fairly clear standards and relatively strong liability standards to offset the incentives of for-profit providers to skimp on quality. Again, the monitoring issues are the same under public or private provision (Abbott 1995; Afifi 1997, 2001; Gauthier and Rogal 2001; Hurst and Jee-Hughes 2001; Kumaranayake 1997, 1998; Kumaranayake and others 2000; Newbrander 1999; Or 2002; Saltman, Busse, and Mossialos 2002; Van Lerberghe and others 1997).

If all the issues are the same under public or private systems, and if the private systems have the potential to improve service by way of competition or at least more-efficient contracting, what rationale may be there for public systems? The core rationale has to do with the widespread suspicion of the profit motive when it comes to providing vital services such as health care. If effective regulatory systems in a country cannot be established to counteract the incentive of for-profit providers to skimp on quality, then maybe the incentive needs to be weakened, such that the natural interest of public servants to provide decent service comes to dominate.

Judging Trust and Competence. Of course, the argument does not imply that health care provision should be public. It implies that health care should be provided by nonprofit organizations, of which the public sector is a variant. Moving to nonprofit provision does not generate better information; it simply promises to establish more trust in the motives of health personnel. If the issue is one of judging whom we want to trust, why should we not leave the decision to individuals? And why would we want to establish monopolies of provision? As long as competition between nonprofit and for-profit providers is allowed, individuals can judge whom to trust. We would, in any case, expect individuals to have the strongest interest in making sure they are served by trustworthy parties, and we expect them to be capable of deciding whom to trust.[2]

If we think individuals require expert handholding in their decisions because their instincts may just not be up to judging whom to trust and their competence,[3] then we can allow public and private rating services to provide competing information on the quality of treatment of service providers. If we believe that such rating cannot be done or is likely to be biased or unfair, then we are simply saying that nobody can do better than the individual.

If we think that we need case-specific rather than general judgments, then we need specific reviews of doctors' decisions, for example, by insurance companies. Again, we can only argue against private and competing provision of such review functions if we think monetary incentives will unduly bias judgment. Indeed, that suspicion arises, for example, in the case of for-profit health maintenance organizations. In that case, we are back to saying that trustworthy reviewers are needed. Nonprofit reviewers should supervise for-profit providers. Still, why individuals should not be able to choose among them is unclear, unless we believe that we can set up a system of benevolent and efficient monopoly stewards and providers in the public sector.

Public Sector Performance and Private Choice in Low-Income Countries. For most poor countries, this discussion is rather academic. Nonprofit provision of health care, including by the state, reduces one form of monetary incentive—namely, the ability to obtain dividends. But it leaves many ways open for individuals to pursue private gain (box 4.7). They may sell drugs on the black market instead of administering them to patients. They may provide lousy service to make their own lives easier. They may extort side-payments precisely from those most vulnerable and in need of care (Delcheva, Balabanova, and McKee 1997).

> *We would rather treat ourselves than go to the hospital where an angry nurse might inject us with the wrong drug.*
>
> —A poor person, Tanzania, 1997

The nonprofit form of incorporation helps if it is accompanied by good monitoring of the nonprofit organization and a general civic spirit in society. Some public sector health systems in low-income countries appear to provide good service, such as in Kerala (India), Sri Lanka, and Costa Rica.

Box 4.7. Public Health Workers in Uganda

In a 1997 study, the conduct of health workers was examined in 12 health units in two districts of Uganda (Bushenyi and Iganga). One of the findings was that health workers in all but two facilities routinely charged users beyond the formally agreed-upon levels, and the drug supply by donors or by the government was routinely used as a source of additional income. The estimate of leakages ranged from 40 to 94 percent of the public supply of drugs to the facilities. The investigators summarized the situation as one in which public health facilities and resources were treated as the private property of the health workers.

Source: Ablo and Reinikka 1998. For more details, see Asiimwe and others 1997.

Their success appears to depend on effective social or political monitoring systems of the effort and quality of health workers (Filmer, Hammer, and Pritchett 1997). As in the case of successful public interventions in other markets, the quality and integrity of civil servants and the degree of local accountability seem to be important. Such success seems to be the exception in low-income countries and is not easily replicable. As evidenced by the plethora of problem cases, it is also hard to recognize ex ante whether in a particular situation the prerequisites for a well-functioning state system exist.

The overwhelming empirical evidence is that public sector provision of health services in low-income countries does not systematically induce a spirit of client service, but often quite horrific service—just as for other public services. Sales of drugs on the black market are rampant in many cases, and many clients have to pay special fees and are mistreated by hospital staff (Filmer, Hammer, and Pritchett 1997). A client survey (Mtemeli 1994, as cited in Filmer, Hammer, and Pritchett 1997) in the Mutasa district of Zimbabwe found that mothers complained about being ridiculed by nurses and forced to wash clothes right after delivery. A full 13 percent of mothers complained about being hit by nurses during delivery. Even 11 percent of nurses said that clients preferred private facilities because they feared being mistreated by nurses.

Health systems have private elements in most industrial countries as well. The mix of public and private financing and provision varies significantly. The options for composing systems that attempt to exploit market-type disciplines are clear. The juxtaposition of concerns about externalities, affordability, natural monopoly, insurance problems, and ability to judge quality create numerous detailed issues. When taken together with the views of entrenched interests, reform becomes hard—witness the troubles of health care reform in the United States (reminiscent of the complications of California's electricity sector reform with its combination of sophisticated debate and inability to deal with simple fundamentals).

Low-income countries are in a somewhat easier situation. Many basic health care services are least plagued by market failure. Individuals are voting with their feet (figure 4.6). Competition among health service providers is clearly beneficial for the vast majority of the poor, and they are willingly paying user fees for the service (Abel-Smith and Rawal 1992; Audibert and Mathonnat 2000; Diop, Yazbeck, and Bitran 1995; Filmer, Hammer, and Pritchett 1997; Kipp and others 2001; Litvack and Bodart 1993).

Private Participation and Markets in Education

Education is quite a different business from health care. However, two broad parts of the picture are similar. In developing and transition economies, private forms of education financing and provision are widespread, particularly in low-income countries (figures 4.7 and 4.8). Yet for decades, the focus of development efforts—as in health—has been on improving public sector performance.

Various concerns with market outcomes are cited to argue the case for public systems:
- Existence of local natural monopolies
- Affordability for poor students and imperfect credit markets
- Externalities from education
- Incentives for private schools to cherry-pick the best students and leave others underserved
- Incentives for rich parents to send their children to schools with other rich children and, thus, to increase social segregation
- Incentives for private schools to neglect the teaching of civic values
- Difficulty for parents or students to assess the need for and the quality of education.

FIGURE 4.6. Use of Private versus Public Facilities by the Poor for Treatment of Acute Respiratory Infections

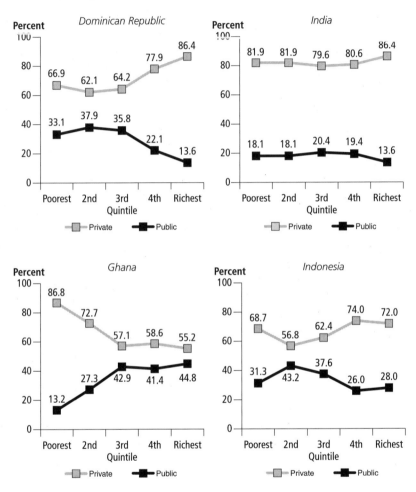

Source: Gwatkin and others 2000.

Affordability, Credit Market Failure, Externalities, and Natural Monopoly. Theoretically, students should be able to fund their education by borrowing against future income. However, future income is difficult to assess, and enforcement of such loan contracts may be problematic. Nevertheless, student loan schemes, particularly for tertiary education, are fruitfully pur-

FIGURE 4.7. Private Expenditure on Education, by Country, as a Percentage of Total Education Expenditure

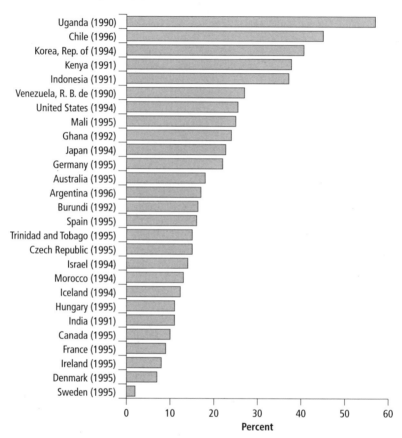

Source: World Bank EDSTATS Data.

sued in a number of countries, as in India recently (Tooley 1999). Beyond this possibility and as argued before for the case of health services, issues of affordability can be tackled by subsidizing the poor and contracting out service provision (Beales 1994a, 1994b; Beales and O'Leary 1993; Fitz and Beers 2001; Goldstone 2001; Hannaway 1999; Hill, Pierce, and Guthrie 1997; Lieberman 1989; Wertz 2000). Various subsidy schemes are possible, including stipends and vouchers (Alderman, Orazem, and Paterno 1996; Cave 2001; Fernández and Rogerson 2001; Kim, Alderman,

FIGURE 4.8. Enrollment in Private Schools, by Country, as a Percentage of Total Enrollment, 1996

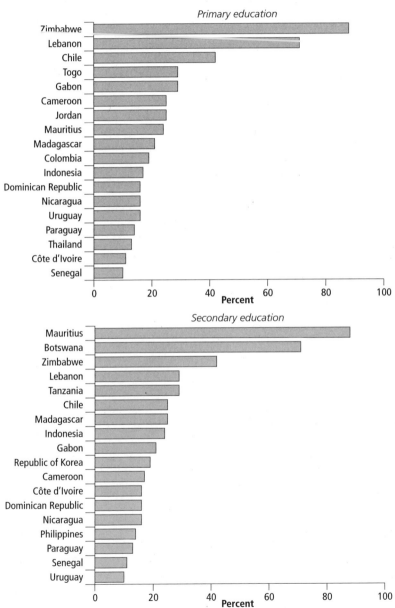

Primary education

Secondary education

Source: United Nations Educational, Scientific, and Cultural Organization (UNESCO) 2000.

and Orazem 1998; Patrinos 2000; Patrinos and Ariasingam 1997; Scobie and Patrinos 2001). Widespread agreement exists among proponents and critics of privatization that the poor can be reached effectively (Carnoy 1997, Friedman 1995, West 1997). In addition to affordability concerns, subsidies may be justified by externalities from basic education. For example, evidence exists that innovations in India during the green revolution were more easily adopted when basic education levels were higher. The way to deal with natural monopoly issues follows the same approach as that set out in the section on contracting out public services.

Cherry-Picking and Segregation. When there is competition, all competitors—whether public or private—will try to enhance profit by raising revenue and lowering costs. Schools have an incentive to select the best students if doing so enhances profit. The best students, in turn, want to go to the schools that offer them a superior quality–price bundle. If schools can discriminate price or quality according to student ability and motivation, then they can actively pursue such strategies. To attract the best, they would have to offer a discount of some type that hurts profit. Attracting the best students has a positive effect on profit only if having them enhances other clients' willingness to pay. That scenario assumes that good students enhance educational achievements of others, which is to some extent the case.

> *School is no good if you don't have connections.*
>
> —A poor person, Macedonia

Many countries maintain private or public schools for gifted students. If we agree to have such schools, the question is whether we allow them to emerge in competition or whether we have a centralized system assigning students to them. It is not clear why centralized systems would be better at assigning students than the market. It may still be effective to use standard tests for all to determine ability, but central allocation of students appears unnecessary. When schools compete freely for good students, we would expect the best students to get discounts, presumably as a function of their test results. This added incentive for performance would tend to improve the system.

We may not want students to cluster in schools with others of similar characteristics, be those characteristics ability or social status. To some extent, there are natural limits to such clustering—namely, the multitude of goals that parents and students pursue in choosing a school. The decision depends not only on characteristics of other students, but also on the quality of the school and its location. Judgments about quality or valuations of different dimensions of quality will vary. Existing school choice experiments suggest that, for example, increased social segregation either is not a significant problem or can be addressed by the use of subsidies, for example, in the form of vouchers (Figlio and Stone 2001; Greene 2000; West 1997).

When parents and students can select a school, that choice becomes more independent of the choice of residential location. Typically, in systems without school choice, students attend schools in their neighborhoods. Whether in public or private systems, people may move into neighborhoods with schools they prefer. They thus have de facto school choice. Rich people always have a broader choice, because they can afford more expensive housing. School choice systems, particularly when combined with vouchers or other types of targeted subsidies for the poor, provide much wider choice for the poor relative to traditional systems. Again, in several systems of school choice, such outcomes have been achieved (Nechyba 2001; Patrinos 2000; Vawda 1997).

Teaching Social Values. Many believe that one of the core reasons to have public schools is to ensure basic civic education that helps integrate a nation or community. Many analysts worry that private schools would not have an interest in teaching social values. Although it is arguable whether, indeed, public schools teach civic values better than private institutions, it is possible to require private as well as public schools to provide ethical education. It is not clear that governments have more control over the teaching in public schools than that in private schools. In countries such as Denmark and the Netherlands, which cannot be suspected of a belief in unfettered markets and where civic education matters, education is largely provided by private, albeit publicly funded schools (James 1990, 1991; Patrinos 2001, 2002; Ritzen, Van Dommelen, and De Vijlder 1997).

Assessing the Need for and the Quality of Education. Assessing the need for and the quality of education is difficult. Some studies suggest that low-income households are less capable of choosing schools than others (Carnoy 1997). Others show that poor families are willing to invest a lot in a better future for their children (Narayan and others 2000b). The widespread willingness to pay for private education among low-income groups in developing countries supports the latter view. Clearly, both schools and individual teachers develop very distinct reputations.

In Kenya, in all districts, poor parents place a very high premium on keeping their children in school. To do so, they would sell their possessions, beg, steal, brew and sell beer, pray,... cajole teachers into letting the children stay in school, pay in installments, put their children to work, and sometimes become destitute trying to keep their children in school.

—A poor person, Kenya

Whatever the capability of individuals to choose, if somebody can better assess schools, then it should be possible to have competing rating services. The argument runs just as in the case of health, where the assessment problem may be harder. In the end, to find systematic advantages in the public provision of education and the restriction of choice, one has to argue that parents and students are unable to choose well and that the nonprofit character and the monopoly of public schools provide incentives to improve service.

Evidence from School Choice. The desolate state of many public education systems in low-income countries demonstrates that choice and private provision rather than public monopoly are valuable and appreciated by clients. Yet the many private systems in low-income countries have hardly been studied—much less compared with—public systems.

Beyond the de facto competition from private providers in poor countries, a number of experiments with school choice and subsidy schemes such as vouchers have by now been conducted, for example, in Chile and Colombia (Angrist and others 2001; Calderón 1996; King and others 1997; Savedoff 1997). Although the evidence is not conclusive, a number of experiments show a cost savings in private schools. Educational achievements may also improve under choice systems, but the findings appear more mixed (Bedi and Garg 2000; Canagarajah and Ye 2001; De and others 1999; Glewwe and Patrinos 1999; Jimenez, Lockheed, and Paqueo 1991; Shah 2001; see also figure 4.9). The most detailed analysis available from the United States on the effects of school choice suggests that greater choice has led to performance improvements (Hanushek and Rivkin 2001; Hepburn 1999; Howell and others 2000; Hoxby 1994, 2001; Peterson and others 2001; Sawhill and Smith 1998). Furthermore, it has actually

FIGURE 4.9. Private Schools Can Deliver Better Education at Lower Cost: Ratio of Private to Public Cost and Test Score Achievement, by Country

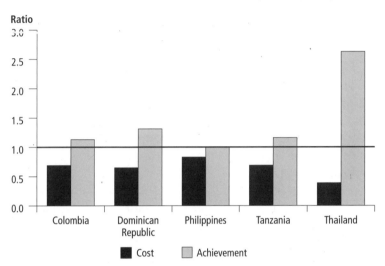

Source: Lockheed and Jimenez 1994.

reduced the cost of education and has led to a greater demand for public schools as these schools improved. In fact, public policies that reduce choice appear to push more people into private schools. Effects of reform barely differ between poor and well-to-do families. However, teacher salaries are more related to performance in systems with greater choice for parents (Hoxby 2000).

Private Provision and Market: Prospects for Reform

All in all, the debate about private participation in the social sectors resembles that about infrastructure during the 1980s. Some high-quality public systems exist. In the past, much ostensible effort has been directed at emulating those systems with little success. Most public systems in low-income countries perform poorly. Individuals opt for private alternatives if they have the choice. Typically, policymakers know little about this subject. Consumer choice, combined with free entry (that is, competition), holds promise for improvement. Where competition is not possible, private disciplines can still be introduced, but with greater difficulty (World Bank 1994a).

123

It is always hard to make the a priori case for competition against a public (or private) monopoly. The monopolist defender of the status quo, always asks, "What will be better after the introduction of competition?" If anybody can come up with a convincing idea, the monopolist's answer is, "Very good, I can do that, too. My monopoly can do anything." But the case for competition ultimately rests on the ability of competitive systems to come up with solutions that nobody has thought of before or that nobody has seriously pursued. Empirically, competition does, indeed, generate innovation (Winston 1993). The innovation may be obvious after the fact, such as the introduction of hub-and-spoke systems in the airline industry after deregulation or in the design of electricity transmission systems, but it took competition to make it happen.

The dynamics of debate are also visible in the fledgling empirical literature that tries to assess the outcome of experiments with new competitive private education schemes. A number of studies have found, for example, that private schools operate at a lower cost. They then analyzed why—for example, lower teacher salaries or higher classroom sizes. And then the argument follows, "Of course, if the public schools had done the same thing they would perform the same way." Yes, but why didn't they?

During the 1990s, interest in school choice and market options to organize education and health care systems increased across the world (OECD 1994). There is latent promise in reform. Yet the politics of reform are complicated. Letting the profit motive loose on vital services creates political tension. Some of the tension is due to resistance of groups associated with the existing system (for example, teachers' unions). Some of it is caused by doubts about the effectiveness of reform. When we look at the social sectors in the same way as we look at other sectors that have undergone market-friendly reform, it appears that much can be gained from bolder experiments.

Reform prospects may be a bit like in the water sector. Benefits from new forms of private participation and competition are not always easy to obtain and may require effective regulation. Technical change does not seem set to force reform, as it did in telecommunications. Deeply held social concerns prevail, as in the debate about the National Health Service in the United Kingdom. In that context, no matter how market-oriented society might otherwise be, there is no clear prospect of decisive reform. At the same time, it is clear that free entry and choice are key features that need to be available for low-income groups to get at least minimum service.

While sophisticated reform discussion proceeds, the poor continue to pay for private services because they value health and education and because they make the best decisions that they can (Narayan and others 2000a).

Notes

1. Note that markets with very high concentration do not necessarily indicate the existence of a natural monopoly or even the exercise of market power. As long as it is possible for new firms to enter the market, such potential competition may be sufficient to curb the exercise of market power (Evans and Kessides 1993).

2. Arguably one of the key reasons humans have been able to develop the most complex division of labor of any species is their ability to judge whether to trust somebody else. It appears that major parts of the brain developed to solve the issue of deciding whom to trust (Ridley 1998).

3. Basic assurance of competence may be obtained through licensing systems for health personnel.

5

Private Sector Development and Pro-Poor Policy Design

Pro-poor policy design requires more than just private sector development components, as in the case of any multidimensional issue. The private sector development agenda can make a significant contribution, but it will not be the magic bullet.

Mechanisms to Promote Diffusion of Best Practice

The potentially biggest hope for poverty reduction comes from mechanisms that transmit best practice to areas where the poor live and work. The private sector development agenda emphasizes the crucial contribution of competition in this regard. Free entry allows new and better entrepreneurs to enter the market. Some would be advanced firms (of any size) that bring best practice. Others would be new and small entrepreneurs from poor areas, who work with the new firm or adopt new methods and techniques. Free entry allows such opportunities for improved methods of production and service delivery to be seized. Choice by customers tests whether, indeed, the opportunity seized brings the benefits that customers want. The threat of exit for entrepreneurs who do not meet customer demand provides an incentive to upgrade practices and be responsive.

Improved and clear assignation of property rights to the poor, as suggested, for example, by Hernando de Soto (2000), can help the poor seize opportunities. Property rights provide owners with a long-term outlook and enable them to raise capital more easily. The potential for redistributing property rights to help the poor is, however, limited by the need to preserve basic protection of rights and contracts such that the incentive to invest is not undermined.

Special assistance to fledgling entrepreneurs through microcredit or business development services may help speed up the diffusion of best practice. Many such efforts to jumpstart markets have had rather mixed success. The likelihood of truly furthering diffusion of best practice appears highest if such support measures are delivered in ways that are consistent with market principles and that do not create unsustainable dependence on subsidies.

These mechanisms, in sum, are the fundamental contributions that the private sector development agenda can make to promote the diffusion processes of best practice. Yet more is required to translate such measures into effective and widespread poverty reduction. Basic infrastructure may be needed to connect remote communities to markets. For example, rural roads plus free entry can go a long way toward providing new opportunities for the poor. It is also clear that the poor need the capability to respond to opportunities. Some minimum level of education and some basic level of social cohesion are important determinants of progress.

The design of pro-poor policies is a case-by-case effort, drawing on the private sector development toolkit in combination with other interventions.

Mechanisms to Enhance Service Delivery

The second basic contribution of the private sector development agenda is the provision of basic services, which, to some degree, may include infrastructure and social services. Free entry and competition are again key policy design elements. In addition, output-based disciplines for contracting out monopoly services can help—provided a meaningful and operational measure of output exists (Brook and S. Smith 2001).

Work on pro-poor design, particularly of private infrastructure schemes, has substantially advanced in recent years (Brook 2000). This effort promises solutions that lead well beyond the overall efficiency effects of well-designed private schemes. Pro-poor infrastructure schemes could be particularly beneficial for women charged with collecting water or fuel wood.

Again, the private sector development agenda provides just elements for the solution of a multidimensional problem. The quality of government institutions is important, for example, for contracting out and regulation, where required. Community participation can help define desirable service standards and outputs. Community organizations or other nonprofit organizations can help in the process of contracting and monitoring (Bray 1999; de Silva 2000; Jimenez and Sawada 1998). Overall, private sector development approaches do not replace the need for a state or for well-functioning communities. However, such approaches can help complement them and, thus, render them more effective.

Subsidies and Choice

To some degree, subsidies may be necessary as part of an overall pro-poor intervention. Subsidies can be designed to be compatible with the market solution in a number of ways. Subsidies are meant to serve the truly needy. They should not excessively undermine incentives for the poor to help themselves. Also, by their nature, subsidies are in infinite demand both by the intended beneficiaries and by others who are interested in diverting them for private gain. Yet study after study of subsidy systems shows that these programs benefit the rich as well as the poor. In many cases, the better-off are the main recipients of subsidies (Castro-Leal and others 1999). Given the large amount of subsidies provided and the evidence of waste and inefficiency, there is every reason to help design more-efficient and better-targeted subsidy delivery systems (Bosch and others 2000; Foster, Gomez-Lobo, and Halpern 2000; Gomez-Lobo, Foster, and Halpern 2000; Yepes 1999).

Subsidies with Consumer Choice

Subsidies may be given to consumers so as to leave them with choice. Such systems require markets for the service to be meaningful. There may simply be a sort of negative income tax, which enhances general incomes of the poor. Or one may want to target the poor, for example, through means-testing. Also, private and public donors are often reluctant to provide general purpose support and prefer to tie donations or subsidies to the consumption of particular goods and services. Partially, that preference reflects donors' wishes to determine what the poor should do with the subsidy, and partially, it represents an attempt to provide the subsidy in a form that makes it unattractive for those who are not in need.

To provide assistance with the purchase of a particular good or service, one can establish voucher systems that still leave choice to the consumer. Voucher systems have been used for education, nursing homes, and business development services (Cave 2001; Patrinos 2000; West 1997). Care needs to be taken that vouchers do not become tradable and do not allow money to be raised for other, unintended consumption. Methods that try to cope with the problem include direct payment to the service provider. In any case, the problem is not peculiar to vouchers. Any service that is rationed, whether through vouchers or otherwise, can effectively be traded.

Subsidies without Consumer Choice

Other subsidy systems may not leave consumers choice—either because the subsidized service is a natural monopoly or because the government provided monopoly rights to some service (for example, public education). Subsidies may be targeted at individuals on the basis of need (means-testing), or they may be available to anybody who buys a particular service. There can still be donor competition, in the sense that donors can decide which of several monopoly services to fund, but individual beneficiaries have no choice in these cases. Choices about service quantity and quality need to be made by some collective mechanism, which includes community participation as an option.

Market mechanisms can still help establish the most-efficient level of subsidy for a particular monopoly service. For example, the right to serve remote infrastructure customers may be auctioned off to the bidder of the lowest subsidy, as in the Chilean telecommunications system (Wellenius 1997). More generally, the service to be provided can be auctioned off among competing providers, be they for-profit or not. Such auctions determine the most-efficient service provider. Such actions are simply an application of the competition for the market discussed in chapter 4. The principles for efficient contracting out apply—in particular, efficient risk-sharing that establishes performance or output goals for the private provider and leaves it to private ingenuity to come up with the most-efficient way to meet such goals.

Provision of Subsidized Service and Competition

Privately provided subsidies tend to be passed on through nonprofit organizations. This structure allows the ability to monitor the use of the donations. When people use a flower service to send a bouquet of flowers to a relative or friend as a gift, they pay for a service that someone else receives and rely on competing for-profit firms to provide the service. Quality of service is easily checked through feedback from the recipients. The providers have an interest in maintaining a good reputation.

When citizens make donations, they help people with whom they are not in direct contact and whom they do not know well enough to be able to interpret any feedback with confidence. In such situations, donors have to delegate some of the monitoring to others—in effect to charitable organizations. Such charities tend to incorporate as nonprofits (Hansman 1981). Nonprofit structures weaken monetary incentives to abuse donations for private gain because profit can no longer be distributed as dividends. By the same token, nonprofit organizations are not subject to the disciplines of the market for corporate control, because there is no equity to be sold.

However, opportunities still exist for insiders in nonprofit organizations to divert funds for private gain by other means—for example, through payment of high salaries or through corrupt contracting practices. The basic discipline on nonprofit organizations comes from information on their behavior and the ability of donors to stop giving to agencies abusing their trust. Both donors and beneficiaries benefit from choice. As in the case of any other private firm, the agency chain from voluntary donor to manager of the charity is more effective than that from taxpayer to aid agency because donors have the choice whether to give and they can choose among competing charities.

Competition among charities is thus, in principle, beneficial because it allows donors and beneficiaries choice. One generic problem may arise. Beneficiaries of donations or subsidies have potentially infinite demand for the service and need to be rationed. In the process, clever beneficiaries may be able to exploit donor competition by receiving multiple, undeserved service. The charity market functions better when information systems exist that allow donors to check whether somebody else has already given to a beneficiary. Also, as in any market, standard terms and conditions for complex donor service may be valuable. Beyond such measures, however, donor coordination or government control over donor services is problematic and amounts to establishing undesirable monopoly power.

Contracts for Efficient Service and Subsidy Delivery

Whatever the degree of choice on the parts of beneficiaries, output-based contracts provide the option for donors to improve provision of a service by shifting performance risk to parties that have strong incentives to perform. Such parties may include for-profit firms, nonprofit organizations, or community organizations. Such contracts require that a meaningful measure exists for truly desired output or performance. (Of course, when misleading measures are used, there are dangers, because what gets measured gets done at the expense of more important matters.) In addition, there will always be quality regulations that constrain the options for the provider, such as environmental and social standards. Also, donors need credible ways to measure output (Vinson 1999; Wellenius 1997).

When output-based contracts are used, part or all of subsidies can be disbursed when service is delivered rather than being used to finance inputs. It is up to service providers to fund themselves in commercial markets to invest and operate. (Markets themselves are the ultimate output-based system because customers pay only when they receive service.)

Suppose grant aid is disbursed on delivery of, say, medical service or education. Such aid provides purchasing power and reduces the price that customers have to pay, possibly to zero. Assuming the same efficiency of delivery had the aid been disbursed for the purchase of inputs, the consumer price would have been equally low.

However, the whole point is that efficiency is likely to be increased when aid is disbursed against actual output. In that case, the cost of capital of commercial financing adds an ostensible cost to the whole production and delivery process. But, as argued before, the cost of capital of public funds is truly no lower than that of private funds, even though apparent costs may be higher. When aid is disbursed against output, the risk for taxpayers that their money is wasted disappears as long as the contract monitoring system works.

Evaluated at the correct risk-adjusted cost of capital, the cost of service delivery under output-based contracts is no worse than that under equally efficient traditional input-based grant financing. This principle is also behind value-for-money tests based on risk-adjusted cost of capital. It does not matter for the analysis whether aid is delivered in the form of grants or loans with an equivalent grant element. The net cost to taxpayers is the same.

The big issue for output-based subsidies is not the cost of capital, but the monitoring issues that arise. As discussed before, monitoring of providers is generally most effective when there is head-to-head competition for customers (and donors) who choose and pay. This system favors general income transfers or voucher systems, when possible. Discipline is weakened when there is no choice. But as long as customers still pay, white elephants and corruption are reduced. Discipline is hardest to achieve when there is no choice for consumers and when taxpayers or donors pay. In that case, the weight of establishing discipline falls largely on the monitoring process. Transparency of monitoring is improved whenever clear output-based contracts can be used.

6

Private Sector Development and Sustainability

Worries that unfettered markets will destroy the environment and undermine the social fabric are as old as markets themselves (Hirschman 1992). Consider, in turn, environmental and social sustainability.

Private Markets and the Environment

Markets for Scarce Resources and Overexploitation of Common Resources

Now all places are accessible, all are documented, all are full of business.... [T]here are such great cities where formerly hardly a hut.... [E]verywhere there is a dwelling, everywhere a multitude, everywhere a government, everywhere there is life.... [W]e are burdensome to the world, the resources are scarcely adequate to us.

—Quintus Septimus Florence Tertillianus, circa A.D. 200,
as quoted in Johnson 2000

Never before in history has the natural environment been under as much stress from humans as today. Worries about depletion of resources and destruction of the ecosphere as a result of rampant growth have increased in recent decades (Daly 1987). At the same time, it has become evident that centrally planned economies have had a worse environmental record than market-based systems. State-owned enterprises often pollute more than private ones, in part because governments have a harder time supervising themselves than regulating arm's-length parties. It thus appears that markets are likely to figure in the solution, but the debate rages over how much markets and private firms operating in them should be controlled.

When goods or factors of production are abundant in the sense that supply exceeds demand, there tend to be no clearly defined property rights for resources. When a resource becomes scarce, it becomes costly to allow all to use the resource. Free entry into fishing, for example, may lead to over-fishing—the well-known "tragedy of the commons" (Hardin 1968). Societies then need a mechanism that limits fishing, so as to avoid over-exploitation of the resource, while providing the freedom to deploy more and more productive methods of fishing. In countries such as Iceland, New Zealand, and Peru this mechanism takes the form of fishing rights (OECD 1992b). Those countries limit the total allowable catch and allocate rights to fish. Entry into fishing is then restricted to those who own or acquire a right to fish. In this sense, property rights restrict free entry (Demsetz 1982; Von Weizsäcker 1980). Property rights establish exclusivity to use an asset even though they may not establish exclusivity of the right to provide a particular service for which the asset may be used.

The allocation of property rights is the prime mechanism underlying markets that renders the use of scarce resources sustainable because property rights are a key tool for limiting overexploitation. At the same time, property rights provide incentives for resource owners to innovate and improve productivity because they profit from the net benefits generated by the use of the resource. The stream of net benefits encompasses all those expected for the life of the asset in question. No other institution in society creates incentives to take a longer view than property rights. Whereas political interests are often driven by short-term perspectives, property rights create, in principle, an indefinite time horizon for the owner and, thus, the incentive to take good care of a resource (box 6.1).

The use of quality regulation and property rights has by now helped improve a number of environmental issues in many countries, particularly industrial economies that use a large amount of resources. Local environmental quality has improved in countries that adopted stricter environmen-

Box 6.1. Windfall Gains and Sustainable Development

In the 17th century, Spain imported gold, which brought inflation and slow growth, while the Netherlands, a country poor in resources, flourished. In the 18th century, Haiti's exports to Europe, mostly of sugar, were worth more than those of the 13 American colonies put together, but by 1804 Haiti became trapped in lasting poverty. In the United States, the resource-rich South lost the Civil War because the North had advanced in industry. In the 19th century, resource-poor countries such as Switzerland and Japan leaped ahead of resource-rich Russia. Many of the star performers during recent decades were the resource-poor countries of East Asia—the Republic of Korea, Singapore, Taiwan (China), and Hong Kong (China)—while the resource-rich countries of Nigeria and the República Bolivariana de Venezuela struggled (The Economist 1995). Are these isolated incidents or realities of resource-based economies?

Studies have shown that the resource-rich developing countries have historically underperformed compared with resource-deficient countries. Jeffrey Sachs and Andrew Warner (1997) found that there is a statistically significant, inverse relationship between natural resource intensity and the growth rate of per capita income. Among resource-rich countries, Malaysia, Thailand, Indonesia, Botswana, and post-1982 Chile were high-growth outliers and achieved rates of saving and investment (relative to gross domestic product) that were comparable to those of the successful manufacturing-driven countries that were deficient in resources. The first three countries did so by diversifying into a wide range of manufactured goods; the other two remained dependent on natural resources (Auty 1998).

The Dutch Disease is often blamed for the misfortunes of the resource-rich countries. Exploiting natural resources requires considerable investment, which can divert resources away from investments in traded goods sectors. The competitiveness of the nonmineral traded goods sectors can also be undermined by an appreciation of the exchange rate attributable to the rapid domestic absorption of windfall gains in a boom. The resource base of the mineral economies can end up being more of a curse than a blessing, a finding confirmed in a study of oil exporting countries by Alan Gelb and others (1988). They found that political pressure for rapid absorption of windfall

(Box continues on the following page.)

Box 6.1. (continued)

gains from the oil shocks was the main reason the potentially beneficial resource endowment impaired the economic performance of the oil exporting countries. Research on the economic causes of civil wars suggests that civil wars are more often fueled by rebel groups competing with national governments for control of valuable resources (Collier 2000).

The challenges facing resource-rich countries are (a) not to rely entirely on the mineral sector but to view it as a bonus that assists competitive diversification; (b) not to treat windfalls as permanent income gains and to, instead, invest them with prudence; (c) to make rent-seeking unpopular by using the revenue from exports to fund effective basic services; and (d) to limit mineral-driven shifts in the exchange rate to safeguard the competitive diversification of the nonmining traded goods sectors. A number of countries have attempted to address these issues by establishing savings funds. Savings funds in the U.S. state of Alaska, Chile, Kuwait, and Norway, have been more successful than those in Oman and the República Bolivariana de Venezuela because of fiscal discipline and sound macroeconomic management in the former jurisdictions (Fasano 2000).

tal standards. International action, for example, under the Montreal Protocol has been effective in curbing emissions of chlorofluorocarbons (CFCs). Some of the methods to limit such emissions make use of tradable rights (for example, in Singapore). Tradable rights and other market-compatible economic incentives have been successfully deployed in countries such as Chile and the United States (OECD 1999a; Thobani 1997). The use of market-based instruments to deal with modern environmental issues is still limited, but history so far suggests that it is possible to introduce new property rights to cope with resource scarcity, as has happened with land, certain fishery rights, and all sorts of commodities.

Over the past 100 years, commodities traded in markets (food, nonfood agricultural commodities, and industrial and mining products) have, on average, declined in price by a factor of five—as measured by the commodity price index published by *The Economist* (see figure 6.1, Economist Intelligence Unit n.d.).

FIGURE 6.1. Intelligence Is Scarce: Natural Resources Are Abundant, 1900–2000

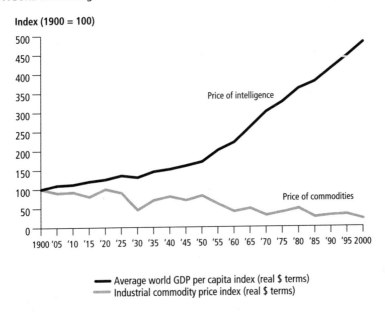

Index (1900 = 100)

Price of intelligence

Price of commodities

— Average world GDP per capita index (real $ terms)
══ Industrial commodity price index (real $ terms)

Source: Economist Intelligence Unit n.d.; Maddison 2001.

Energy prices have remained broadly stable over the century, but they dropped significantly when adjusted for improved quality (figure 6.2). Hence, despite unprecedented growth of the world economy in the 20th century and equally unprecedented population growth, relevant scarcity has declined for services provided by resources that are traded in markets (Crafts 2000; de Long 2000).

The main current worries about environmental problems tend to concern resources to which property rights are not assigned and resources that are not traded. The most notable problem, the emission of greenhouse gases, affects the ultimate resource, the ecosphere. The current degradation of local environments in developing countries and of the ecosphere overall proceeds. Solutions include the use of mechanisms making best use of private markets and property rights.

The historical record so far shows that markets are compatible with protection of the environment. Market mechanisms using tradable property

FIGURE 6.2. Real Consumer Fuel Prices in the United Kingdom, by Year

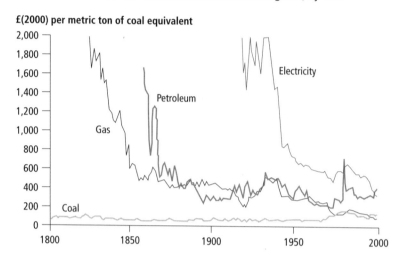

Source: Based on Fouquet and Pearson 1999; revised in 2003. Reprinted with permission.

rights or equivalent instruments can actually help resolve the issues. Markets are not the solution in themselves. Demand for environmental protection must emerge from citizens in the political process and from consumers in the market. Rules and rights must be established for markets to do their work.

Change and Innovation

The Scope for Beneficial Change. There is, of course, always the argument that the very economic growth and increase in wealth made possible by markets have now reached such proportions that the end is near. Doomsday predictions are always about. All we can say is that there is, as yet, no difficulty in outlining benign scenarios for the future of a world of markets. Although world population more than tripled during the 20th century, population projections have declined significantly over the years, with central estimates of peak world population in the order of 9 billion people—just 50 percent more than the 6 billion today. The new low variant of United

Nations population predictions assumes that fertility decline will slow at a lesser rate than in recent decades. Still, under these assumptions, world population would actually decline after about 2040 and drop to about 5 billion in 100 years (Cohen 1995; United Nations 2001).

Technical progress and, thus, the ability to conserve resources or to find new ways of delivering services show no sign of abating. Energy technologies such as fuel cells or solar power exist. One or the other of these technologies will make a serious contribution to resource conservation. Whole fields of technical advances are likely to make contributions, such as communications, information technology, new materials, and nanotechnology and biotechnology. Plausible visions—for example, of environmentally friendly solutions based on biotechnology and nanotechnology—are not in short supply (Dyson 1999; Von Weizsäcker and others 1997). Environmental capitalism is being embraced by activists, who essentially argue that markets need to be structured such that they take environmental effects into account—exactly what well-defined tradable property rights do best (Hawken, Lovins, and Lovins 1999).

The Dilemma of Innovation. Whether one is an optimist or a pessimist, change and innovation are inevitable. Pessimists tend to emphasize the demand side and want life-styles to be changed. Optimists tend to believe supply-side innovation will meet demand. Whatever the mix, we need a system that promotes effective innovation. Private markets are arguably the most-efficient innovation machines ever known (Marx 1867). Innovation itself may, of course, ultimately create more problems than it solves. Witness the fears of Bill Joy, the information-technology whiz-kid and guru of Sun Microsystems. Joy worries that, within decades, self-replicating artificial mechanisms and organisms will threaten humans (Joy 2000). In the end, there is no compelling argument—only fear and hope. We just do not know what will happen.

Private Markets and the Social Fabric

Whether the world and humans will do well and whether we will ultimately be able to master new challenges depends on functioning societies. Will markets help or hinder?

Incentives to Exploit and Skimp on Quality

It is clear that a decent social fabric is essential for markets to function well. A growing literature on social capital or similar concepts makes the point persuasively (Burawoy 1997; Collier 1998; Evans 1997; Fox 1997; Fukuyama 1995, 2000; Grootaert 1999; Heller 1997; Helliwell and Putnam 1995; Kähkönen 1999; Knack 1999; Knack and Keefer 1997; La Porta and others 1996b; Ostrom 1997; Van Bastelaer 1999). Critics of markets then argue that the profit motive destroys the trust that holds the social fabric together (Hirsch 1976). The classic critique by Richard Titmus (1971) makes the key points based on empirical comparison of the market for blood donations in the United Kingdom with that for blood purchase in the United States. Although amounts of blood raised in both systems did not differ dramatically, purchased blood was significantly more often infected with hepatitis than donated blood. The lure of profit undermined civic behavior. The Chicago school struck back by studying blood purchase systems in more detail, controlling for applicable liability rules. Those researchers found the best results in terms of generating supply of good-quality blood obtained when blood was purchased under strict liability rules (Kessel 1974). The underlying issue is generic to market transactions. The profit motive creates high-powered incentives to skimp on quality. Strong quality monitoring is necessary to offset that incentive. When quality is relatively easily observable, buyer beware rules will do, maybe combined with obligations to provide consumers with specific information. When quality is hard to judge and consequences may be catastrophic, stronger rules and standards (for example, strict liability) may be required. If such strong rules cannot be implemented, the power of incentives may not be reduced, leading to the use of voluntary supply and nonprofit organizations (Laffont and Tirole 1993).

It is easy to come up with examples in which high-powered incentives of private firms led to quality problems or outright exploitation. Most social critiques of the market are based on them. However, such examples in themselves are no argument against the use of markets. It is equally easy for powerful government officials to become corrupt. The more fundamental critique has to show that markets erode the ability of society to impose sensible rules. This argument is the same as saying that competition and social cooperation cannot coexist in the long run (box 6.2).

Box 6.2. The Price of Everything and the Value of Nothing

Opponents of the market often paraphrase Oscar Wilde, saying that market advocates "know the price of everything and the value of nothing." Indeed, market advocates like to use price mechanisms to deal with problems of scarcity.

When something is in greater supply than total demand, there is no scarcity. The price is zero, or rather there is no price. But when demand exceeds supply at a price of zero, that supply is, by definition, scarce and needs to be allocated somehow among all those who would like to have a bit. Market advocates tend to argue that property rights to the scarce commodity or service should be established and that trading in free markets should determine the price at which total demand is equal to total supply.

Sometimes, essential goods become dramatically scarce—food in war time, gasoline during an oil crisis, and so on. If prices are left to allocate supply, the rich will get what they need, but the poor will be left with little. Hence, we often see ration coupons that are issued for essential items in time of crisis on a relatively equal basis to citizens. The poor thus are assured that they get as much food or gasoline as the rich.

Typically, the poor are best off if they can decide whether to use their coupons for the purchase of the rationed good or whether to sell the coupon and to purchase something else instead. Whenever trade in coupons is allowed, the outcome is the same as if the coupons did not exist; they simply become an income subsidy for the poor (Schelling 1984) and the free market mechanism for allocating scarce goods and services. In such cases, the issue is, thus, not whether the price mechanism should be used, but whether and how to subsidize the poor.

But there are cases where tradability of rations can sensibly be considered illegitimate. For example, in the 19th century, U.S. citizens observed reasonably well the obligation to serve in the military. However, when the Militia Act of 1862 introduced the provision that one could buy out the obligation to serve by providing a substitute, voluntary enlistment collapsed (Calabresi and Bobbit 1978). In that case, the introduction of a market undermined the functioning of a system to allocate responsibility.

Some situations require cooperation, and everybody is expected to provide his or her fair share. Others are legitimately left to the price system. This

(Box continues on the following page.)

143

> **Box 6.2.** (continued)
>
> *observation should not be surprising. The coexistence between cooperation and competition is critical for economic development. Markets themselves require a certain level of cooperation or trust. The precise boundary between cooperation and competition is often hotly debated and shifts as new markets are introduced, for example, for pollution permits. Prices are often the right mechanism to value scarce resources, but we also need to know when to value competition and when to value cooperation.*

So far, history shows that human societies have developed vastly more complex forms of cooperation and division of labor than any other species (Ridley 1998). Markets have not introduced greed into the world. They have been a key part of the evolution of an ever more-complex division of labor. If greed were a corroding force in the long run, no social trust and altruism would be left after thousands of years of history dominated by ruthless rulers.

Humans may follow incentives and ride roughshod over others, but they also have inclinations to behave cooperatively. Laboratory games and decision analysis by so-called prospect theory suggest that humans show dispositions to cooperate that are inconsistent with narrow-minded egoism.[1] To some extent, cooperative behavior may actually be hard-wired in the brain. People who lose a certain part of the brain (for example, because of an accident) have been found to change their behavior into completely uncaring pursuit of narrow self-interest (Fukuyama 1999; Ridley 1998).

Some argue that humans need to rely more on altruism. Yet pure altruism is a derived virtue. Somebody has to have selfish wishes first for the altruist to even know what to do—namely, to fulfill that person's wishes (Nagel 1979). A system based on altruism needs a framework that spells out which selfish wish is acceptable and which one is not. The same problem occurs in setting rules for markets—for example, environmental or social standards. Conceptually, competitive markets and long-term relationships under rules of reciprocity are equivalent: indefinite repeated interaction among well-informed people leads to the same trades that would be generated by markets in which prices reflect preferences and production possibilities among the same people (Kurz 1977).

As Simmel (1955) states:

> The aim for which competition occurs within a society is presumably always the favor of one or more third persons. Each of the competing parties therefore tries to come as close to that third one as possible. Usually, the poisonous, divisive, destructive effects of competition are stressed and, in exchange, it is merely pointed out that it improves economic welfare. But in addition, it has, after all, this immense [effect on the society]. Competition compels the wooer ... to go out to the wooed, come close to him, establish ties with him, find his strengths and weaknesses and adjust to them....
>
> Innumerable times [competition] achieves what usually only love can do: the divination of the innermost wishes of the other, even before he himself becomes aware of them. Antagonistic tension with his competitor sharpens the businessman's sensitivity to the tendencies of the public, even to the point of clairvoyance, in respect to future changes in the public's tastes, fashion, interests.... Modern competition is described as the fight of all against all, but at the same time it is the fight for all....
>
> ... In short, [competition] is a web of a thousand sociological threads by means of conscious concentration on the will and feeling and thinking of fellowmen.... Once the narrow and naïve solidarity of primitive social conditions yielded to decentralization ... man's effort toward man, his adaptation to the other seems possible only at the price of competition, that is, of the simultaneous fight against a fellowman for a third one (pp. 61–63).

Traditional gift exchange economies are based on systems of mutual obligations that are sustained by indefinite repeated interaction (Mauss 2000; Sahlin 1972). When humans interact for indefinite periods, they have an interest in playing by the rules, lest they be punished (for example, outcast). Analysis of social norms across all types of societies suggests that at least two key norms may be universal: reciprocity and the obligation to help members of society who are in need through no fault of their own (Moore 1978). Indefinite long-term relationships can sustain and explain such norms even when only modest amounts of information flow and outcasting is possible (Greif 1989).

As long as exiting from a relationship does not wipe out reputational concerns, markets are compatible with long-term relationships. Yet they offer extra choice and, thus, better incentives to innovate and perform than alternative systems (Allen and Gale 2000). The classic argument for the civilizing forces of markets was made more than 200 years ago by Samuel Ricard (1781):

> Commerce attaches [men] one to another through mutual utility. Through commerce the moral and physical passions are superseded by interest.... Commerce has a special character, which distinguishes it from all other professions. It affects the feelings of men so strongly that it makes him who was proud and haughty suddenly turn supple, bending and serviceable. Through commerce, man learns to deliberate, to be honest, to acquire manners, to be prudent and reserved in both talk and action. Sensing the necessity to be wise and honest in order to succeed, he flees vice, or at least his demeanor exhibits decency and seriousness so as not to arouse any adverse judgment on the part of present and future acquaintances; he would not dare make a spectacle of himself for fear of damaging his credit standing and thus society may well avoid a scandal which it might otherwise have to deplore (p. 463).

Race to the Bottom—Race to the Top: Corporate Responsibility

The modern world has created more interaction among more people from far-flung places. But information is also flowing like never before—there are fewer and fewer places to hide. Herein lies a powerful force capable of sustaining cooperation based on reputational concerns, even while unified global rules and a single world government are absent.

The different rules and behaviors in different jurisdictions clash in the process of globalization. People interact across borders. They visit, they marry, they trade, and they wage war. As interaction increases, tradeoffs increase. Tradeoffs require rules to settle them. When rules and enforcement mechanisms differ among jurisdictions, processes are set in motion that lead to a new set of common overarching rules. De facto, the nations of this world are competing protective agencies, to use the expression of Robert Nozick (1974), the conservative philosopher of the libertarian minimal state. If such a system is to work reasonably harmoniously in the longer run, competition among different ways of settling tradeoffs is unsustainable, and a single system emerges. It is noteworthy that during the current globalization episode since the 16th century, economic integration went hand in hand with the rise of the human rights movement, notably the antislavery movement of the 18th and 19th centuries. The human rights movement stands for decent and nondiscriminatory treatment of individuals anywhere in the world and, thus, intrinsically conflicts with traditional sovereign power.

One process leading to global rules relies on corporate responsibility (box 6.3). More and more corporations operate in multiple jurisdictions. Laws and regulations governing products and organizational behavior may differ between them, and some rules may not exist in some jurisdictions. Large visible corporations are subject to increasing scrutiny. Various stakeholders (pressure groups, consumers, labor, and investors) observe their behavior. Corporations then have an increasing interest in maintaining good reputations. To maintain relevant reputations, they find that it may not be good enough to obey the law in each jurisdiction where they operate. Stakeholders demand that corporations stretch goals that exceed minimum standards in some countries. When there is competition, reputational pressure on corporations has the most power, because then consumers or

---

Box 6.3. The Business Case for Corporate Responsibility

It is clear that a corporation should obey the laws and regulations of its host country. When a corporation is asked to observe higher standards than those provided in the law of its host country, one would expect that this added responsibility would entail extra costs and risks that would lower profits. Lower profits, in turn, might reduce investment and job creation in the host country.

Not so, say some advocates of corporate responsibility. Consumers may be willing to pay more for products made in a socially and environmentally responsible fashion, and investors may be happy with lower returns from such companies. In addition, the search for more responsible methods of operation may yield innovations that improve quality or reduce costs. In the presence of such effects, the pursuit of social and environmental responsibility would also be the key to profitability.

If there is money in corporate responsibility, we can trust the private sector to find it. Currently, numerous attempts are under way to construct portfolios of ethical companies and to sell them to investors. Some appear to have out-

(Box continues on the following page.)

Box 6.3. (continued)

performed the market recently. Yet it remains to be seen whether that finding was a coincidence or a trend. For example, many ethical portfolios were weighted toward nonpolluting, new economy stocks in the telecommunications media and technology areas. Now, after the decline in valuations of such stocks, the picture may look different. In any case, we can be sure the market will exploit every ounce of profit that is in ethical behavior.

Higher standards do sometimes impose extra costs. Advocates of corporate responsibility say that private companies still need to shoulder these costs. In fact, these costs should be viewed as fees for the license to operate. By being unethical, companies theoretically lose their legitimacy and ultimately have to cease operations. That theory may hold true in some cases. In such cases, the company in question earns sufficient rents to pay the license fee.

In practice, companies asked to demonstrate responsible behavior tend to be large multinationals. In the absence of effective competition, the productivity advantages of being large offer some scope to pay the license fee, which is one way to dissipate rents. Large firms can thus become the forerunners of better social standards. They may initially adopt the standards because they can afford to because of lack of competition. As competition intensifies, they then become lobbyists for higher standards, which might benefit all. The mechanism and the arguments are not new at all. For example, they are already contained in the story of an English traveler in 1817 who noted that the Spanish and Portuguese profited from the voluntary prohibition of the slave trade by his own country. Because of the low price they were paying for slaves, the Spanish and Portuguese would have "the means to sell cheaper than we can in foreign markets, not only sugar and coffee, but all tropical products" (Braudel 1979, p. 440). The complaint sounds familiar today when companies worry that more demanding labor standards may place them at a competitive disadvantage. As in the past, we can hope that, in the end, workers will be treated better and that such worries will be laid to rest as all firms adhere to improved standards.

The current corporate responsibility debate reflects the absence of agreed and enforceable global norms. It is a second-best way of dealing with business ethics, holding both promise and danger. The big issue is to come to global agreements on norms and ways to enforce them and to allow competition to produce jobs.

investors have choice and can cast out a corporation and punish it with loss of the gains from trade. The existence of private markets and competitive global markets provides a mechanism to improve global standards.

Many fear, however, that global competition leads to a race to the bottom, eroding social and environmental standards (box 6.4). Indeed, we can find—as usual—a number of cases where high-powered incentives lead corporations to misbehave.[2] For example, there is a certain degree of inefficient tax competition (Devereux and Griffith 1998; Hines 1999; Morisset and Pirnia 2000). Yet, overall, the evidence also indicates a race to the top. Corporations do not just seek to minimize cost; they also want to maximize profit. When jurisdictions offer a productive environment, firms prefer to operate there instead of some tax-free wasteland (Eskeland and Harrison 1997). As discussed previously, some form of institutional or social capability is important for strong economic performance. Corporations are, thus, most likely to invest in jurisdictions where such capability exists. Such capabilities are, in turn, associated with the rule of law, the protection of property, and adequate quality regulation. A number of empirical studies from Canada and Switzerland, which are members of the Organisation for Economic Co-operation and Development (OECD), and from developing countries suggest that, indeed, the race is to the top and that competition among jurisdictions is beneficial (OECD 1998b; World Bank 2001b). Markets and demands for quality of life by citizens interact to produce this race to the top, which did not take place among centrally planned economies and their state-owned firms.

Balance of Power, Openness, and Sociodiversity

No matter what social system we favor, we have to confront the question of who guards the guardians of the rules. Belief in salvation from enlightened and efficient dictators seems thoroughly misguided. For example, merchant law has developed from the interaction of competitors with a mutual interest in trade. Compare this interaction to the attitude of autocratic rulers to the law, as expressed by the Chinese Kang Hsi emperor (1661–1722), who declared:

> Lawsuits would increase to a frightful amount if people were not afraid of tribunals and if they felt confident of always finding in them ready and perfect justice.... I desire, therefore, that those who have recourse to the tribunals should be treated without any pity and in

Box 6.4. Racing to the Bottom

The race to the bottom hypothesis has been tested in a recent study that analyzes air quality trends in the United States and the three largest recipients of foreign direct investment (FDI) among the developing countries: Brazil, China, and Mexico. The evidence shows that, instead of racing toward the bottom, major cities in these countries have experienced significant improvements in air quality (figures 6.3 and 6.4). The improvements in the developing countries have occurred in an era of economic liberalization, industrial growth, and rapid expansion of foreign investment flows, thus contradicting the concerns that free trade and capital flows tend to erode global environmental standards. Furthermore, the reductions in air pollution in Mexico City and Los Angeles have occurred even though these cities are dominant industrial centers that are most strongly affected by the North American Free Trade Agreement.

Evidence from numerous studies suggests that an environmental race to the bottom is unlikely for the following reasons:

- *Pollution control costs matter to factory owners and managers, but they are generally not a critical factor in location decisions.*

- *Where regulations are weak or absent, nongovernmental organizations (NGOs) and community groups pursue informal regulation (threat of social, political, or physical sanctions) to convince polluters to compensate the community or reduce pollution.*

FIGURE 6.3. Air Pollution in Metropolitan Areas of the United States, 1988–97

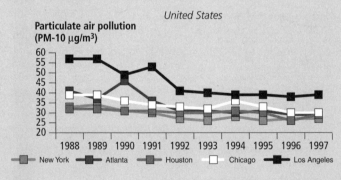

FIGURE 6.4. Urban Air Pollution and Foreign Direct Investment in Brazil, China, and Mexico, 1985–97

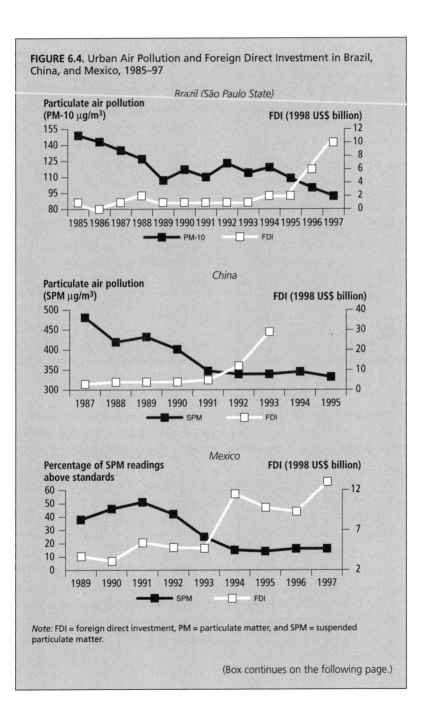

Note: FDI = foreign direct investment, PM = particulate matter, and SPM = suspended particulate matter.

(Box continues on the following page.)

Box 6.4. (continued)

- *At the national level, governments display a tendency to tighten regulation as incomes grow.*
- *Local businesses control pollution because abatement reduces costs.*
- *Because of the scrutiny of consumers and environmental NGOs, multinational firms generally adhere to environmental standards of the Organisation for Economic Co-operation and Development in their developing-country operations.*

Source: Wheeler 2000.

such a manner that they should be disgusted with law and tremble to appear before a magistrate (Finer 1997, p. 556).

Some form of balance of power to restrain abuse of power seems needed. If so, competition is clearly one of the most-effective forms of introducing balance of power. Competition in markets and among jurisdictions gives greater power to citizens and lets the powerful work in their interest.

Competition among jurisdictions can be achieved by allowing people to migrate. For example, in China, internal migration has given hundreds of millions of people more hope. If people are not allowed to migrate, competition among jurisdictions can still be obtained by importing better governance. Contracting out the currency or customs service or other public services can, to some extent, improve governance. When services are contracted out competitively, the winning bidder will usually maximize the use of local resources—including staff—by providing training and better discipline. The incentives for capacity building under contracting out are typically stronger than under other arrangements. The same broad rules for contracting across borders apply as for contracting out public services generally (see chapter 5).

Competition among jurisdictions also holds promise for improved overall social rules for another reason. We know from social choice theory that it is highly unlikely that all citizens will agree on common rules without some element of coercion (Arrow 1970). Not all rules across jurisdictions will ever be the same, and not all rules will command legitimacy. Allowing multiple jurisdictions to flourish to the extent possible provides greater scope for people to sort themselves into communities of their choice and to develop new rules. However much we may aspire to more uniform global rules, there will probably be reason to innovate and one day find new ways to organize the society.

Albert Hirschman (1992) summarized the old and continuing debates about the market and society in the following way: Some argue that market forces are powerful and good. They think markets improve the social fabric, as the search for profitable trade promotes cooperation. Others argue that markets are powerful and bad. For them the profit motive will undermine the social fabric and destroy markets in the process.

Another set of analysts argues that feudal forms of society preceding capitalism are the real drivers of development. Some of them claim that vested interests from the past prevent effective reform. For them capitalism is too weak to realize its progressive role. Finally, there are those who think that the very diversity of feudal society contained the seeds for social and technical innovation, not a rule-based market society. After all, it was the diversity of feudal Europe that gave rise to the modern world (Berman 1983; Jones 1987; Landes 1998).

Assuming that we are skeptical of absolute power and that society will need continued social and technical innovation, effective mechanisms to establish balance of power would seem necessary, as well as openness for change. Just as there is value in biodiversity, there is, presumably, value in sociodiversity. Competition then sounds like part of the policy menu.

Notes

1. See Kahneman and Tversky (1979), Ridley (1998), and Thaler (1992). The exceptions are experiments conducted with economics students. These students appear to have been led to believe that textbook models assuming self-serving rationality are a full, accurate, and desirable description of actual human behavior (Frank, Gilovich, and Regan 1993).

2. The same incentive problem plagues many governments. High-powered incentives facing officials make them behave without concern for the common good, most obviously in countries where heads of state or warlords pursue wealth from mining and from oil and gas extraction rather than looking out for citizens' welfare (Collier 2000).

7

Policy and the Country Context for Reform

Basic Thrust for a Private Sector Development Policy

The Danish philosopher Søren Kierkegaard said, "Life can only be understood backwards, but it has to be lived forwards" (Hannay 1996, p. 161). The correct strategy or policy cannot be proven; it has to be decided on.

The analysis in the previous chapters suggests that

- Sound private sector development is, first and foremost, a function of a sound policy, including the necessary basic institutional underpinnings. An effective state, as well as functioning communities, is needed for a truly beneficial investment climate.
- Special public interventions to help private firms seem to have weak or mixed results. Overall, it appears that, as for the case of aid effectiveness in general, special support to the private sector is most successful when policy and institutional development is substantially on the right track, but, otherwise, it is typically ineffective.
- Several decades of emphasis by the development community on public sector provision and financing of many services seen as public services (infrastruc-

ture and social services) have led to a neglect of private alternatives that provide poor people with greater choice and better service.

- The deployment of taxpayer-funded subsidies needs basic, clear disciplines—that is, transparent, unbundled subsidy delivery under hard budget constraints, accompanied by clear measurements of cost-effectiveness.

A common theme runs through these basic approaches to policymaking. They take their clue from the very reason for the success of markets: the empowerment of decentralized decisionmakers within a framework of sound policy and hard budget constraints. In particular, there is no clear case for microengineering markets based on public servants' notions of needs and resource gaps.

A Taxonomy of Private Sector Development Interventions

The broad scope of activities for private sector development is summarized in the taxonomy of private sector development interventions in table 7.1. In existing competitive markets, there are all the arguments to improve competition and private provision. In addition, new competitive markets can be created from time to time to deal with a variety of issues such as pollution. However, where natural monopolies exist, the introduction of

TABLE 7.1. Taxonomy of Private Sector Development Interventions

Indicator	Improving existing markets by improving regulations	Creating new markets by creating tradable property rights	Improving natural monopolies through user fees and private provision	Improving natural monopolies through tax financing and private provision
Characteristics	Openness, competition	Privatization, corporate governance, emission rights	Transmission grids, water pipelines	Roads, tax administration, vehicle registration
Monitoring	Consumer choice, user pays	Consumer choice, user pays	Performance standards, user pays	Performance standards
Firm-level interventions	Access to funding and advice, political risk mitigation			

market-type disciplines becomes harder. It is hardest when taxpayers are called to pay for services provided by natural monopolies. While not all goods and services can be privately funded, all of them can, in principle, be provided privately and have been at some time in history somewhere in the world with varying success. The monitoring and regulatory schemes require more government involvement the further one moves from competitive markets to tax-funded monopolies. Wherever governments choose to have private firms as providers, there is a potential case for firm-level intervention to support adequate supply response, as long as adequate disciplines constrain abuse of taxpayer support.

Beyond outlining a broad thrust for private sector development and characterizing the scope of private sector development activities, we find the real issues lie in how to get from the starting point in each country to a well-functioning market economy. It may be relatively easy to agree on a broad goal for policy, but how to get there is typically contentious. What guidance is there for solving such transition issues?

Timing and Sequencing

There are some general rules about desirable timing and sequencing of policy measures. For example:

- When deregulating prices, policymakers should ensure that there is effective freedom of entry of new firms. Otherwise, incumbents may be able to charge excessive prices.
- Before privatizing, policymakers should ensure that market structures have been put in place that allow the maximum of desirable competition to take place. Then they should establish a sensible regulatory regime to deal with remaining issues requiring regulatory intervention. After doing so, they should privatize.
- When the rights of minority shareholders are not well protected, policymakers should privatize through trade sales to strategic investors, but they should not float the company on a market or use vouchers.

This book has set out a number of such rules in the course of discussion—for example, the disciplines to be put in place for contracting out public services. Although such rules should certainly be considered, the politics of the country in question may render optimal sequencing difficult. Sometimes, half-hearted measures may be better than none at all. Even in the case of the Russian Federation, where many privatizations did not yield many visible gains, it remains unclear what better realistic alternative to privatization could have been selected. Policymakers were aware of the issues and chose a politically feasible option, which may yet yield benefits (Dabrowski, Gomulk, and Rostowski 2001). British gas was privatized as a monopoly when it was politically feasible. Competition was introduced later. Yet in other cases, half-baked reform has backfired. For example, many independent power projects have been undertaken without setting consumer prices at adequate levels. Such practices led to massive failures—for example, during the 1997 Asian crisis—and renewed obligations for governments.

Is it possible to design a typology of governments that would help provide practical guidance? At a general level, it is possible to say that the weaker the government system, the stronger the case for choice for citizens and free entry for entrepreneurs. Some people argue that private markets should be introduced only after a series of preconditions are met, such as functioning institutions, basic rule of law, and good regulation. From this point of view, markets are a luxury good—too sophisticated for the poor. The evidence suggests that free entry and choice help the poor escape from dysfunctional public services and dysfunctional regulation in all sectors—even in the natural monopoly areas of infrastructure. Markets are basic needs, not luxury goods. It is true that, in some cases, the private sector may be no better or may even be worse than the public sector, but the issue then is why such private parties can exert their power. The reason is invariably some form of monopoly power and consequent limits on choice and free entry. The case for private sector development set out in this book is not a case for private services per se. The mafia is private after all. It is a case for competitive markets, where citizens have choice and opportunity and where their property is protected.

Beyond the general relationship between governance and free entry and choice, country typologies are of dubious use for policymaking. Consider the case of El Salvador. El Salvador emerged from a vicious 12-year civil war in 1992. Economic policies undertaken by the elected government emphasized macrostability and open, deregulated markets. By 1998, just 6 years after the end of civil war, El Salvador had seen a significant increase in per capita income as well as an increase in the human development index, a broader indicator of the quality of life. El Salvador made this achievement while reducing debt burdens to such a degree that the tiny country was one of only three countries in Latin America with an investment grade rating (from Moody's), and it obtained its rating before Mexico. The case of El Salvador shows that open markets are compatible with social and political advance. However, many policymakers in similar situations would not have opted for the sort of program adopted by El Salvador and would have chosen a more-cautious approach on the argument that preconditions for markets were not right at the end of the civil war.

More generally, many of the country cases that we now recognize as successes followed policies that were quite idiosyncratic and that were not necessarily recommended by standard wisdom. They include such divergent cases as Chile, China, Estonia, the Republic of Korea, Taiwan (China), and Vietnam. What many of the successful countries have in common is that they chose some form of market economy, but the details varied substantially. It is, thus, unlikely that any country typology will provide much insight for practical policymakers. What does matter are willingness to listen to people and scope to experiment within the framework of first principles. The ability to analyze a specific historical situation on the basis of first principles is probably the best one can generally do. Hence, a policy should be based on first principles and a reasoned interpretation of facts, as attempted in this book, that may then help frame debate in specific cases. Of course, there is always some debate about first principles, because our knowledge of both theory and facts of economic policymaking is highly incomplete.

No Cookbook

Not only is our knowledge incomplete, but we also know that incomplete reforms can go a long way, even if they eventually run into trouble. Witness, for example, Japan and Korea. In other cases, approaches that have not worked well in the past may yet hold some potential. For example, the experience with publicly funded support schemes for small and medium-size enterprises has generally been somewhat disappointing—if there has been any evaluation at all. Still, there may be some new schemes, such as matching grants, that can work if done right. We have only limited ability to provide general guidance on how complete reforms need to be in a particular case so as to be beneficial. And we do not know which policy innovation will be successful in the future.

Overall, there is a clear problem with simplistic policy advice such as just privatize, just unbundle, and so on. It is neither possible nor advisable to prepare a cookbook for private sector development. The best we can do is debate first principles, improve our knowledge about what works and what does not through good research, and argue about episodes and case studies to sharpen our judgment in the manner of the Harvard Business School.

Establishing Credibility

Whatever precise solution is chosen in a particular case, an issue that typically looms large is how to establish the credibility of chosen policies. The power of vested interest may lead to half-hearted reforms, which, in turn, may create rent-seeking. Serious reforms create incentives to perform (figure 7.1). When governments have credibility, even gradual reforms may be seen as serious. People and firms then try to position themselves to perform well in the ultimate reform environment. However, when governments face doubts about their true intentions, opposing bodies and detractors are quick to exploit rent-seeking opportunities and build new positions of power able to thwart reform further. Hence, systems where governance is strong can afford gradual solutions, whereas, in weak governance environments, more drastic action tends to be required.

FIGURE 7.1. Credibility and per Capita GDP Growth, Percent per Year

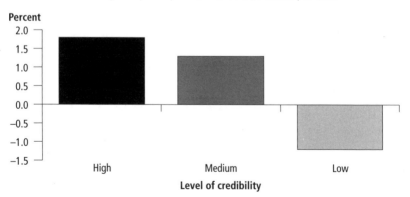

Source: World Bank 1997.

It is useful to recall that, for individuals or institutions that start from a position of weak credibility, establishing credibility generally requires two things: (a) a reasonably genuine recognition of the problem on the part of the individual or the government, and (b) the use of commitment mechanisms. Typically, commitment is not generated by nice policy statements or New Year's resolutions, but by drastic actions, which tie the hands of policymakers, reduce their discretion, and amount to throwing away the key to the past.

Policy Dilemmas

Also, we need to recognize that there are several inescapable dilemmas for reform. First, societies with weak governance are likely to have the most-distorted policy environments. Reforms are, thus, likely to have a relatively drastic effect on income distribution. Yet for purposes of establishing credibility, drastic reform may precisely be the remedy of choice. Second, the danger of getting stuck on the road to reform is high in countries with weak governance, as is the danger of corruption, as has been highlighted, for example, in the case of contracting out public services. Third, concern for the poor who suffer from bad governance induces well-meaning helpers to provide support and resources, which may be used ineffectively or be abused by vested interests. Finally, in a number of cases, reliance on foreign firms or governments may provide a shortcut to effective reform. However, this shortcut may be difficult to accept politically and, when accompanied by subsidies, can undermine incentives to reform.

Disciplines on Aid Agencies

All in all, there is no way around country-specific solutions on how to tackle the private sector development agenda. Discretionary decisions are inescapable. What the consideration of private sector development approaches then suggests is that we should seek generic disciplines that allow local knowledge and initiative to be tapped while providing an overall discipline on the use of resources. This process implies that the same principles that aid agencies use to make recommendations to client countries should also be applied to the way aid agencies themselves are structured and operate.

Official aid agencies are state owned and benefit from support by taxpayers through financing guarantees, tax exemptions, or explicit subsidies. The agencies are supposed to support poverty reduction and to use their privileges and subsidies to this effect. Typically, the decisionmaking is discretionary in the sense that agency management judges programs and activities on their developmental effect and allocates funds accordingly.

Whether such judgments are made well is hard for supervisory bodies of the agencies or the public at large to evaluate. The question then arises whether agencies can be given general mandates and constraints that can be more easily monitored. Two basic types of constraints are feasible: rate-of-return constraints and subsidy disciplines.

Rate-of-Return Constraints

Suppose an agency is given the mandate to remedy the type of market failures discussed in chapter 3. These failures mean that the private sector leaves good deals on the table that the agency then finances. They do not imply that subsidies are needed. In fact, subsidies would invite waste. If the agency truly meets its goal, it should be able to earn a commercial rate of return. If it does not, by implication it supports too many deals that are not worth funding. Such an agency would have the mandate to remedy certain types of market failures in developing countries. It would be asked to complement private markets and not substitute for them, and it would be asked to make a return sufficient to fund itself in private markets.

A rate-of-return discipline does not mean that the developmental mandate is abandoned. Developmental interventions by an agency subject to rate-of-return constraints should benefit other private parties by improving the investment climate and, thus, investment opportunities. Such benefits are not captured by the agency itself. Nevertheless, all these justifications assume that the agency would pick up good deals left on the table by the private sector in the following sense: Because of its special standing, the agency has a lower risk-adjusted cost of capital than private firms.[1] It can thus undertake some projects that are not attractive to private firms. Such projects will exist for a while, until the investment climate has improved to such a degree that the private sector undertakes a broad range of projects, with no worthwhile projects left for the agency (figure 7.2).

But there is no argument that substandard deals should be financed just because they require subsidies, in the sense that the agency should be con-

FIGURE 7.2. The Cost of Capital and the Role of Direct Financial Support to Private Firms by Development Banks

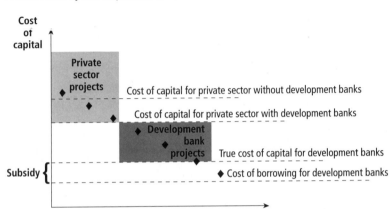

tent with average returns of less than its own risk-adjusted cost of capital. If one were to go this route, one would effectively unbundle any subsidy contained in the agencies' products. In case the agency is owned by either the government or charitable shareholders, profits so earned could then be used explicitly to subsidize those activities that are deemed to require subsidies under the disciplines discussed below. For example, the agency could go beyond funding demonstration projects and could work directly on improving the investment climate for entrepreneurs. The issue, then, is whether to bundle work on demonstration projects with such policy work or whether to assign these activities to separate agencies. One key consideration in this regard is the following: any work on improving the investment climate is targeted at governments and aims to persuade them to adjust policy or implementation practices.

The question arises as to what type of agency is best able to nudge governments toward improving the investment climate. Consider at one end of the spectrum the for-profit private sector. Investors typically let governments know in more or less explicit fashion what policies they would like to see in place. However, investors, particularly large ones, will often ask for special deals that are not in the public interest.

At the other end of the spectrum, government-owned institutions may have a better incentive to promote public interest concerns. However, government-owned institutions are also likely to be more diplomatic than private investors and less inclined to assess the seriousness of government promises about policy change in the same uncompromising manner as private investors. Thus, public institutions may, for example, agree to support policy change with a loan even when the recipient government is not terribly serious about reform. The financial position of such public institutions does not suffer much from a misjudgment about policy intentions if taxpayers in the client country support the policy regardless of what happens.

On the spectrum of institutions between the private markets and the fully taxpayer-supported agencies like the World Bank are other institutions such as the European Bank for Reconstruction and Development and the International Finance Corporation. They have a better incentive to watch their investments because taxpayers in client countries do not guarantee repayment. At the same time, they are government-sponsored institutions with a greater concern about public interest than many private investors have. Overall, the question is which type of institution has the best mix of incentives to assess government intentions dispassionately while promoting policy and interventions that are in the public interest.

This debate is also relevant to the issue of writing political risk guarantees that cover government behavior, such as expropriation or breach of contract. Such guarantees back the words and promises of governments. They are in demand by private firms when there is doubt in the ability or willingness of governments to honor their commitments. Political risk insurers must have a way of diversifying or reducing political risk that private investors do not have. At the same time, they should retain incentives to assess dispassionately the likelihood that governments will honor their commitments.

Subsidy Disciplines

A number of activities of aid agencies may require subsidies. The first question is whether subsidies should be made transparent and how transparency may be achieved. Subsidies embedded in aid activities can be calculated. Transparency is further enhanced when subsidies are unbundled, as they would be in private competitive markets. Then the subsidies provided for a particular activity could be calculated with some precision. In addition, results could be assessed. The aid agency would then report the subsidy dependence of its different activities and, thus, provide donors with additional tools for judging performance. When results are well defined and can be monitored, output-based contracts can be written. Aid agencies themselves could then be remunerated for such activities, at least partially on a success fee basis. In addition, the activities of aid agencies that allocate subsidies could be based more on participatory approaches to help improve responsiveness to the concerns of intended beneficiaries.

Greater transparency could thus be obtained by clearly defining the mandates of aid agencies in relation to the constraints that are to be imposed. Three basic types of agencies could be envisaged: (a) those subject to commercial rate of return constraints; (b) those subject to output-based contractual disciplines remunerated partially on a success fee basis; and (c) agencies delivering subsidies or subsidized services, the effect of which is hard to measure.

Competition

As in attempts to introduce good corporate governance, a key issue is the possibility of failure. Without possible failure, all these more-commercial constraints remain meaningless. Sunset clauses might be used to enable donors more easily to close agencies or programs that appear problematic. However, donors may at times find it hard to decide explicitly to close an agency even in the presence of such clauses. As in the case of private markets, a potential remedy of choice is real competition. De facto, aid agencies compete for tax funds and other donations already. Concerns about donor coordination often obscure this. Yet, as discussed above, the true coordination issues are standardization of procedures and accounting, as well as information sharing about services received by aid beneficiaries. Beyond these issues, competition among agencies may be valuable, as it provides choice for both ultimate donors and recipients. The situation is analogous to that of private financial institutions; one would not want them to coordinate but to compete. Donors can decide whether to pool resources by giving them to their favorite agency, and beneficiaries can decide whose solicitations to entertain.

Note

1. The need for special standing rules out full privatization—hence, the difficulties that the Commonwealth Development Corporation (CDC) has experienced with attempted privatization.

8

Conclusions

The role of entrepreneurs and markets is critical for poverty reduction, because the key to rapid poverty reduction lies in transmitting advances in technology or organizational improvements across the world. Freedom for entrepreneurs to enter markets and adapt products and production processes to local circumstances is essential for the purpose. Choice by consumers renders entrepreneurs responsive to what citizens want. When entrepreneurs are free to enter and consumers have choice, competition reigns. Competition provides opportunity to introduce better products and services, as well as better production and delivery processes. It also provides a check on monopoly power of entrepreneurs and their firms.

Markets with workable competition require sound institutional underpinnings to reap their full potential. Countries need a system of property rights and regulations addressing concerns about the quality of goods and services, as well as processes for producing and delivering those goods and services. The combination of competition based on a system of property rights with quality regulations that restrict the exercise of these rights in the public interest is the way to channel the powerful incentives of private entrepreneurs into socially useful directions.

The system of property rights and quality regulation needs to be developed and enforced by public agencies, most notably the state. Competitive markets are not a way to replace the state; they require an effective state to function at their best. In turn, by delegating decisions to competitive markets, the state can become more effective and can concentrate on essential functions, such as ensuring the rule of law, the sanctity of property rights and contracts, and the institution of social and environmental regulations.

For the symbiosis of markets and state to work well, it is also necessary that individuals be capable of responding to the opportunities created by markets. Hence, health and education are important. Furthermore, a minimum of social cohesion and an absence of civil strife are required.

While the full power of markets only comes to the fore when embedded in an effective state, one should not wait to establish markets until all ideal preconditions are fulfilled. Free entry and choice—and hence competition—are particularly valuable for individuals when governance systems are weak. Competition helps create a system of balance of power that underlies effective states that are responsive to their citizens.

Within this overall context, this book sketches out the basic ways to introduce markets in parts of the economy where competition can clearly reign (for example, manufacturing and farming). It also presents the existing evidence for the effectiveness of policies such as trade liberalization and privatization. Although many hopes in such policies have turned out to be overly optimistic, and although political abuse has clearly happened, the weight of the evidence suggests that such policies have been beneficial compared with realistic alternatives.

The issue then becomes whether the state can jumpstart markets and help, in particular, poor citizens benefit more rapidly from access to markets and the diffusion of best practice that markets can bring. Here the evidence suggests that many public programs for private firms—including those for small and medium-size enterprises and particularly those for subsidized financing—have delivered only mediocre results. Hope lies in reinforcing market forces rather than substituting for them, through programs such as vouchers for business development services. A balance needs to be struck between allowing experimentation in this regard and imposing disciplines that prevent waste of public subsidies.

Beyond these observations, the issue is how far states can and should delegate activity to the market. In principle, such delegation can make sense when there is a reasonable case that an adequate level of competition can be introduced, which would create incentives that would improve on those under state ownership. It is by now clear that there is significant scope to introduce markets into many infrastructure businesses. Yet in those areas where natural monopoly features dominate (for example, water pipelines) it becomes harder to establish the right framework for private provision to improve on state provision because the state will need to institute reasonably efficient regulation of monopolies. Nevertheless, several studies now show that private participation is feasible in a range of middle- and low-income countries. Where regulatory capacity is so weak that regulation of the private provision is not practical, the response is not necessarily a fallback to state provision. In the face of failed integrated state monopolies, small-scale free entry options and choice for customers seem promising in areas such as telecommunications, water, and electricity.

As it happens, governments across the world have experimented with private participation in infrastructure over the past decade. Policy has been less adventurous in the social sectors. At the same time, the nature of basic health services and education is such that poor people in low-income countries actually often depend on private service options because of the failure of public systems. There would thus appear to be a large scope for improvement by exploiting more aggressively the potential for market solutions. The regulatory issues are in part similar to those in the infrastructure sectors and are in part a function of the special nature of social services, particularly issues of insurance and goals of society. Still, many options for improving on current performance of health and education systems appear to be unexploited.

Having characterized the approaches to tapping the potential in markets for development, we must ask how pro-poor interventions that improve on hopes for automatic trickle-down can be engineered, whether in the market or in the public sector. The design of such interventions requires market solutions to be combined with other measures. For example, rural education, rural roads, and free entry would be key interventions enabling rural populations to benefit from markets.

Even if we are convinced that markets can help and that the poor can be reached and served with the help of markets, the question remains whether the profit motive and the growth it engenders will end up undermining the natural environment and the social cohesion that underlies well-functioning markets. Yet evidence suggests that market mechanisms are part of the solution rather than part of the problem. Again, the key is finding the right balance between cooperation and competition that distinguishes sound markets. To give up on the mechanism of competition would severely curtail options to deal with environmental problems and would risk setting back the enabling of citizens because one would lose a key mechanism for establishing balance of power.

All these general points on markets need to be translated into action to solve country-specific problems. It is not possible to derive cookbook-type recommendations for engineering pro-poor market development. Thinking based on first principles needs to be combined with an assessment of the political and social conditions in the country or area in question to design practical interventions. If one takes this view, the question then is whether one can impose disciplines on those who design and implement these interventions such that they have scope for experimentation and for adaptation to local circumstances and yet do not squander taxpayers' money and achieve the goals of development.

To some extent, such disciplines can be borrowed from markets and applied to aid agencies. After all, the power of markets comes, in good part, from their ability to allow experimentation, to benefit from dispersed and local knowledge, and to adapt to local conditions. This book suggests two basic market-type disciplines: (a) disbursing aid when a service is delivered—thus shifting performance risk from taxpayers to private investors—and (b) providing rate-of-return targets for aid agencies that help jumpstart private entrepreneurship, for example, in small and medium-size enterprises through financial support. Beyond these approaches, the establishment of development goals, the deployment of subsidies, and ways to deal with effects of interventions on communities and the environment should benefit from better use of consultation and participation processes and from greater transparency about the size and application of subsidies and the measurement of results.

References

Aarland, K., and K. Robinson. 1999. "National Management Regimes in European Fisheries." In A. Hatcher and K. Robinson, eds., *The Definition and Allocation of Use Rights in European Fisheries: Proceedings of the Second Workshop Held in Brest, France, 5–7 May.* Portsmouth, United Kingdom: Centre for the Economics and Management of Aquatic Resources.

Abbott, Thomas, A., ed. 1995. *Health Care Policy and Regulation.* Boston: Kluwer Academic Publishers.

Abed, George T., and Hamid R. Davoodi. 2000. "Corruption, Structural Reforms, and Economic Performance in the Transition Economies." Working Paper WP/00/132. International Monetary Fund, Washington, D.C.

Abel-Smith, Brian, and Pankaj Rawal 1992. "Can the Poor Afford 'Free' Health Services? A Case Study of Tanzania." *Health Policy and Planning* 7(4): 329–41.

Ablo, Emmanuel, and Ritva Reinikka. 1998. "Do Budgets Really Matter? Evidence from Public Spending on Education and Health in Uganda." Policy Research Working Paper 1926. World Bank, Washington, D.C.

Abramson, Wendy B. 1999. "Partnerships between the Public Sector and Nongovernmental Organizations: Contracting for Primary Health Care Services: A State of the Practice Paper." Abt Associates, Bethesda, Md.

Abrantes, Alexandre. 1999. "Contracting Public Health Care Services in Latin America." World Bank, Washington, D.C. Processed.

Acemoglu, Daron, and James A. Robinson. 2000. "Political Losers as a Barrier to Economic Development." *American Economic Review* 90(2): 126–30.

Afifi, Nihal Hafez. 1997. "International Comparative Review of Health Care Regulatory Systems." *Partnership for Health Technical Report 11.* Abt Associates, Bethesda, Md.

———. 2001. "Harnessing Private Participation in the Health Sector through Active Regulation." Background paper from a training course, "Private Participation and Health Services Performance," held in June 2001. World Bank, Health, Nutrition, and Population Team, Washington, D.C.

Akerlof, George. 1970. "The Market for 'Lemons': Quality Uncertainty and the Market Mechanism." *Quarterly Journal of Economics* 54(3): 488–500.

———. 1976. "The Economics of the Rat-Race and Other Woeful Tales." *Quarterly Journal of Economics* 90: 599-617.

Alderman, Harold, Peter F. Orazem, and Elizabeth M. Paterno. 1996. "School Quality, School Cost, and the Public/Private School Choices of Low-Income Households in Pakistan." Development Economics Research Group Working Paper Series on Impact Evaluation of Education Reforms, Paper No. 2. World Bank, Washington, D.C.

Allen, Franklin, and Douglas Gale. 2000. *Comparing Financial Systems.* Cambridge, Mass.: MIT Press.

Anand, Sudhir, and Martin Ravallion. 1993. "Human Development in Poor Countries: On the Role of Private Incomes and Public Services." *Journal of Economic Perspectives* 7(1): 133–50.

Angrist, Joshua, Eric Bettinger, Erik Bloom, Elizabeth King, and Michael Kremer. 2001. "Vouchers for Private Schooling in Colombia: Evidence from a Randomized Natural Experiment." Working Paper 8343. National Bureau of Economic Research, Cambridge, Mass.

Arnason, R. 1996. "On the Individual Transferable Quota Fisheries Management System in Iceland." *Reviews in Fish Biology and Fisheries* 6(1): 63–90.

Arrow, Kenneth J. 1970. *Social Choice and Individual Values.* 2nd ed. New Haven, Conn.: Yale University Press.

Aseno-Okyere, W. Kwadwo, Adote Anum, Isaac Osei-Akoto, and Augustina Adukonu. 1998. "Cost Recovery in Ghana: Are There Any Changes in Health Care Seeking Behavior?" *Health Policy and Planning* 13(2): 181–88.

Ashton, Toni. 1998. "Contracting for Health Services in New Zealand: A Transaction Cost Analysis." *Social Science & Medicine* 46(3): 357–67.

Asiimwe, Delius, Francis Mwesigye, Barbara McPake, and Pieter Streefland. 1997. "Informal Health Markets and Formal Health Financing in Uganda." In Sara Bennett, Barbara McPake, and Anne Mills, eds., *Private Health Providers in Developing Countries: Serving the Public Interest?* London: Zed Books.

Aubert, Vilhelm, ed. 1969. *Sociology of Law: Selected Readings.* London: Penguin.

Audibert, Martine, and Jacky Mathonnat. 2000. "Cost Recovery in Mauritania: Initial Lessons." *Health Policy and Planning* 15(1): 66–75.

Audretsch, David B. 2002. "The Dynamic Role of Small Firms: Evidence from the U.S." *Small Business Economics* 18(1–3): 13–40.

Auty, Richard M. 1998. "Resource Abundance and Economic Development." Research for Action 44. UNU World Institute for Development Economics Research, Helsinki.

Aw, Bee Yan. 2002. "Productivity Dynamics of Small and Medium Enterprises in Taiwan." *Small Business Economics* 18(1–3): 69–84.

Bacon, Robert. 1994. "Restructuring the Power Sector: The Case of Small Systems." Public Policy for the Private Sector Note 10. World Bank, Washington, D.C.

Baker, Bill, and Sophie Tremolet. 2000. "Regulation of Quality of Infrastructure Services in Developing Countries." Paper presented at the International Conference on Infrastructure for Development: Private Solutions and the Poor, London, May 31–June 2.

Baldwin, Robert E. 2000. "Trade and Growth: Still Disagreement about the Relationships." Economics Department Working Paper 264. Organisation for Economic Co-operation and Development, Paris.

Barnett, Steven. 2000. "Evidence on the Fiscal and Macroeconomic Impact of Privatization." Working Paper WP/00/130. International Monetary Fund, Washington, D.C.

Barr, Nicholas. 1993. *The Welfare State*. London: Weidenfeld and Nicolson.

Barrientos, Armando, and Peter Lloyd-Sherlock. 2000. "Reforming Health Insurance in Argentina and Chile." *Health Policy and Planning* 15(4): 417–23.

Barro, Robert J. 2000. "Inequality and Growth in a Panel of Countries." *Journal of Economic Growth* 5(1): 87–120.

Bartone, Carl R., Luiz Leite, Thelma Triche, and Roland Schertenleib. 1991. "Private Sector Participation in Municipal Solid Waste Service: Experiences in Latin America." *Waste Management and Research* 9(6): 495–509.

Barzel, Yoram. 1989. *Economic Analysis of Property Rights*. Cambridge, United Kingdom: Cambridge University Press.

Batra, Geeta, and Syed Mahmood. 2001. "Direct Support to Private Firms: Evidence on Effectiveness." World Bank, Private Sector Advisory Services, Washington, D.C. Processed.

Batra, Geeta, and Hong Tan. 1995. *Enterprise Training in Developing Countries: Incidence, Productivity Effects, and Policy Implications.* Washington, D.C.: World Bank.

Batstone, C. J., and B. M. H. Sharp. 1999. "New Zealand's Quota Management System: The First Ten Years." *Marine Policy* 23(2): 177–90.

Bayliss, Kate, and David Hall. 2002a. "Another PSIRU Critique of Another Version of the World Bank Private Sector Development Strategy." PSIRU Report. London: Public Services International Research Unit, University of Greenwich.

———. 2002b. "Glimpses of an Alternative—The Possibility of Public Ownership in the World Bank's Latest PSD Strategy Paper." PSIRU Report. London: Public Services International Research Unit, University of Greenwich.

———. 2002c. "Unsustainable Conditions—The World Bank, Privatization, Water and Energy." PSIRU Report. London: Public Services International Research Unit, University of Greenwich.

Beales, Janet R. 1994a. "Doing More with Less: Competitive Contracting for School Support Services." Reason Public Policy Institute, Los Angeles. Processed.

———. 1994b. "A Private-Practice Option for Educators." Reason Public Policy Institute, Los Angeles. Processed.

Beales, Janet R., and John O'Leary. 1993. "Making Schools Work: Contracting Options for Better Management." Policy Study 169. Reason Public Policy Institute, Los Angeles.

Bedi, Arjun S., and Ashish Garg. 2000. "The Effectiveness of Private versus Public Schools: The Case of Indonesia." *Journal of Development Economics* 61: 463–94.

Ben-David, Dan. 1999. "Trade, Growth and Disparity among Nations." In Dan Ben-David, Hakan Nordstrom, and L. Alan Winters, eds., *Trade, Income Disparity, and Poverty.* Special Studies 5. Geneva: World Trade Organization.

Bennett, Sara, Barbara McPake, and Anne Mills, eds. 1997. *Private Health Providers in Developing Countries: Serving the Public Interest?* London: Zed Books.

Berman, Harold Joseph. 1983. *Law and Revolution: The Formation of the Western Legal Tradition.* Cambridge, Mass.: Harvard University Press.

Bernal, P., and B. Aliagna. 1999. "ITQ's in Chilean Fisheries." In A. Hatcher and K. Robinson, eds., *The Definition and Allocation of Use Rights in European*

Fisheries: Proceedings of the Second Workshop Held in Brest, France, 5–7 May. Portsmouth, United Kingdom: Centre for the Economics and Management of Aquatic Resources.

Bernal, Richard L., and Winsome J. Leslie. 1999. "Privatization in the English-Speaking Caribbean: An Assessment." *CSIS Policy Papers on the Americas* 10(7).

Bertranou, Fabio. 1999. "Are Market-Oriented Health Insurance Reforms Possible in Latin America? The Cases of Argentina, Chile, and Colombia." *Health Policy* 47: 19–36.

Biggs, Tyler. 1999. "A Microeconomic Evaluation of the Mauritius Technology Diffusion Scheme." RPED Discussion Paper 108. World Bank, Washington, D.C.

Blomstrom, Magnus, and Ari Kokko. 1996. "The Impact of Foreign Investment on Host Countries: A Review of the Empirical Evidence." Policy Research Working Paper 1745. World Bank, Washington, D.C.

Blundell, Richard, Rachel Griffith, and John Van Reenen. 1995. "Dynamic Count Data Models of Technological Innovation." *Economic Journal* 105: 333–44.

Boardman, Anthony E., and Aidan R. Vining. 1989. "Ownership and Performance in Competitive Environments: A Comparison of the Performance of Private, Mixed, and State-Owned Enterprises." *Journal of Law and Economics* 32: 1–33.

Borenzstein, Eduardo, José De Gregorio, and Jong-Wha Lee. 1998. "How Does Foreign Direct Investment Affect Economic Growth?" *Journal of International Economics* 45: 115–35.

Bosch, Christophe, Kirsten Hommann, Claudia Sadoff, and Lee Travers. 2000. "Water, Sanitation, and Poverty." *Poverty Reduction Strategy Sourcebook.* Washington, D.C.: World Bank.

Boubakri, Narjess, and Jean-Claude Cosset. 1998. "The Financial and Operating Performance of Newly Privatized Firms: Evidence from Developing Countries." *Journal of Finance* 53: 1081–110.

———. 1999. "Does Privatization Meet the Expectations? Evidence from African Countries." Working Paper. Ecole des HEC, Montreal.

Braudel, Ferdinand. 1979. *Civilization and Capitalism: 15th–18th Century,* vol. 3. New York: Harper and Row.

Bray, Mark. 1999. "Community Partnerships in Education: Dimensions, Variations, and Implications." Comparative Education Research Center, University of Hong Kong, Hong Kong, China. Processed.

Brealey, Richard A., Ian A. Cooper, and Michael A. Habib. 1997. "Investment Appraisal in the Public Sector." *Oxford Review of Economic Policy* 13(4): 12–28.

Brook, Penelope J. 2000. "Better Energy Services for the Poor: Issues, Challenges and Opportunities for the Private Sector." Paper presented at the International Conference on Infrastructure for Development: Private Solutions and the Poor, London, May 31–June 2.

Brook, Penelope J., and Suzanne Smith, eds. 2001. *Contracting for Public Services: Output-Based Aid and Its Applications.* Washington, D.C.: World Bank.

Brook, Penelope J., and Warrick Smith. 2001. "Improving Access to Infrastructure Services by the Poor: Institutional and Policy Responses." World Bank, Private Sector Advisory Services, Washington, D.C. Processed.

Brook, Penelope J., and Nicola Tynan. 1999. "Reaching the Urban Poor with Private Infrastructure." Public Policy for the Private Sector Note 188. World Bank, Washington, D.C.

Broomberg, Jonathan, Anne Mills, and Patrick Masobe. 1997. "To Purchase or to Provide? The Relative Efficiency of Contracting Out versus Direct Public Provision of Hospital Services in South Africa." In Sara Bennett, Barbara McPake, and Anne Mills, eds., *Private Health Providers in Developing Countries: Serving the Public Interest?* London: Zed Books.

Brunetti, Aymo, Gregory Kisunko, and Beatrice Weder. 1998. "How Businesses See Government: Responses from Private Sector Surveys in 69 Countries." Discussion Paper 33. International Finance Corporation, Washington, D.C.

Bubnova, Nina. 2000. "Governance Impact on Private Investment: Evidence from the International Patterns of Infrastructure Bond Risk Pricing." Technical Paper 488. World Bank, Washington, D.C.

Burawoy, Michael. 1997. "The State and Economic Involution: Russia through a China Lens." In Peter Evans, ed., *State-Society Synergy: Government and Social Capital in Development.* Research Series 94. Berkeley, Calif.: University of California–Berkeley.

Burke, James. 1995. *Connections.* New York: Little, Brown.

Burnside, Craig, and David Dollar. 1997. "Aid, Policies, and Growth." Policy Research Working Paper 1777. World Bank, Washington, D.C.

Calabresi, Guido, and Philip Bobbit. 1978. *Tragic Choices.* New York: W. W. Norton.

Calderón, Alberto. 1996. "Voucher Program for Secondary Schools: The Colombian Experience." Human Capital Development and Operations Policy Working Papers. World Bank, Washington, D.C.

Canagarajah, Sudharshan, and Xiao Ye. 2001. "Public Health and Education Spending in Ghana in 1992–98: Issues of Equity and Efficiency." Research Working Paper 2579. World Bank, Washington, D.C.

Caprio, Gerard Jr., and Asli Demirgüç-Kunt. 1998. "The Role of Long-Term Finance: Theory and Evidence." *World Bank Research Observer* 13(2): 171–89.

Carnaghan, Robert, and Barry Bracewell-Milnes. 1993. "Testing the Market: Competitive Tendering for Government Services in Britain and Abroad." Research Monograph 49. Institute of Economic Affairs, London.

Carnoy, Martin. 1997. "Is Privatization through Education Vouchers Really the Answer? A Comment on West." *World Bank Research Observer* 12(1): 105–16.

Castro-Leal, Florencia, Julia Dayton, Lionel Demery, and Kalpana Mehra. 1999. "Public Social Spending in Africa: Do the Poor Benefit?" *World Bank Research Observer* 14(1): 49–72.

Cave, Martin. 2001. "Voucher Programmes and Their Role in Distributing Public Services." *OECD Journal on Budgeting* 1(1): 59–88.

Caves, Richard E. 1998. "Industrial Organization and New Findings on the Turnover and Mobility of Firms." *Journal of Economic Literature* 36(4): 1947–82.

———. 1999. "Spillovers from Multinationals in Developing Countries: The Mechanisms at Work." Working Paper 247. William Davidson Institute, Ann Arbor, Mich.

Chadwick, Edwin. 1859. "Results of Different Principles of Legislation in Europe." *Journal of the Royal Statistical Society,* Series A22: 381–420.

Chisari, Omar, Antonio Estache, and Carlos Romero. 1999. "Winners and Losers from Utility Privatization in Argentina: Lessons from a General Equilibrium Model." Working Paper 3. Centro de Estudios Económicos de la Regulación, Buenos Aires.

Churchill, Anthony A. 1995. "Beyond Project Finance." *Electricity Journal* 8(5): 36–44.

Claessens, Stijn, Simeon Djankov, and L. Lang. 2000. "East Asian Corporations: Heroes or Villains?" Discussion Paper 409. World Bank, Washington, D.C.

Clague, Christopher, Philip Keefer, Stephen Knack, and Mancur Olson. 1999. "Contract Intensive Money: Contract Enforcement, Property Rights, and Economic Performance." *Journal of Economic Growth* 4: 185–211.

Clarke, George R. G., Claude Menard, and Ana Maria Zuluage. 2000. "The Welfare Effects of Private Sector Participation in Guinea's Urban Water Supply." Policy Research Working Paper 2361. World Bank, Washington, D.C.

Cohen, Joel E. 1995. *How Many People Can the Earth Support?* New York: W. W. Norton.

Collier, Paul. 1998. "Social Capital and Poverty." Social Capital Initiative Working Paper 4. World Bank, Washington, D.C.

———. 2000. *Economic Causes of Civil Conflict and Their Implications for Policy.* Washington, D.C.: World Bank.

Collier, Paul, and David Dollar. 2000. "Can the World Cut Poverty in Half? How Policy Reform and Effective Aid Can Meet the International Development Goals." Policy Research Working Paper 2403. World Bank, Washington, D.C.

Collier, Paul, and Jan Willem Gunning. 1999. "Explaining African Economic Performance." *Journal of Economic Literature* 37(1): 64–111.

Collier, Paul, and Anke Hoeffler. 1998. "On Economic Causes of Civil War." *Oxford Economic Papers* 50: 563–73.

Collignon, Bernard, and Marc Vezina. 2000. "Independent Water and Sanitation Providers in African Cities: Full Report of a Ten-Country Study." Working Paper. United Nations Development Programme–World Bank Water and Sanitation Program, Washington, D.C. Available at http://www.wsp.org. Last accessed March 12, 2003.

Collins, David, Jonathan D. Quick, Stephen N. Musau, Daniel Kraushaar, and Ibrahim M. Hussein. 1996. "The Fall and Rise of Cost Sharing in Kenya: The Impact of Phased Implementation." *Health Policy and Planning* 11(1): 52–63.

Colombo, Francesca. 2001. "Towards More Choice in Social Protection? Individual Choice of Insurer in Basic Mandatory Health Insurance in Switzerland." Labor Market and Social Policy Occasional Paper No. 53. Organisation for Economic Co-operation and Development, Paris.

Conn, Catherine P., and Veronica Walford. 1998. "An Introduction to Health Insurance for Low-Income Countries." Health Systems Resource Centre, U.K. Department for International Development, London. Processed.

Courcelle-Seneuil, Jean-Gustave. 1869. *Tratado Teorico I Practico de Economía Política.* Paris: Librería de Rosa y Bouret.

Crafts, Nicholas. 2000. "Globalization and Growth in the Twentieth Century." Working Paper WP/00/44. International Monetary Fund, Washington, D.C.

Cramton, Peter C. 1995. "Money Out of Thin Air: The Nationwide Narrowband PCS Auction." *Journal of Economics and Management Strategy* 4: 267–343.

Cutler, David M., and Sarah Reber. 1996. "Paying for Health Insurance: The Trade-Off between Competition and Adverse Selection." Working Paper No. 5796. National Bureau of Economic Research, Cambridge, Mass.

Cutler, David M., and Richard J. Zeckhauser. 1999. "The Anatomy of Health Insurance." Working Paper No. 7176. National Bureau of Economic Research, Cambridge, Mass.

Dabrowski, Marek, Stanislaw Gomulk, and Jacek Rostowski. 2001. "Whence Reform? A Critique of the Stiglitz Perspective." *Journal of Policy Reform* 4(4): 291–324.

Daly, Herman E. 1987. "The Economic Growth Debate: What Some Economists Have Learned but Many Have Not." *Journal of Environmental Economics and Management* 14: 1–14.

Davidse, W. 1999. "Lessons from Twenty Years of Experience with Property Rights in the Dutch Fishery." In A. Hatcher and K. Robinson, eds., *The Definition and Allocation of Use Rights in European Fisheries: Proceedings of the Second Workshop Held in Brest, France, 5–7 May.* Portsmouth, United Kingdom: Centre for the Economics and Management of Aquatic Resources.

De, Anuradha, Jean Dreze, Shiva Kumar, Claire Noronha, Pushpendra, Anita Rampal, Meera Samson, and Amarjeet Sinha. 1999. *Public Report on Basic Education in India (PROBE).* New Delhi: Oxford University Press.

de Capitani, Alberto, and Douglass C. North. 1994. "Institutional Development in Third World Countries: The Role of the World Bank." HRO Working Paper 42. World Bank, Washington, D.C.

Deininger Klaus, and Hans Binswanger. 1999. "The Evolution of the World Bank's Land Policy: Principles, Experience, and Future Challenges." *World Bank Research Observer* 14(2): 247–76.

Deininger, Klaus, and Gershon Feder. 1999. "Land Policy in Developing Countries." World Bank Rural Development Note 3. World Bank, Washington, D.C.

Deininger, Klaus, and Lyn Squire. 1997. "Economic Growth and Income Inequality: Reexamining the Links." *Finance & Development* (March): 38–41.

de Jonquieres, Guy. 2000. "NGOs Winning in Battle to Sway Public Opinion." *Financial Times,* December 6.

Delcheva, Evgenia, Dina Balabanova, and Martin McKee. 1997. "Under-the-Counter Payments for Health Care: Evidence from Bulgaria." *Health Policy* 42: 89–100.

de Long, Bradford J. 2000. "Cornucopia: The Pace of Economic Growth in the Twentieth Century." Working Paper 7602. National Bureau of Economic Research, Cambridge, Mass.

de Long, Bradford J., and A. Michael Froomkin. 2000. "Speculative Microeconomics for Tomorrow's Economy." In Brian Kahin and Hal Varian, eds., *Internet Publishing and Beyond: The Economics of Digital Information and Intellectual Property.* Cambridge, Mass.: MIT Press.

Demirgüç-Kunt, Asli, and Vojislav Maksimovic. 1996. "Financial Constraints, Uses of Funds, and Firm Growth: An International Comparison." Policy Research Working Paper 1671. World Bank, Washington, D.C.

Demsetz, Harold. 1982. "Barriers to Entry." *American Economic Review* 72(1): 47–57.

de Silva, Samantha. 2000. *Community-Based Contracting: A Review of Stakeholder Experience.* Washington, D.C.: World Bank.

de Soto, Hernando. 1989. *The Other Path: The Invisible Revolution in the Third World.* New York: Harper and Row.

———. 2000. *The Mystery of Capital: Why Capitalism Triumphs in the West and Fails Everywhere Else.* New York: Basic Books.

Devereux, Michael P., and Rachel Griffith. 1998. "Taxes and the Location of Production: Evidence from a Panel of U.S. Multinationals." *Journal of Public Economics* 68(3): 335–67.

Dinar, Ariel, and Gabriel Keynan. 1998. "The Cost and Performance of Paid Agricultural Extension Services." Policy Research Working Paper 1931. World Bank, Washington, D.C.

Diop, François P., A. Yazbeck, and R. Bitran. 1995. "The Impact of Alternative Cost Recovery Schemes on Access and Equity in Niger." *Health Policy and Planning* 10: 223–40.

Djankov, Simeon, and Peter Murrell. 2002. "Enterprise Restructuring: A Quantitative Survey." *Journal of Economic Literature* 40(3): 739–92.

Djankov, Simeon, Rafael La Porta, Florencio Lopez-de-Silanes, and Andrei Shleifer. 2000. "The Regulation of Entry." *Quarterly Journal of Economics* 117(1): 1–37.

Dollar, David, and Aart Kraay. 2000a. "Growth Is Good for the Poor." Policy Research Working Paper 2587. World Bank, Washington, D.C.

———. 2000b. "Property Rights, Political Rights, and the Development of Poor Countries in the Post-Colonial Period." World Bank, Development Research Group, Washington, D.C. Processed.

———. 2001. "Trade, Growth, and Poverty." Policy Research Working Paper 2199. World Bank, Washington, D.C.

Domberger, Simon, and John Piggott. 1994. "Privatization Policies and Public Enterprise: A Survey." In Matthew Bishop, John Kay, and Colin P. Mayer, eds., *Privatization and Economic Performance.* Oxford, United Kingdom: Oxford University Press.

Drabek, Zdenek, and Warren Payne. 1999. "The Impact of Transparency on Foreign Direct Investment." Staff Working Paper ERAD-99-02. World Trade Organization, Geneva.

Dror, David M., and Christian Jacquier. 1999. "Micro-insurance: Extending Health Insurance to the Excluded." *International Social Security Review* 52(1): 71–97.

Drucker, Peter F. 1998. "The Discipline of Innovation." *Harvard Business Review* (November–December): 149–57.

d'Souza, Juliet, and William L. Megginson. 1999. "The Financial and Operating Performance of Newly Privatized Firms in the 1990s." *Journal of Finance* 54(4): 1397–438.

Dyson, Freeman J. 1998. *Imagined Worlds.* Cambridge, Mass.: Harvard University Press.

———. 1999. *The Sun, the Genome, and the Internet: Tools of Scientific Revolutions.* Oxford, United Kingdom: Oxford University Press.

Earle, John S., and Saul Estrin. 1998. "Privatization, Competition, and Budget Constraints: Disciplining Enterprises in Russia." Working Paper 128. Stockholm Institute of Transition Economics, Stockholm.

Easterly, William. 2001. *The Elusive Quest for Growth: Economists' Adventures and Misadventures in the Tropics.* Cambridge, Mass.: MIT Press.

Easterly, William, and Ross Levine. 2000. "It's Not Factor Accumulation: Stylized Facts and Growth Models." *World Bank Economic Review* 15(2): 177–219.

The Economist. 1995. "Ungenerous Endowments." December 23.

———. 2001. "Poverty and Property Rights." March 31–April 6, 20–22.

Economist Intelligence Unit. n.d. "EIU Commodity Price Index." World Commodity Forecasts. Available from EIU Data Services at http://eiu.com. Last accessed March 13, 2003.

Edwards, Sebastian. 1997. "Openness, Productivity, and Growth: What Do We Really Know?" Working Paper 5978. National Bureau of Economic Research, Cambridge, Mass.

Ehrhardt, David. 2000. "Impact of Market Structure on Service Options for the Poor." Paper presented at the International Conference on Infrastructure for Development: Private Solutions and the Poor, London, May 31–June 2.

Ehrlich, Isaac, George Gallais-Hamonno, Zhiqiang Liu, and Randall Lutter. 1994. "Productivity Growth and Firm Ownership: An Empirical Investigation." *Journal of Political Economy* 102: 1006–38.

Elmeskov, Jorgen, and Stefano Scarpetta. 2000. "New Sources of Economic Growth in Europe." Paper presented at the Organisation for Economic Co-operation and Development Economic Conference on the New Millennium—Time for a New Economic Paradigm, Vienna, June 15–16.

England, Roger. 2000. "Contracting and Performance Management in the Health Sector: A Guide for Low- and Middle-Income Countries." Department for International Development, Health Systems Resource Centre, London. Processed.

Ensor, Tim. 1999. "Developing Health Insurance in Transitional Asia." *Social Science & Medicine* 48(7): 871–79.

Eskeland, Gunnar S., and Ann E. Harrison. 1997. "Moving to Greener Pastures? Multinationals and the Pollution-Haven Hypothesis." Policy Research Working Paper 1744. World Bank, Washington, D.C.

Estache, Antonio, Andres Gomez-Lobo, and Danny Leipziger. 2000. "Utility Privatization and the Needs of the Poor in Latin America: Have We Learned Enough to Get It Right?" Policy Research Working Paper 2407. World Bank, Washington, D.C.

European Bank for Reconstruction and Development. 2000. *Transition Report 2000*. London.

Evans, Peter. 1997. "Introduction: Development Strategies across the Public–Private Divide." In Peter Evans, ed., *State-Society Synergy: Government and Social Capital in Development*. Research Series 94. Berkeley, Calif.: University of California–Berkeley.

Evans, William N., and Ioannis N. Kessides. 1993. "Localized Market Power in the U.S. Airline Industry." *Review of Economics and Statistics* (February): 66–75.

Evenson, R. E. 1998. "Economic Impact Studies of Agricultural Research and Extension." Yale University, New Haven, Conn. Processed.

Fasano, Ugo. 2000. "Review of the Experience with Oil Stabilization and Savings Funds in Selected Countries." Working Paper WP/00/112. International Monetary Fund, Washington, D.C.

Feder, Gershon, Anthony Willett, and Willem Zijp. 1999. "Agricultural Extension: Genetic Challenges and Some Ingredients for Solutions." Policy Research Working Paper 2129. World Bank, Washington, D.C.

Fernández, Raquel, and Richard Rogerson. 2001. "Vouchers: A Dynamic Analysis." Paper presented at the National Bureau of Economic Research Conference on the Economics of School Choice, Florida Keys, Florida, February 22–24.

Figlio, David N., and Joe A. Stone. 2001. "Can Public Policy Affect Private School Cream-Skimming." Occasional Paper No. 31. National Center for the Study of Privatization in Education, Columbia University, New York.

Filmer, Deon, Jeffrey Hammer, and Lant Pritchett. 1997. "Health Policy in Poor Countries: Weak Links in the Chain." Policy Research Working Paper 1874. World Bank, Washington, D.C.

Finer, Samuel E. 1997. *The History of Government from the Earliest Times*, vol. 1–3. Oxford, United Kingdom: Oxford University Press.

Fitz, John, and Bryan Beers. 2001. "Education Management Organization and the Privatization of Public Education: A Cross-National Comparison of the U.S.A. and the U.K." Occasional Paper No. 22. National Center for the Study of Privatization in Education, Columbia University, New York.

Foley, Fritz C. 2001. "The Effects of Having an American Parent: An Analysis of the Growth of U.S. Multinational Affiliates." Paper presented at the World Bank Financial Economic Series Seminar, Washington, D.C., April 18.

Foreman-Peck, James, and Robert Millward. 1994. *Public and Private Ownership of British Industry 1820–1990.* Oxford, United Kingdom: Clarendon Press.

Foster, Vivien, and Osvaldo Irusta. 2001. "Does Infrastructure Reform Work for the Poor? A Case Study on the Twin Cities of La Paz and El Alto." World Bank, Public–Private Infrastructure Advisory Facility, Washington, D.C.

Foster, Vivien, Andres Gomez-Lobo, and Jonathan Halpern. 2000."Designing Direct Subsidies for the Poor—A Water and Sanitation Case Study." Public Policy for the Private Sector Note 211. World Bank, Washington, D.C.

Fouquet, Roger, and Peter J. G. Pearson. 1999. "Long-Run Energy Prices in the United Kingdom (1500–1996)." Paper presented at the British Institute of Energy Economics Conference on A New Era for Energy? Price Signals, Industry Structure, and Environment, St John's College, Oxford, United Kingdom, September 20–21.

Fox, Jonathan. 1997. "How Does Civil Society Thicken? The Political Construction of Social Capital in Rural Mexico." In Peter Evans, ed., *State-Society Synergy: Government and Social Capital in Development.* Research Series 94. Berkeley, Calif.: University of California–Berkeley.

Frank, Robert H., Thomas Gilovich, and Dennis T. Regan. 1993. "Does Studying Economics Inhibit Cooperation?" *Journal of Economic Perspectives* 7(2): 159–71.

Frankel, Jeffrey L., and David Romer. 1999. "Does Trade Cause Growth?" *The American Economic Review* 89: 379–99.

Frantzen, Dirk. 2000. "R&D, Human Capital and International Technology Spillovers: A Cross-Country Analysis." *Scandinavian Journal of Economics* 102(1): 57–75.

Friedman, Milton. 1995. "Public Schools: Make Them Private." Briefing Paper No. 23. Cato Institute, Washington, D.C.

Frydman, Roman, Cheryl Gray, Marek Hessel, and Andrej Rapaczynski. 1999a. "The Limits of Discipline: Ownership and Hard Budget Constraints in the Transition Economies." Transition Economics Series 5. Vienna: Institute for Advanced Studies.

————. 1999b. "When Does Privatization Work? The Impact of Private Ownership on Corporate Performance in Transition Economies." *Quarterly Journal of Economics* 114(4): 1153–91.

Fukuyama, Francis. 1995. *Trust: The Social Virtues and the Creation of Prosperity.* New York: Free Press.

————. 1999. *The Great Disruption: Human Nature and the Reconstitution of Social Order.* New York: Simon and Schuster.

————. 2000. "Social Capital and Civil Society." Working Paper WP/00/74. International Monetary Fund, Washington, D.C.

Galal, Ahmed, Leroy Jones, Pankaj Tandoon, and Ingo Vogelsang. 1994. *Welfare Consequences of Selling Public Enterprises: An Empirical Analysis.* Washington, D.C.: World Bank.

Gallup, John Luke, Steven Radelet, and Andrew Warner. 1998. "Economic Growth and the Income of the Poor." Harvard Institute for International Development, Cambridge, Mass. Processed.

Gautam, Madhur. 2000. *Agricultural Extension: The Kenya Experience.* Washington, D.C.: World Bank.

Gauthier, Anne K., and Deborah L. Rogal. 2001. "The Challenge of Managed Care Regulation: Making Markets Work." Academy for Health Services Research and Health Policy, Changes in Health Care and Financing and Organization Program, Washington, D.C. Processed.

Gaynor, Martin, Deborah Haas-Wilson, and William B. Vogt. 1998. "Are Invisible Hands Good Hands? Moral Hazard, Competition, and the Second Best in Health Care Markets." Working Paper No. 6865. National Bureau of Economic Research, Cambridge, Mass.

Gelb, Alan, and others. 1988. *Oil Windfalls: Blessing or Curse.* Oxford, United Kingdom: World Bank and Oxford University Press.

Geroski, Paul A. 1990. "Innovation, Technological Opportunity, and Market Structure." *Oxford Economic Papers* 42(3): 586–602.

Gertler, Paul J., and Orville Solon. 2000. "Who Benefits from Social Health Insurance in Developing Countries?" University of California–Berkeley, National Bureau of Economic Research, and University of the Philippines. Processed.

Gertler, Paul J., and Jeffrey Hammer. 1997. "Strategies for Pricing Publicly Provided Health Services." Policy Research Working Paper 1762. World Bank, Washington, D.C.

Glaeser, Edward L. 1998. "Are Cities Dying?" *Journal of Economic Perspectives* 12(2): 139–60.

Glaeser, Edward L., and Andrei Shleifer. 2001. "Legal Origins." Working Paper 8272. National Bureau of Economic Research, Cambridge, Mass.

Glewwe, Paul, and Harry A. Patrinos. 1999. "The Role of the Private Sector in Education in Vietnam: Evidence from the Vietnam Living Standards Survey." *World Development* 27(5): 887–902.

Goldstone, David. 2001. "Output-Based Education: The Evolution of Contracts for Schools in the U.K." In Penelope J. Brook and Suzanne Smith, eds., *Contracting for Public Services: Output-Based Aid and Its Applications.* Washington, D.C.: World Bank.

Gomez-Ibanez, José and John R. Meyer, eds. 1993. *Going Private: The International Experience with Transport Privatization.* Washington, D.C.: Brookings Institution Press.

Gomez-Lobo, Andres, Vivien Foster, and Jonathan Halpern. 2000. "Infrastructure Reform, Better Subsidies, and the Information Deficit." Public Policy for the Private Sector Note 212. World Bank, Washington, D.C.

Graham, Carol, and Stefano Pettinato. 2000. *Happiness and Hardship: Opportunity and Insecurity in New Market Economies.* Washington, D.C.: Brookings Institution Press.

Graham, Edward M., and Erika Wada. 2001. "Foreign Direct Investment in China: Effects on Growth and Economic Performance." Institute for International Economics, Washington, D.C. Processed.

Grant, Simon, and John Quiggin. 1998. "The Equity Premium Puzzle and the Privatization Paradox." Paper presented at the Industry Economics Conference, Australian National University, Canberra, July 6–7.

Gray, Philip. 2001. "Private Participation in Infrastructure: A Review of the Evidence." World Bank, Private Sector Advisory Services, Washington, D.C. Processed.

Greene, Jay P. 2000. "A Survey of Results from Voucher Experiments: Where We Are and What We Know." Civic Report 11. Manhattan Institute for Policy Research, New York.

Greenwald, Bruce C., and Joseph E. Stiglitz. 1986. "Externalities in Economies with Imperfect Information and Incomplete Markets." *Quarterly Journal of Economics* 101: 229–64.

Greif, Avner. 1989. "Reputation and Coalitions in Medieval Trade: Evidence of the Maghribi Traders." *Journal of Economic History* 49(December): 857–82.

Greif, Avner, Paul Milgrom, and Barry R. Weingast. 1994. "Coordination, Commitment, and Enforcement: The Case of the Merchant Guild." *Journal of Political Economy* 102(4): 745–76.

Grootaert, Christian. 1999. "Social Capital, Household Welfare, and Poverty in Indonesia." Research Working Paper 2148. World Bank, Washington, D.C.

Guasch, I. Luis, and Robert W. Hahn. 1999. "The Costs and Benefits of Regulation: Implications for Developing Countries." World Bank Research Observer 14(1): 137–58.

Gugerty, Mary Kay, and Michael Kremer. 2000. "Outside Funding of Community Organizations: Benefiting or Displacing the Poor?" Working Paper 7896. National Bureau of Economic Research, Cambridge, Mass.

Gugerty, Mary Kay, and C. Peter Timmer. 1999. "Growth, Inequality, and Poverty Alleviation: Implications for Development Assistance." CAER II Discussion Paper 50. Harvard Institute for International Development, Cambridge, Mass.

Guiso, Luigi, Luigi Zingales, and Paolo Sapienza. 2000. "The Role of Social Capital in Financial Development." Discussion Paper 2383. Centre for Economic Policy Research, London.

Gupta, Sanjeev, Hamid Davoodi, and Rosa Alonso-Terme. 1998. "Does Corruption Affect Income Inequality and Poverty?" Working Paper WP/98/76. International Monetary Fund, Washington, D.C.

Gwatkin, Davidson R., Shea Rustein, Kiersten Johnson, Rohini P. Pandle, and Adam Wagstaff. 2000. "Socio-Economic Differences in Health, Nutrition, and Population." World Bank, Demographic and Health Survey Program, Washington, D.C.

Haddad, Brent M. 1997. "Putting Markets to Work: The Design and Use of Marketable Permits and Obligations." Public Management (PUMA) Occasional Paper 19. Organisation for Economic Co-operation and Development, Paris.

Hallberg, Kristin. 2000. "A Market-Oriented Strategy for Small and Medium-Scale Enterprises." Discussion Paper 40. International Finance Corporation, Washington, D.C.

Hannay, Alastair, trans. 1996. Søren Kierkegaard Papers and Journals: A Selection. New York: Penguin.

Hannaway, Jane. 1999. "Contracting as a Mechanism for Managing Education Services." CPRE Policy Briefs. University of Pennsylvania, Philadelphia.

Hansman, Henry. 1981. "Consumer Perceptions of Non-Profit Enterprise: Reply." Yale Journal of Law (June): 1633–38.

Hansman, Henry, and Reinier Kraakman. 2000. "The End of History for Corporate Law." Discussion Paper 280. Harvard Law School, Center for Law, Economics, and Business, Cambridge, Mass.

Hanushek, Eric A., and Steven G. Rivkin. 2001. "Does Public School Competition Affect Teacher Quality?" Paper presented at the National Bureau of Economic Research Conference on the Economics of School Choice, Florida Keys, Florida, February 22–24.

Hardin, Garrett. 1968. "Tragedy of the Commons." *Science* 162: 1243–48.

Harris, Milton, and Art Raviv. 1990. "Capital Structure and the Informational Role of Debt." *Journal of Finance* 45(June): 321–49.

Harrison, Ann, and Gordon Hanson. 1999. "Who Gains from Trade Reform? Some Remaining Puzzles." Working Paper 6915. National Bureau of Economic Research, Cambridge, Mass.

Havrylyshyn, Oleh, and Donal McGettigan. 1999. "Privatization in Transition Countries: A Sampling of the Literature." Working Paper WP/99/6. International Monetary Fund, Washington, D.C.

Havrylyshyn, Oleh, and John Odling-Smee. 2000. "Political Economy of Stalled Reform." *Finance & Development* 37(3): 7–9.

Hawken, Paul, Amory Lovins, and L. Hunter Lovins. 1999. *Natural Capitalism: Creating the Next Industrial Revolution.* Boston: Little, Brown.

Heller, Patrick. 1997. "Social Capital as a Product of Class Mobilization and State Intervention: Industrial Workers in Kerela, India." In Peter Evans, ed., *State-Society Synergy: Government and Social Capital in Development.* Research Series 94. Berkeley, Calif.: University of California–Berkeley.

Helliwell, John F., and Robert D. Putnam. 1995. "Economic Growth and Social Capital in Italy." *Eastern Economic Journal* 21(3): 295–307.

Hellman, Joel. 1998. "Winners Take All: The Politics of Partial Reform in Post-communist Transitions." *World Politics* 50(January): 203–34.

Hellwig, Martin. 2000. "On the Economics and Politics of Corporate Finance and Corporate Control." In Xavier Vives, ed., *Corporate Governance: Theoretical and Empirical Perspectives.* Cambridge, United Kingdom: Cambridge University Press.

Hendricks, Lutz. 2002. "How Important Is Human Capital for Development? Evidence from Immigrant Earnings." *American Economic Review* 92(1): 198–219.

Hepburn, Claudia R. 1999. The Case for School Choice: Models from the United States, New Zealand, Denmark, and Sweden." Fraser Institute, Vancouver, B.C. Processed.

Hill, Paul T., Lawrence Pierce, and James Guthrie. 1997. *Reinventing Public Education: How Contracting Can Transform America's Schools.* Chicago: University of Chicago Press.

Hines, James R. Jr. 1999. "Lessons from Behavioral Response in International Taxation." *National Tax Journal* 52(2): 305–22.

Hirsch, Fred. 1976. *Social Limits to Growth.* Cambridge, Mass.: Harvard University Press.

Hirschman, Albert. 1992. *Rival Views of Market Society and Other Recent Essays.* Cambridge, Mass.: Harvard University Press.

Hoskins, Lee, and Ana I. Erias. 2002. "Property Rights: The Key to Economic Growth." In Gerald P. O'Driscoll Jr., Kim R. Holmes, and Mary Anastasia O'Grady, eds., *The 2002 Index of Economic Freedom.* Washington, D.C.: Heritage Foundation.

Howell, William G., Patrick J. Wolf, Paul E. Peterson, and David E. Campbell. 2000. "Test-Score Effects of School Vouchers in Dayton, Ohio; New York City; and Washington, D.C.: Evidence from Randomized Field Trials." Paper presented at the annual meeting of the American Political Science Association, Washington, D.C., September.

Hoxby, Caroline. 1994. "Do Private Schools Provide Competition for Public Schools?" Working Paper 4978. National Bureau of Economic Research, Cambridge, Mass.

———. 2000. "Does Competition among Public Schools Benefit Students and Taxpayers?" *American Economic Review* (December): 1209–38.

———. 2001. "School Choice and School Productivity (or Could School Choice be a Tide That Lifts All Boats?)" Paper presented at the National Bureau of Economic Research Conference on the Economics of School Choice, Florida Keys, Florida, February 22–24.

Hurst, Jeremy, and Melissa Jee-Hughes. 2001. "Performance Measurement and Performance Management in OECD Health Systems." Labor Market and Social Policy Occasional Paper No. 47. Organisation for Economic Co-operation and Development, Directorate for Education, Employment, Labor and Social Affairs, Paris.

Institute for Health Sector Development. 2000. "Contracting for Primary Medicines Care Management in Albania: Lessons Learned and Transferable Principles." Issues Note. Institute for Health Sector Development, London.

International Confederation of Free Trade Unions, Trade Union Advisory Committee, and International Trade Secretariats. 2001. "Combating Growing World Inequality and Renewed Threats of International Financial Instability." Statement presented at the spring 2001 meetings of the International Monetary Fund and World Bank, Washington, D.C., April 29–30.

Irwin, Timothy, Michael Klein, Guillermo E. Perry, and Mateen Thobani, eds. 1997. *Dealing with Public Risk in Private Infrastructure.* Washington, D.C.: World Bank, Latin American and Caribbean Studies.

Izaguirre, Ada Karina. 2002. "Private Infrastructure: A Review of Projects with Private Participation, 1990–2001." Public Policy for the Private Sector Note 250. World Bank, Washington, D.C.

Jack, William G. 2001. "Health Insurance Reform in Four Latin American Countries: Theory and Practice." Policy Research Working Paper 2492. World Bank, Washington, D.C.

Jacobzone, Stéphane. 2000. "Pharmaceutical Policies in OECD Countries: Reconciling Social and Industrial Goals." Labor Market and Social Policy Occasional Paper No. 40. Organisation for Economic Co-operation and Development, Directorate for Education, Employment, Labor and Social Affairs, Paris.

James, David. 2001. "Cooperation, Competition, and the 'Science of Pricing' in the Political Risk Insurance Marketplace: Overview." In Theodore Moran, ed., *International Political Risk Management: Exploring New Frontiers.* Washington, D.C.: World Bank.

James, Estelle. 1990. "Private Education and Redistributive Subsidies in Australia." In William T. Gormley, ed., *Privatization and Its Alternatives.* Madison, Wis.: University of Wisconsin Press.

———. 1991. "Public Policies toward Private Education: An International Comparison." *International Journal of Educational Research* 15(5): 359–76.

———. 1996. "New Systems for Old Age Security: Theory, Practice, and Empirical Evidence." Policy Research Working Paper 1766. World Bank, Washington, D.C.

———. 1999. "Coverage under Old-Age Security Programs and Protection for the Uninsured—What Are the Issues?" Policy Research Working Paper 2163. World Bank, Washington, D.C.

Janovsky, J. 1986. "Les Parcs de Technologie en R.F.A., en France et au Royaume-Uni." AREPIT Série Etudes 16. Association de Recherche Économique en Propriété Intellectuelle et Transferts Techniques, Paris.

Jimenez, Emmanuel. 1987. *Pricing Policy in the Social Sectors.* Baltimore and London: Johns Hopkins University Press.

Jimenez, Emmanuel, and Yasayuki Sawada. 1998. "Do Community-Managed Schools Work? An Evaluation of El Salvador's EDUCO Program." Development Economics Research Group Working Paper Series on Impact Evaluation of Education Reforms, Paper No. 8. World Bank, Washington, D.C.

Jimenez, Emmanuel, Marlaine Lockheed, and Vicente Paqueo. 1991. "The Relative Efficiency of Private and Public Schools in Developing Countries." *World Bank Research Observer* 6(2): 205–18.

Johnson, Gale. 2000. "Population, Food, and Knowledge." *American Economic Review* 90(1): 1–14.

Jones, Charles I. 1999. "Was an Industrial Revolution Inevitable? Economic Growth over the Very Long Run." Working Paper 7375. National Bureau of Economic Research, Cambridge, Mass.

Jones, E. L. 1987. *The European Miracle: Environments, Economies, and Geopolitics in the History of Europe and Asia.* 2nd ed. Cambridge, United Kingdom: Cambridge University Press.

Jones, Leroy, Yahya Jammal, and Nilgun Gokur. 1999. "Impact of Privatization in Côte d'Ivoire." Boston Institute for Developing Economies, Boston. Processed.

Jonsson, Gunnar, and Arvind Subramanian. 2000. "Dynamic Gains from Trade: Evidence from South Africa." Working Paper WP/00/45. International Monetary Fund, Washington, D.C.

Joskow, Paul L., Richard Schmalensee, and Elizabeth M. Bailey. 1998. "The Market for Sulfur Dioxide Emissions." *American Economic Review* (September): 669–85.

Joy, Bill. 2000. "Why the Future Doesn't Need Us." *Wired Magazine* 8(04).

Kähkönen, Satu. 1999. "Does Social Capital Matter in Water and Sanitation Delivery? A Review of Literature." Social Capital Initiative Working Paper 9. World Bank and IRIS Center, Washington, D.C.

Kahn, Alfred. 1970. *The Economics of Regulation: Principles and Institutions.* New York: Wiley.

Kahneman, Daniel, and Amos Tversky. 1979. "Prospect Theory: An Analysis of Decision under Risk." *Econometrica* 47: 263–92.

Kaufmann, Daniel, Pablo Zoido-Lobaton, and Young Lee. 2000. "Governance and Anti-Corruption in Ecuador: Survey Evidence." World Bank, World Bank Institute, Washington, D.C. Processed.

Keane, Michael P., and Eswar S. Prasad. 2000. "Inequality, Transfers, and Growth: New Evidence from the Economic Transition in Poland." Working Paper WP/00/117. International Monetary Fund, Washington, D.C.

Keesing, Don B., and Andrew Singer. 1990. "How Support Services Can Expand Manufactured Exports: New Methods of Assistance" Policy Research Working Paper 544. World Bank, Washington, D.C.

Kelly, Jack. 2000. "Safety at a Price: Security Is a Booming, Sophisticated, Global Business." *PG News Article*, February 13. Available at http://www.postgazette.com/headlines/20000213security1.asp. Last accessed February 28, 2003.

Kessel, Reuben A. 1974. "Transfused Blood, Serum Hepatitis, and the Coase Theorem." *Journal of Law and Economics* 17(2): 265–89.

Khan, Mohsin. 2000. "Financial Development and Economic Growth—An Overview." Working Paper WP/00/209. International Monetary Fund, Washington, D.C.

Kikeri, Sunita, and John Nellis. 2002. "Privatization in Competitive Sectors: The Record to Date." Policy Research Working Paper 2860. World Bank, Washington, D.C.

Kim, Jooseop, Harold Alderman, and Peter Orazem. 1998. "Can Private School Subsidies Increase Schooling for the Poor? The Quetta Urban Fellowship Program." Development Economics Research Group Working Paper Series on Impact Evaluation of Education Reforms, Paper No. 11. World Bank, Washington, D.C.

King, Elizabeth M., Laura Rawling, Marybell Gutierrez, Carlos Pardo, and Carlos Torres. 1997. "Colombia's Targeted Education Voucher Program: Features, Coverage, and Participation." Development Economics Research Group Working Paper Series on Impact Evaluation of Education Reforms, Paper No. 3. World Bank, Washington, D.C.

Kipp, Walter, Jimmy Kamugisha, Phil Jacobs, Gilbert Burnham, and Tom Rubaale. 2001. "User Fees, Health Staff Incentives, and Service Utilization in Kabarole District, Uganda." *Bulletin of the World Health Organization* 79: 1032–37.

Klaassen, Ger. 1999. "Emissions Trading in the European Union: Practice and Prospects." In Steve Sorrell and Jim Skea, eds., *Pollution for Sale: Emissions*

Trading and Joint Implementation. Cheltenham, United Kingdom: Edward Elgar.

Klein, Michael. 1997. "The Risk Premium for Evaluating Public Projects." *Oxford Review of Economic Policy* 13(4): 29–42.

———. 1998a. "Network Industries." In Dieter Helm and Tim Jenkinson, eds., *Competition in Regulated Industries.* Oxford, United Kingdom: Oxford University Press.

———. 1998b. "Rebidding for Concessions." Public Policy for the Private Sector Note 161. World Bank, Washington, D.C.

———. 1999. "The Asian Crisis and Structural Change in Energy Markets." In Eugene McCarthy and Felix Martin, eds., *Energy and Development Report 1999.* Washington, D.C.: World Bank.

———. 2000. "Why Large Size Adds to Value: A Comment on Dennis Mueller's Paper." *International Journal of Global Energy Issues* 13(4): 425–31.

Klein, Michael, and Neil D. Roger. 1994. "Back to the Future: The Potential in Infrastructure Privatization." In Richard O'brien, ed., *Finance and the International Economy 8, American Express Bank Review Prize Essays.* New York: Oxford University Press.

Knack, Stephen. 1999. "Social Capital, Growth and Poverty: A Survey of Cross-Country Evidence." Social Capital Initiative Working Paper 7. World Bank and IRIS Center, Washington, D.C.

Knack, Stephen, and Philip Keefer. 1997. "Does Social Capital Have an Economic Payoff? A Cross-Country Investigation." *Quarterly Journal of Economics* 112(4): 1251–88.

Komives, Kristin, Dale Whittington, and Xun Wu. 2000. "Infrastructure Coverage and the Poor: A Global Perspective." Paper presented at the International Conference on Infrastructure for Development: Private Solutions and the Poor, London, May 31–June 2.

Kumaranayake, Lilani. 1997. "The Role of Regulation: Influencing Private Sector Activity within Health Sector Reform." *Journal of International Development* 9(4): 641–49.

———. 1998. "Effective Regulation of Private Sector Health Service Providers." Paper presented at the World Bank Mediterranean Development Forum II, Morocco, September 3–6.

Kumaranayake, Lilani, Sally Lake, Phare Mujina, Charles Hongoro, and Rose Mpembeni. 2000. "How Do Countries Regulate the Health Sector? Evidence from Tanzania and Zimbabwe." *Health Policy and Planning* 15(4): 357–67.

Kurz, Mordecai. 1977. "Altruistic Equilibrium." In Bela Balassa and Richard Nelson, eds., *Economic Progress, Private Values, and Public Policy: Essays in Honor of William Fellner.* Amsterdam: North-Holland.

Kwoka, John E. Jr. 1996. *Power Structure: Ownership, Integration, and Competition in the U.S. Electricity Industry.* Boston: Kluwer Academic Publishers.

Laffont, J. J., and J. Tirole. 1993. *A Theory of Incentives in Regulation and Procurement.* Cambridge, Mass.: MIT Press.

Landes, David. 1998. *The Wealth and Poverty of Nations: Why Are Some So Rich and Others So Poor?* New York: W. W. Norton.

Lanjouw, Peter. 1999. "The Rural Non-Farm Sector: A Note on Policy Options." World Bank, Development Economics Research Group, Washington, D.C. Processed.

La Porta, Rafael, and Florencio Lopez-de-Silanes. 1997. "The Benefits of Privatization: Evidence from Mexico." Working Paper 6215. National Bureau of Economic Research, Cambridge, Mass.

La Porta, Rafael, Florencio Lopez-de-Silanes, Andrei Shleifer, and Robert W. Vishny. 1996a. "Law and Finance." Working Paper 5661. National Bureau of Economic Research, Cambridge, Mass.

———. 1996b. "Trust in Large Organizations." Working Paper 5864. National Bureau of Economic Research, Cambridge, Mass.

Lewis, Maureen A. 1993. "User Fees in Public Hospitals: Comparison of Three Country Case Studies." *Economic Development and Cultural Change* 41(3): 513–32.

Lieberman, Myron. 1989. *Privatization and Educational Choice.* New York: St. Martin's Press.

Liedholm, Carl. 2002. "Small Firm Dynamics: Evidence from Africa and Latin America." *Small Business Economics* 18(1–3): 227–42.

Litvack, Jennie, and Claude Bodart. 1993. "User Fees Plus Quality Equals Improved Access to Health Care: Results of a Field Experiment in Cameroon." *Social Science & Medicine* 37(3): 369–83.

Lockheed, Marlaine E., and Emmanuel Jimenez. 1994. "Public and Private Secondary Schools in Developing Countries: What Are the Differences and

Why Do They Persist?" Human Capital Working Paper 43. World Bank, Washington, D.C.

Loevinsohn, Benjamin. 2000a. "Contracting for the Delivery of Primary Health Care in Cambodia: Design and Initial Experience of a Large Pilot Test." *WBI Online Journal.* Washington, D.C.: World Bank. Available at http://www.worldbank.org/wbi/healthflagship/journal.html. Last accessed March 12, 2003.

————. 2000b. "Practical Issues in Contracting for Primary Health Care Delivery: Lessons from Two Large Projects in Bangladesh." *WBI Online Journal.* Washington, D.C.: World Bank. Available at http://www.worldbank.org/wbi/healthflagship/journal.html. Last accessed March 12, 2003.

Lovei, Magda. 1999. "Environmental Implications of Privatization." Pollution Management in Focus Discussion Note 5. World Bank, Washington, D.C.

Maas, Peter. 2001. "Ayn Rand Comes to Somalia." *Atlantic Monthly* 287(5): 30–31.

Macedo, Roberto. 2000. "Privatization and the Distribution of Assets and Income in Brazil." Economic Reform Project Working Paper 14. Carnegie Endowment, Washington, D.C.

Maddison, Angus. 2001. *The World Economy: A Millennial Perspective.* Paris: Organisation for Economic Co-operation and Development.

Mahboobi, Ladan. 2001. "Recent Privatization Trends." *Financial Market Trends* 79: 43–65.

Marek, Tonia, Issakha Diallo, Biram Ndiaye, and Jean Rakotosalama. 1999. "Successful Contracting of Prevention Service: Fighting Malnutrition in Senegal and Madagascar." *Health Policy Planning* 14(4): 382–9.

Marx, Karl. 1867. *Capital: A Critique of Political Economy.*

Matusz, Steven J., and David Tarr. 1999. "Adjusting to Trade Policy Reform." Policy Research Working Paper 2142. World Bank, Washington, D.C.

Mauro, Paulo. 1995. "Corruption and Economic Growth." *Quarterly Journal of Economics* 110(3): 682–712.

Mauss, Marcel. 2000. *The Gift: The Form and Reason for Exchange in Archaic Societies.* New York: W. W. Norton.

Mayer, Colin P. 1989. "Myths of the West: Lessons from Developed Countries for Development Finance." Policy Research Working Paper 301. World Bank, Washington, D.C.

McKinsey Global Institute. 1994. *Latin American Productivity.* Washington, D.C.

———. 1997. *Removing Barriers to Growth and Employment in France and Germany.* Washington, D.C.

———. 1998a. *Driving Productivity and Growth in the U.K. Economy.* Washington, D.C.

———. 1998b. *Productivity-Led Growth for Korea.* Washington, D.C.

———. 1998c. *Productivity—The Key to an Accelerated Development Path for Brazil.* Washington, D.C.

———. 1999. *Unlocking Economic Growth in Russia.* Washington, D.C.

———. 2000. *Why the Japanese Economy Is Not Growing: Microbarriers to Productivity Growth.* Washington, D.C.

———. 2001. *India—The Growth Imperative: Understanding the Barriers to Rapid Growth and Employment Creation.* Washington, D.C.

———. 2002. *Thailand—Prosperity Through Productivity.* Washington, D.C.

McMillan, John. 1994. "Selling Spectrum Rights." *Journal of Economic Perspectives* 8(Summer): 145–62.

———. 1995. "China's Nonconformist Reforms." In Edward P. Lazear, ed., *Economic Transition in Eastern Europe and Russia: Realities of Reform.* Stanford, Calif.: Hoover Institution Press.

McPake, Barbara, and Charles Hongoro. 1995. "Contracting Out of Clinical Services in Zimbabwe." *Social Science & Medicine* 41(1): 13–24.

Megginson, William L., and Jeffrey M. Netter. 2001. "From State to Market: A Survey of Empirical Studies of Privatization." *Journal of Economic Literature* 39(2): 321–89.

Megginson, William L., Robert C. Nash, and Matthias Van Randenborgh. 1994. "The Financial and Operating Performance of Newly Privatized Firms: An International Empirical Analysis." *Journal of Finance* 49(2): 403–52.

Mellitt, Brian. n.d. "Restructuring by Privatization: The U.K. Experience." In *Proceedings of the Conference of the Institution of Engineers.* Australia: Institution of Engineers. Processed.

Milgrom, Paul, Douglass C. North, and Barry Weingast. 1990. "The Role of Institutions in the Revival of Trade: Law Merchants, Private Judges, and the Champagne Fairs." *Economics & Politics* 2(1): 1–24.

Mody, Ashoka, and Fang-Yi Wang. 1997. "Determinants of Industrial Growth in Coastal China, 1986–9." *World Bank Economic Review* 11(2): 293–325.

Moore, Barrington. 1978. *Injustice: The Social Base of Obedience and Revolt.* Stamford, Conn.: Ray Freiman.

Moran, Theodore. 2001. "Cooperation, Competition, and the 'Science of Pricing' in the Political Risk Insurance Marketplace: Overview." In Theodore Moran, ed., *International Political Risk Management: Exploring New Frontiers.* Washington, D.C.: World Bank.

Morduch, Jonathan. 1999. "The Microfinance Promise." *Journal of Economic Literature* 37(4): 1569–1614.

Morisset, Jacques, and Neda Pirnia. 2000. "How Tax Policy and Incentives Affect Foreign Direct Investment: A Review." Policy Research Working Paper 2509. World Bank, Washington, D.C.

Mtemeli, D. N. 1994. "An Investigation into Why Women in Muttasa District Prefer to Deliver at Home and Not in Health Institutions." Processed.

Nagel, Thomas. 1979. *The Possibility of Altruism.* Princeton, N.J.: Princeton University Press.

Narayan, Deepa, and Patti Petesch. 2002. *Voices of the Poor: From Many Lands.* Washington, D.C.: World Bank.

Narayan, Deepa, Robert Chambers, Meera K. Shah, and Patti Petesch. 2000a. *Voices of the Poor: Crying Out for Change.* Washington, D.C.: World Bank.

Narayan, Deepa, Raj Patel, Kai Schafft, Anne Rademacher, and Sarah Koch-Schulte. 2000b. *Voices of the Poor: Can Anyone Hear Us?* Washington, D.C.: World Bank.

Nechyba, Thomas J., 2001. "Introducing School Choice into Multi-District Public School Systems." Paper presented at the National Bureau of Economic Research Conference on the Economics of School Choice, Florida Keys, Florida, February 22–24.

Nellis, John. 1999. "Time to Rethink Privatization in Transition Economies?" Discussion Paper 38. International Finance Corporation, Washington, D.C.

Newbery, David M., and Michael G. Pollitt. 1997. "The Restructuring and Privatization of Britain's CEGB—Was It Worth It?" *Journal of Industrial Economics* 45(3): 269–303.

Newbrander, William. 1999. "Accreditation of Providers for the National Health Insurance Fund of Tanzania." Management Sciences for Health, Boston. Processed.

Newbrander, William, Carlos J. Cuellar, and Barbara K. Timmons. 2000. "The PROSALUD Model for Expanding Access to Health Services." *WBI Online Journal*. Washington, D.C.: World Bank. Available at http://www.worldbank.org/wbi/healthflagship/journal.html. Last accessed March 12, 2003.

Nickell, Stephen J. 1996. "Competition and Corporate Performance." *Journal of Political Economy* 104(4): 724–46.

Nickell, Stephen J., Daphne Nicolitsas, and Neil Dryden. 1997. "What Makes Firms Perform Well?" *European Economic Review* 41: 783–96.

Noll, Roger, Mary Shirley, and Simon Cowan. 2000. "Reforming Urban Water Systems in Developing Countries." In Anne Krueger, ed., *Economic Policy Reform: The Second Stage*. Chicago: University of Chicago Press.

North, Douglas. 1982. *Structure and Change in Economic History*. New York: W.W. Norton.

Nozick, Robert. 1974. *Anarchy, State, and Utopia*. New York: Basic Books.

Nugent, Jeffrey B., and Seung-Jae Yhee. 2002. "Small and Medium Enterprises in Korea: Achievements, Constraints, and Policy Issues." *Small Business Economics* 18(1–3): 85–119.

Ogunbekun, I., O. Adeyi, Anne-Marie Wouters, and R. H. Morrow. 1996. "Costs and Financing of Improvements in the Quality of Maternal Health Services through the Bamako Initiative in Nigeria." *Health Policy and Planning* 11(4): 369–84.

Olson, Mancur. 1996. "Big Bills Left on the Sidewalk: Why Some Nations Are Sick and Others Poor." *Journal of Economic Perspectives* 10(2): 3–24.

————. 2000. *Power and Prosperity: Outgrowing Communist and Capitalist Dictatorships*. New York: Basic Books.

Or, Zeynep. 2002. "Improving the Performance of Health Care Systems: From Measures to Action—A Review of Experiences in Four OECD Countries." Labor Market and Social Policy Occasional Paper No. 57. Organisation for Economic Co-operation and Development, Paris.

Organisation for Economic Co-operation and Development. 1992a. "Health-Care Reform." In *OECD Economic Surveys: United States*. Paris.

———. 1992b. "Property Rights Modifications in Fisheries." Public Management (PUMA) Occasional Papers: Market-Type Mechanisms Series No. 3. Paris.

———. 1994. *School: A Matter of Choice.* OECD Center for Educational Research and Innovation, Paris.

———. 1997a. "Best Practice Guidelines for Contracting Out Government Services." Public Management Service (PUMA) Policy Brief No. 2. Paris.

———. 1997b. "Small Businesses, Job Creation, and Growth: Facts, Obstacles, and Best Practices." Paris. Processed.

———. 1998a. "Contracting Out Government Services: Best Practice Guidelines and Case Studies." Public Management (PUMA) Occasional Papers 20. Paris.

———. 1998b. *OECD Economic Outlook* (June). Paris.

———. 1999a. "Economic Instruments for Pollution Control and Natural Resources Management in OECD Countries: A Survey." Working Party on Economic and Environmental Policy Integration, Paris.

———. 1999b. "OECD Principles of Corporate Governance." SG/CG(99)5. Directorate for Financial, Fiscal and Enterprise Affairs, Paris.

———. 2001. *Private Health Insurance in OECD Countries: Compilation of National Reports.* Paris: Insurance and Private Pensions Unit, Financial Affairs Division, Directorate for Financial, Fiscal and Enterprise Affairs.

Ostrom, Elinor. 1990. *Governing the Commons: The Evolution of Institutions for Collective Action.* New York: Cambridge University Press.

———. 1997. "Crossing the Great Divide: Coproduction, Synergy, and Development" In Peter Evans, ed., *State-Society Synergy: Government and Social Capital in Development.* Research Series 94. Berkeley, Calif.: University of California–Berkeley.

Palmer, Natasha. 2000. "The Use of Private-Sector Contracts for Primary Health Care: Theory, Evidence, and Lessons for Low-Income and Middle-Income Countries." *Bulletin of the World Health Organization* 78(6): 821–29.

Patrinos, Harry A. 2000. "Market Forces in Education." *European Journal of Education* 35(1): 61–80.

———. 2001. "School Choice in Denmark." World Bank, Human Development Network, Education Team, Washington, D.C. Processed.

————. 2002. "Private Provision and Public Finance: Education in the Netherlands." World Bank, Human Development Network, Education Team, Washington, D.C. Processed.

Patrinos, Harry A., and Lakshmanan Ariasingam. 1997. *Decentralization of Education: Demand-Side Financing.* Washington, D.C.: World Bank.

Peterson, Paul E., William G. Howell, Patrick J. Wolf, and David E. Campbell. 2001. "School Vouchers: Results from Randomized Experiments." Paper presented at the National Bureau of Economic Research Conference on the Economics of School Choice, Florida Keys, Florida, February 22–24.

Petrazzini, Ben A., and Theodore H. Clark. 1996. "Costs and Benefits of Telecommunications Liberalization in Developing Countries." Working Paper. Hong Kong University of Science and Technology, Hong Kong, China.

Pfeffermann, Guy P. 2000. *Paths Out of Poverty: The Role of Private Enterprise in Developing Countries.* Washington D.C.: International Finance Corporation.

Pfeffermann, Guy P., and Gregory Kisunko. 1999. "Perceived Obstacles to Doing Business: Worldwide Survey Results." International Finance Corporation, Washington, D.C. Processed.

Pinto, Brian, Marek Belka, and Stefan Krajewski. 1993. "Transforming State Enterprises in Poland: Evidence on Adjustment by Manufacturing Firms." *Brookings Papers on Economic Activity* 1: 213–70.

Pohl, Gerhard, Robert E. Anderson, Stijn Claessens, and Simeon Djankov. 1997. "Privatization and Restructuring in Central and Eastern Europe: Evidence and Policy Options." Technical Paper 368. World Bank, Washington, D.C.

Porter, Michael, E. 1990. *The Competitive Advantage of Nations.* New York: Free Press.

Porter, Michael E., and Mariko Sakakibara. 2001. "Competing at Home to Win Abroad: Evidence from Japanese Industry." *Review of Economics and Statistics* 83(2): 310–22.

Preker, Alexander S., April Harding, and Phyllida Travis. 2000. "Make or Buy Decisions in the Production of Health Care Goods and Services: New Insights from Institutional Economics and Organizational Theory." *Bulletin of the World Health Organization* 78(6): 779–90.

Pritchett, Lant. 1996. "Where Has All the Education Gone?" Policy Research Working Paper 1581. World Bank, Washington, D.C.

Proudhon, Pierre-Joseph. 1970. *What Is Property? An Inquiry into the Principle of Right and of Government.* Translated from the French by Benjamin R. Tucker. New York: Dover.

Purcell, Dennis L., and Jock R. Anderson. 1997. *Agricultural Extension and Research: Achievements and Problems in National Systems.* Oxford, United Kingdom: Oxford University Press.

Rajan, Raghuram, and Luigi Zingales. 1998. "Financial Dependence and Growth." *American Economic Review* 88(3): 559–86.

Ravallion, Martin. 1995. "Growth and Poverty: Evidence for Developing Countries in the 1980s." *Economic Letters* 48: 411–17.

———. 1997a. "Can High-Inequality Developing Countries Escape Absolute Poverty?" *Economic Letters* 56: 51–57.

———. 1997b. "Good and Bad Growth: The Human Development Reports." *World Development* 25(5): 631–38.

———. 2000. "Growth, Inequality, and Poverty: Looking Beyond Averages." Policy Research Working Paper 2558. World Bank, Washington, D.C.

Ravallion, Martin, and Shaohua Chen. 1997. "What Can New Survey Data Tell Us about Changes in Distribution and Poverty?" *World Bank Economic Review* 11(2): 357–82.

Ravallion, Martin, and Gaurav Datt. 1999. "When Is Growth Pro-Poor? Evidence from the Diverse Experiences of India's States." Policy Research Working Paper 2263. World Bank, Washington, D.C.

Renard, Vincent. 1999. "Application of Tradable Permits to Land-Use Management." In *Implementing Domestic Tradable Permits for Environmental Protection.* Paris: Organisation for Economic Co-operation and Development.

Reuter, Peter. 1984. *Disorganized Crime: Illegal Markets and the Mafia.* Cambridge, Mass.: MIT Press.

Ricard, Samuel. 1781. *Traite Generale du Commerce.* Amsterdam: E. von Harrevelt and A. Soetens.

Ridley, Matt. 1998. *The Origins of Virtue: Human Instincts and the Evolution of Cooperation.* New York: Penguin.

Ritzen, Jozef M., Jan Van Dommelen, and Frans J. De Vijlder. 1997. "School Finance and School Choice in the Netherlands." *Economics of Education Review* 16(3): 329–35.

Rodriguez, Francisco, and Dani Rodrik. 2000. "Trade Policy and Economic Growth: A Skeptic's Guide to the Cross-National Evidence." In Ben Bernank and Kenneth Rogoff, eds., *NBER Macroeconomic Annual 2000.* Cambridge, Mass.: MIT Press.

Rodrik, Dani. 1999a. "Institutions for High-Quality Growth: What They Are and How to Acquire Them." Working Paper 7540. National Bureau of Economic Research, Cambridge, Mass.

———. 1999b. *The New Global Economy and Developing Countries: Making Openness Work.* Baltimore, Md.: Johns Hopkins University Press.

Roemer, Michael, and Mary Kay Gugerty. 1997. "Does Economic Growth Reduce Poverty?" CAER I Discussion Paper 5. Harvard Institute for International Development, Cambridge, Mass.

Roger, Neil. 1999. "Recent Trends in Private Participation in Infrastructure." Public Policy for the Private Sector Note 196. World Bank, Washington, D.C.

Romer, Paul. 1993. "Ideas and Things." *The Economist.* September 11, 70–72.

Rosegrant, Mark W., and Renato Gazmuri Schleyer. 1994. "Reforming Water Allocation Policy through Markets in Tradable Water Rights: Lessons from Chile, Mexico, and California." Discussion Paper 6. International Food Policy Research Institute, Washington, D.C.

Rosen, James E. 2000. "Contracting for Reproductive Health Care: A Guide." World Bank, Health, Nutrition, and Population team, Washington, D.C.

Rosenberg, Nathan, and L. E. Birdzell Jr. 1927. *How the West Grew Rich: The Economic Transformation of the Industrial World.* New York: Basic Books.

Runolfson, Birgir. 1999. "ITQs in Icelandic Fisheries: A Rights-Based Approach to Fisheries Management." In A. Hatcher and K. Robinson, eds., *The Definition and Allocation of Use Rights in European Fisheries: Proceedings of the Second Workshop Held in Brest, France, 5–7 May.* Portsmouth, United Kingdom: Centre for the Economics and Management of Aquatic Resources.

Sachs, Jeffrey D., and Andrew Warner. 1995. "Economic Reform and the Process of Global Integration." *Brookings Papers on Economic Activity* 1: 1–118.

———. 1997. "Natural Resource Abundance and Economic Growth." Center for International Development and Harvard Institute for International Development, Cambridge, Mass. Processed.

Sachs, Jeffrey, Clifford Zinnes, and Yair Eilat. 2000. "The Gains from Privatization in Transition Economies: Is Change of Ownership Enough?" CAER Discussion Paper 63. Harvard Institute for International Development, Cambridge, Mass.

Sahlin, Marshall. 1972. *Stone Age Economics*. Chicago: Aldine-Atherton.

Saltman, Richard B., Reinhard Busse, and Elias Mossialos. 2002. *Regulating Entrepreneurial Behavior in European Health Care Systems*. Buckingham, United Kingdom: Open University Press.

Savedoff, William. 1997. "Social Services Viewed through New Lenses: Agency Problems in Education and Health in Latin America." Research Network Working Paper R-318. Inter-American Development Bank, Washington, D.C.

Sawhill, Isabel V., and Shannon L. Smith. 1998. "Vouchers for Elementary and Secondary Education." Paper prepared for a conference of the Urban Institute, the Brookings Institution, and the Committee for Economic Development, October 2–3.

Schelling, Thomas. 1984. *Choice and Consequence*. Cambridge, Mass.: Harvard University Press.

Schneider, Pia. 2000. "Development and Implementation of Prepayment Schemes in Rwanda." Technical Report No. 45. Abt Associates, Bethesda, Md.

Scobie, Tanya D., and Harry A. Patrinos. 2001. *Investing in Private Education: IFC's Strategic Directions*. Washington, D.C.: International Finance Corporation.

Shah, Parth J. 2001. "New Education Policy: Choice and Competition." India Policy Institute, Hyderabad, India. Processed.

Sharma, Suneeta, and David R. Hotchkiss. 2001. "Developing Financial Autonomy in Public Hospitals in India: Rajasthan's Model." *Health Policy* 55: 1–18.

Shaw, R. Paul, and Charles C. Griffin. 1995. *Financing Health Care in Sub-Saharan Africa through User Fees and Insurance*. Washington, D.C.: World Bank.

Sheaff, Rod, and Andrew Lloyd. 1999. "From Competition to Cooperation: Service Agreements in Primary Care—A Handbook for Professionals and Managers." University of Manchester, National Primary Care Research and Development Center, Manchester, United Kingdom.

Sheshinski, Eytan, and Luis Felipe Lopez-Calva. 1999. "Privatization and Its Benefits: Theory and Evidence." Development Discussion Paper 698. Harvard Institute for International Development, Cambridge, Mass.

Shirley, Mary, and Claude Menard. 2000. "Cities Awash: Reforming Water Supply in Developing Countries." World Bank, Development Research Group, Washington, D.C. Processed.

Shirley, Mary, and Patrick Walsh. 2000. "Public vs. Private Ownership: The Current State of the Debate." Policy Research Working Paper 2420. World Bank, Washington, D.C.

Simmel, George. 1955. *Conflict and the Web of Group-Affiliations*. New York: Free Press.

Slack, Katherine, and William D. Savedoff. 2001. "Public Purchaser–Private Provider Contracting for Health Services: Examples from Latin America and the Caribbean." Sustainable Development Department Technical Paper Series. Inter-American Development Bank, Washington, D.C.

Slaughter, Anne-Marie. 1997. "The Real New World Order." *Foreign Affairs* 76(5): 183–97.

Smith, Adam. 1776. *The Wealth of Nations*.

Smith, Warrick. 1997a. "Utility Regulators—The Independence Debate." Public Policy for the Private Sector Note 127. World Bank, Washington, D.C.

———. 1997b. "Utility Regulators—Decisionmaking Structures, Resources, and Start-up Strategy." Public Policy for the Private Sector Note 129. World Bank, Washington, D.C.

———. 2000. "Regulating Infrastructure for the Poor: Perspectives on Regulatory System Design." Paper presented at the International Conference on Infrastructure for Development: Private Solutions and the Poor, London, May 31–June 2.

Snodgrass, Donald, and Tyler Biggs. 1996. *Industrialization and the Small Firm: Patterns and Policies*. International Center for Economic Growth, San Francisco, Calif.

Solo, Tova Maria. 1998. "Competition in Water and Sanitation: The Role of Small-Scale Entrepreneurs." Viewpoint No. 165. World Bank, Washington, D.C.

Srinivasan, T. N. 2000. "Growth, Poverty Reduction, and Inequality." Yale University, New Haven, Conn. Processed.

Srinivasan, T. N., and Jagdish Bhagwati. 1999. "Outward Orientation and Development: Are Revisionists Right?" Yale University and Columbia University, New Haven, Conn., and New York. Processed.

Stern, Nicholas. 2001. *A Strategy for Development.* World Bank, Washington, D.C.

Stiglitz, Joseph E. 1989. "Markets, Market Failures, and Development." *American Economic Review* 79(2): 197–203.

———. 1998. "More Instruments and Broader Goals: Moving toward the Post-Washington Consensus." Paper presented at the 1998 WIDER Annual Lecture, Helsinki, January 7.

———. 1999. "Whither Reform? Ten Years of the Transition." Paper presented at the Annual World Bank Conference on Development Economics, Washington, D.C., April 28–30.

Stover, Charles, Karen Quigley, and Daniel L. Kraushaar. 1996. "Guidelines for Setting Up a Managed Health Care Plan." Management Sciences for Health, Boston. Processed.

Sutton, John. 2000. "Rich Trades, Scarce Capabilities: Industrial Development Revisited." *Keynes Lecture in Economics.* London: British Academy.

Tan, Hong. 2001. "Impact Evaluation of Mexico's SME Training Program." WBI Working Paper. World Bank, Washington, D.C.

Tanzi, Vito, and Hamid Davoodi. 1997. "Corruption, Public Investment, and Growth." Working Paper WP/97/139. International Monetary Fund, Washington, D.C.

Thaler, Richard H. 1992. *The Winner's Curse: Paradoxes and Anomalies of Economic Life.* Princeton, N.J.: Princeton University Press.

Thobani, Mateen. 1997. "Formal Water Markets: Why, When, and How to Introduce Tradable Water Rights." *World Bank Research Observer* 12(2): 161–79.

Thomas, Vinod, and John Nash. 1991. *Best Practices in Trade Policy Reform.* New York: Oxford University Press.

Thorsnes, Paul, and Gerald P. W. Simons. 1999. "Letting the Market Preserve Land: The Case for a Market-Driven Transfer of Development Rights Program." *Contemporary Economic Policy* 17(2): 256–66.

Timmer, C. Peter. 1997. "How Well Do the Poor Connect to the Growth Process?" CAER Discussion Paper 17. Harvard Institute for International Development, Cambridge, Mass.

Titmus, Richard. 1971. *The Gift Relationship: From Human Blood to Social Policy.* New York: Pantheon Books.

Tooley, James. 1999. "The Global Education Industry." Studies in Education No. 7. Institute of Economic Affairs and International Finance Corporation, London.

Tybout, James. 2000. "Manufacturing Firms in Developing Countries: How Well Do They Do and Why?" *Journal of Economic Literature* 38(1): 11–45.

Umali-Deininger, Dina. 1997. "Public and Private Agricultural Extension: Partners or Rivals?" *World Bank Research Observer* 12(2): 203–24.

United Nations. 2001. *World Population Prospects: The 2000 Revision.* New York: Population Division, Department of Economic and Social Affairs.

United Nations Conference on Trade and Development. 2000. "Bilateral Investment Treaties: 1959–1999." *UNCTAD/ITE/IIA/2.* New York.

United Nations Development Programme. 2000. *Human Development Report 2000.* New York: Oxford University Press.

United Nations Educational, Scientific, and Cultural Organization. 2000. *World Education Report 2000: The Right to Education.* Paris.

Van Bastelaer, Thierry. 1999. "Does Social Capital Facilitate the Poor's Access to Credit? A Review of the Microeconomic Literature." Social Capital Initiative Working Paper 8. World Bank and IRIS Center, Washington, D.C.

Van der Mheen, Henk, and Henrik Nilsson. 1997. "Information Channels for Fish Farming Extension in Eastern Province of Zambia." *Aquatic Resource Management Programme Newsletter* 24(January). Food and Agriculture Organization.

Van Lerberghe, W., W. Ammar, R. El Rashidi, A. Sales, and A. Mechbal. 1997. "Reform Follows Failure: Unregulated Private Care in Lebanon." *Health Policy and Planning* 12(4): 296–311.

Vawda, Ayesha. 1997. "Brazil: Stipends to Increase School Enrollment and Decrease Child Labor." World Bank, Washington, D.C.

Vining, Aidan R., and Steven Globerman. 1999. "Contracting Out Health Care Services: A Conceptual Framework." *Health Policy* 46: 77–96.

Vinson, Elisa. 1999. *Governing-for-Results and Accountability: Performance Contracting in Six State Human Services Agencies.* Washington D.C.: Urban Institute.

Von Weizsäcker, C. C. 1980. "A Welfare Analysis of Barriers to Entry." *Bell Journal of Economics* 11: 399–420.

Von Weizsäcker, C. C., Ernst Ulrich, Amory B. Lovins, and L. Hunter Lovins. 1997. *Factor Four: Doubling Wealth, Halving Resource Use.* London: Earthscan.

Wallis, Paul. 1999. "Transferable Fishing Quotas: Experience in OECD Countries." In *Implementing Domestic Tradable Permits for Environmental Protection*. Paris: Organisation for Economic Co-operation and Development.

Webb, Michael, and David Ehrhardt. 1998. "Improving Water Services through Competition." Water Resources Occasional Paper 6. United Kingdom Department for International Development, London.

Wei, Shang-Jin. 1995. "The Open Door Policy and China's Rapid Growth: Evidence from City-Level Data." In Takatoshi Ito and Anne O. Krueger, eds., *Growth Theories in Light of the East Asian Experience*. Chicago and London: University of Chicago Press.

———. 1999. "Does Corruption Relieve Foreign Investors of the Burden of Taxes and Capital Controls?" Policy Research Working Paper 2209. World Bank, Washington, D.C.

Wellenius, Björn. 1997. "Extending Telecommunications Service to Rural Areas —The Chilean Experience: Awarding Subsidies through Competitive Bidding." Public Policy for the Private Sector Note 105. World Bank, Washington, D.C.

———. 2000. "Extending Telecommunications beyond the Market." Public Policy for the Private Sector Note 206. World Bank, Washington, D.C.

Wertz, Richard D. 2000. "Issues and Concerns in the Privatization and Outsourcing of Campus Services in Higher Education." Occasional Paper No. 10. National Center for the Study of Privatization in Education, Columbia University, New York.

West, Edwin G. 1997. "Education Vouchers in Practice and Principle: A World Survey." *World Bank Research Observer* 12(1): 83–104.

West, Gerald T., and Keith Martin. 2001. "Political Risk Investment Insurance: The Renaissance Revisited." In Theodore Moran, ed., *International Political Risk Management—Exploring New Frontiers*. Washington, D.C.: World Bank.

Wheeler, David. 2000. "Racing to the Bottom? Foreign Investment and Air Pollution in Developing Countries" Policy Research Working Paper 2524. World Bank, Washington, D.C.

Williamson, Jeffrey G. 1987. "Is Inequality Inevitable under Capitalism? The American Case." In P. L. Berger, ed., *Capitalism and Equality in America*. New York: Hamilton Press.

Williamson, Oliver. 1975. *Markets and Hierarchies: Analysis and Antitrust Implications*. New York: Free Press.

Willis, Carla Y., and Charlotte Leighton. 1995. "Protecting the Poor under Cost Recovery: The Role of Means Testing." *Health Policy and Planning* 10(3): 241–56.

Winston, Clifford. 1993. "Economic Deregulation: Days of Reckoning for Micro-economists." *Journal of Economic Literature* 31(3): 1263–89.

Winters, L. Alan. 1999. "Trade and Poverty: Is There a Connection?" In Dan Ben-David, Hakan Nordstrom, and L. Alan Winters, eds., *Trade, Income Disparity, and Poverty*. Special Studies 5. Geneva: World Trade Organization.

World Bank. 1989. "Argentina Agricultural Sector Review, Volume II: Technical Annex." Report No. 7733-AR. Country Department I, Latin America and the Caribbean Region, Washington, D.C.

———. 1993a. "The East Asian Miracle: Economic Growth and Public Policy." Policy Research Report. Oxford, United Kingdom: Oxford University Press.

———. 1993b. *World Development Report: Investing in Health*. Washington, D.C.

———. 1994a. "Averting the Old Age Crisis: Policies to Protect the Old and Promote Growth." Policy Research Report. Washington, D.C.

———. 1994b. "Environmental Liability and Privatization in Central and Eastern Europe." Report No. 11686-ECA. Washington, D.C.

———. 1994c. *World Development Report: Infrastructure for Development*. Washington, D.C.

———. 1995. "Directed Credit." DEC Policy Review Note. Washington, D.C.

———. 1997. *World Development Report 1997: The State in a Changing World*. Washington, D.C.

———. 1998. "Project Appraisal Document on a Proposed Loan to the Republic of Peru for an Urban Property Rights Project." Report No. 18245PE. Washington, D.C.

———. 2000a. *Can Africa Claim the 21st Century?* Washington, D.C.

———. 2000b. "Decentralizing Agricultural Extension: Lessons and Good Practice." Agricultural Knowledge and Information Systems Good Practice Note. Washington, D.C.

———. 2000c. *India: Policies to Reduce Poverty and Accelerate Sustainable Development*. Washington, D.C.

———. 2000d. *Making Transition Work for Everyone: Poverty and Inequality in Europe and Central Asia*. Washington, D.C.

———. 2000e. *Reforming Public Institutions and Strengthening Governance: A World Bank Strategy.* Washington, D.C.

———. 2000f. *World Development Report 2000/2001: Attacking Poverty.* Washington, D.C.

———. 2001a. "Colombia—Water Sector Reform Assistance Project." Report No. 21868 CO. Washington, D.C.

———. 2001b. *Global Development Finance: Building Coalitions for Effective Development Finance.* Washington, D.C.

———. 2001c. *Global Economic Prospects.* Washington, D.C.

———. 2001d. "Finance for Growth: Policy Choices in a Volatile World." Policy Research Report. Washington, D.C.

———. 2001e. *World Development Report 2001/2002: Institutions for Markets.* Washington, D.C.

———. 2002a. *Global Development Finance: Financing the Poorest Countries.* Washington, D.C.

———. 2002b. *Global Economic Prospects.* Washington, D.C.

———. 2002c. *Improving the Investment Climate in India.* Washington, D.C.

World Health Organization. 2000. *The World Health Report 2000.* Geneva.

Wouters, Annemarie. 1995. "Improving Quality through Cost Recovery in Niger." *Health Policy and Planning* 10(3): 257–70.

———. 1998. "Alternative Provider Payment Methods: Incentives for Improving Health Care Delivery." *PHR Primer for Policymakers.* Bethesda, Md.: Partnership for Health Reform Resource Center, Abt Associates.

Yepes, Guillermo. 1999. "Do Cross-Subsidies Help the Poor to Benefit from Water and Wastewater Services?" UNDP–World Bank Water and Sanitation Program Working Paper. World Bank, Washington, D.C.

Young, Alwyn. 1992. "A Tale of Two Cities: Factor Accumulation and Technical Change in Hong Kong and Singapore." In Olivier J. Blanchard and Stanley Fischer, eds., *NBER Macroeconomic Annual.* Cambridge, Mass.: National Bureau of Economic Research.

———. 1994. "The Tyranny of Numbers: Confronting the Statistical Realities of the East Asian Growth Experience." Working Paper 4680. National Bureau of Economic Research, Cambridge, Mass.

Index